PRAISE FOR *WEB3 IN FINANCIAL*

At last, a book on how blockchain is transforming financial services that is as accessible as it is timely. Rita Martins' practical tour through the evolution, technology, use cases and jargon of crypto, make this book a must-read for leaders who perceive changes in the financial system, but don't know how to grasp them.

Dante Disparte, Chief Strategy Officer and Head of Global Policy, Circle

Web3 in Financial Services is a must-read for anyone in financial services. Rita Martins provides an accessible, comprehensive, well-rounded and balanced introduction to blockchain's role in finance, drawing on insights from industry experts and practical real-life use cases. The book brilliantly contextualizes Web3's place in shaping financial services.

Sendi Young, Advisory Board Member, Payments Association and former Europe MD and UK Board Director, Ripple

Finance has long faced disruption from emerging technologies, but today's innovations offer unprecedented challenges and opportunities. Rita Martins expertly simplifies intricate concepts, making it a must-read for anyone looking to embrace decentralized technologies and succeed in the digital era.

Steve Suarez, CEO, HorizonX and former Global Head of Innovation, HSBC

Web3 has become indispensable in the financial sector. Rita Martins' *Web3 in Financial Services* provides a comprehensive overview of the opportunities and challenges ahead. It's accessible to anyone who wants to empower themselves to transform tomorrow's world.

Laurent Marochini, Head of Innovation, Société Générale Securities Services

Web3 in Financial Services masterfully dissects the evolving synergy between traditional finance and the innovative realm of DeFi through Web3 technologies. With a focus on digital identity as the cornerstone for secure and accessible financial transactions, the book offers a forward-looking perspective on how these two worlds are not just coexisting but are becoming increasingly intertwined, presenting a compelling vision of a future where finance is more inclusive and resilient. A roadmap for navigating the integration of traditional financial systems with the transformative potential of DeFi and Web3, signalling a new era of financial innovation and cooperation. Indispensable for emerging leaders and strategic thinkers alike.
Nitin Gaur, Global Head of Digital Assets and Technology Design, State Street

Rita Martins leverages her extensive experience in financial services to produce a very accessible and comprehensive tour of the developments facilitated by blockchain technology. Her interviews with key players in the industry lead to a thorough analysis of where the industry has come from, and where it is going.
Keith Bear, Fellow, Cambridge Centre for Alternative Finance

Web3 in Financial Services is an essential guide for finance professionals seeking to understand the transformative landscape of crypto and blockchain. Insightful real-world examples demystify key concepts and drive the discussion towards practical applications, unveiling the true potential of blockchain.
Jess Houlgrave, CEO, WalletConnect

Web3 in Financial Services

How blockchain, digital assets and crypto are disrupting traditional finance

Rita Martins

KoganPage

First published in Great Britain and the United States in 2024 by Kogan Page Limited

2nd Floor, 45 Gee Street
London
EC1V 3RS
United Kingdom

8 W 38th Street, Suite 902
New York, NY 10018
USA

www.koganpage.com

Kogan Page books are printed on paper from sustainable forests.

ISBNs

Hardback   978 1 3986 1581 6
Paperback 978 1 3986 1571 7
Ebook   978 1 3986 1582 3

British Library Cataloguing-in-Publication Data

A CIP record for this book is available from the British Library.

Library of Congress Control Number

2024934066

Typeset by Integra Software Services, Pondicherry
Print production managed by Jellyfish
Printed and bound by CPI Group (UK) Ltd, Croydon CR0 4YY

CONTENTS

PART FOUR

Moving forward 237

ABOUT THE AUTHOR

Rita Martins is a strategic senior leader with a distinguished track record in financial services, fintech and Web3. She serves on the advisory boards of a range of startups at the intersection of finance and DeFi, blockchain, digital assets and crypto.

Previously, Rita was the Global Head of FinTech Partnerships at HSBC, where she played a key role in incubating and accelerating disruptive technologies, creating significant advancements in the fintech landscape. Her extensive background also includes strategy and digital transformation roles at Accenture and Ernst & Young, where she led large-scale digital transformation projects, helping clients achieve strategic milestones.

Rita holds a master's degree in business administration with a major in finance. She grew up in Portugal and currently lives in London.

PART ONE

Early days

Web3 and financial services

01

Introduction

VENTURING BEYOND BANKS

Meet Sophie, one of the best university teachers in the UK. Loved by her executive students, her classes were always filled to the brim. Business leaders would rearrange their demanding schedules to ensure they never missed a session.

But Sophie dreamed of reaching students beyond the walls of her traditional school, wanting to share her knowledge with business leaders across the globe. She envisioned her own online course that could reach leaders from diverse backgrounds, coming together to learn and share ideas. But, she faced a challenge: she did not have the funding available to pursue her dreams.

One day, encouraged by one of her friends who had done the same, she decided to take the jump: she quit her secure job and launched her own business. Initially, she struggled to operate with online conferencing tools, but her determination led her to master those tools quickly. Sophie worked tirelessly to create the content, hired designers for engaging imagery and leveraged the latest AI for real-time translation. Her classes were live in under two months, and the response was overwhelming.

Within the first year, Sophie expanded her business to include other teachers and diverse topics. The growth was so impressive that it caught the attention of John, a banker and one of Sophie's long-time students.

'I am very impressed with your progress, Sophie,' John said one day. 'But I keep wondering, how could you secure a loan so quickly to start your business? Usually, it takes months for new businesses to get loans, and some banks do not even provide loans for small businesses.'

Sophie smiled, 'I didn't go to a bank, John. I got my funds from my community. By tokenizing and fractionalizing my house and using it as collateral, I was able to secure the funding I needed quickly. In exchange, the community receives 30 per cent of my revenues in perpetuity.'

This fictional story is not a vision of the future but an illustration of what is already happening across the world. Many small business owners and entrepreneurs no longer need a loan from a bank to start their businesses. Instead, they are using decentralized solutions. The same is happening across other areas of financial services. Retail clients buy their coffees using Bitcoin, not fiat currency. Wealthy clients invest in cryptocurrencies using decentralized exchanges and trading platforms, not traditional investment banks. And migrant people use Web3 rails instead of fintech companies to send money home to their family members.

Web3 is decentralizing the financial system rails and disrupting how money and every single financial instrument is recorded and transacted. It is enabling a more capital-efficient way for nation-states to move currency globally. Disrupting every single team, product and player in financial services.

Decision and governance powers have moved from the hands of a few financial players to global communities. Enabled by the power of social networks, individuals of all ages, backgrounds and educations are now coming together online and digitally to build the new financial economy. In this new economy, financial processes run without the need for human interaction or intermediaries.

Digital identity will be at the centre of this new financial system. By leveraging both information from the real world, for example your ID or driving licence, and information that is stored within the blockchain, often referred to as on-chain data such as interactions, investments and tokenized assets, decentralized identity has the potential to include underserved and underrepresented communities into financial systems. As opposed to the existing internet, users will be able to own and control their data and identities, as well as with whom they share them and how much they share.

While, until recently, built and operated on the sidelines, Web3 in financial services is now becoming a recognized opportunity for many. To remain competitive, financial services leaders must prioritize building knowledge and capabilities today.

Disruptive innovation

History is full of tales of innovation. For decades, new technology and concepts have disrupted existing players, business models and global industries.

Early reactions to the internet were a mix of excitement and scepticism. Many didn't fully understand its potential, seeing it as a niche tool used primarily by academics and researchers. Others were afraid of the impact it could have on society, such as the prospect of an always-online culture, leading some to declare they would never use it. However, contrary to original beliefs, the internet has profoundly transformed society far beyond a limited niche. It has unlocked unprecedented new businesses, radically reshaping industries worldwide.

The rise of e-commerce platforms like Amazon, enabled by the internet, dramatically altered the retail industry for ever, allowing customers to shop from the comfort of their homes, offering a wider variety of products at lower prices, pushing bricks-and-mortar stores to either close or move online. Companies like Netflix and Spotify revolutionized how users consume media. Netflix shifted the paradigm from cable TV and DVD rentals to streaming services, while Spotify transformed music from CDs and downloads to streaming. Social media platforms like Facebook, Twitter and LinkedIn changed how people connected and communicated, disrupting traditional media, marketing and global communication.

Those stories are not just about transforming industries but also about the ability to adapt to changing consumer preferences and technological advancements. Traditional players who were not able to adapt and leverage new technologies faced significant financial challenges and potential bankruptcies. Many initially ignored the idea of new innovative models or products, then tried to block them and later started to adopt them. Blockbuster executives allegedly laughed at the idea of buying Netflix in 2000 for $50 million. Netflix is now a company worth more than $150 billion, while Blockbuster is no longer an active business.[1] More recently, traditional taxi drivers were first dismissive of the Uber company and later seen on television using physical force to stop Uber drivers from moving their cars. Currently, Uber is courting traditional cabs to be added to their platform.

Now, we are at a new intersection of global disruption due to Web3. This new iteration of the internet, in which new decentralized services and solutions are built on the blockchain, has the potential to disrupt a number of industries. Gaming, entertainment, retail, social media, logistics and financial services are just a few examples.

As we turn our gaze to the financial sector, it is clear that blockchain is positioned to be the next frontier in the technological disruption. Web3, with its emphasis on decentralized solutions, promises to redefine and democratize financial services, similar to how Spotify and Netflix democratized access to music and entertainment. In fact, Web3 is already delivering on its promise, with many live use cases in financial services. While, initially, some traditional institutions dismissed this new technological innovation, many are now embracing the benefits and even taking the lead in creating new solutions that benefit their businesses and their clients' needs.

Web3 innovation: from scepticism to embrace

Let's go back to 2017, when Bitcoin dominated the news, led by a sharp increase in its price followed by an infamous crash. During this time, a wall existed between Web3 and traditional financial services. Both worlds were operated without much acknowledgement or many intersections.

Traditional financial institutions were particularly doubtful about Bitcoin. Jamie Dimon, CEO of J.P. Morgan, famously called Bitcoin a 'fraud',[2] and Larry Fink, CEO of BlackRock, called it an 'index of money laundering'.[3] At the time, many other major leaders shared the scepticism, with crypto seen as a speculative asset fraught with risks and uncertainties.

But, as the years progressed and the technology matured, so did the perception within the financial sector. Financial institutions and leaders started to explore and consider the potential of the underlying technology (blockchain) for improving transaction efficiencies, reducing costs and enhancing security. The walls between the worlds started to crumble.

Financial institutions started to study this space, via internal research and development, incubators or joining industry consortiums. In 2015, more than 25 banks collaborated with the blockchain consortium led by the R3 startup to understand how to apply blockchain technology to enterprise use cases. The list of partners included some big names, such as Goldman Sachs and Santander, both of which had already made some investments in the blockchain space; Goldman Sachs invested in Circle and Santander invested in Ripple.[4]

After a few years of internal research and learning, enterprise solutions started to emerge from traditional institutions. In 2019, Fidelity announced the launch of its Bitcoin crypto custody services, and J.P. Morgan launched JPM Coin, a blockchain-based bank account. The years from 2021 to 2023 were full of new initiatives and launches pioneered by big incumbents from custody, payments, tokenization and exchange-traded funds (ETFs) submissions. Currently, all major players such as Fidelity, J.P. Morgan, HSBC, Morgan Stanley, Citi, Barclays and Goldman Sachs now have dedicated teams for digital assets, blockchain technology and digital identity applications.

Fintech companies have also embraced this new technology. Revolut and Robinhood started to offer crypto trading in 2017 and 2018 respectively. In 2022, both companies partnered with the Polygon blockchain protocol, exploring further Web3 services. PayPal started to enable crypto checkout for merchants in 2021 and announced the launch of its stablecoin in 2023.[5]

Perhaps the most telling sign of this shift in the traditional world was the growing interest of central banks worldwide. In 2023, 130 countries were exploring central bank digital currencies (CBDCs).[6]

In the 'new world', Web3 native startups continued to build and create new innovative solutions over the years. A whole new world of decentralized finance solutions emerged, grabbing the attention and interest of many tech-savvy users and professionals in traditional financial institutions. In 2021, Mary Catherine Lader left her job as a managing director at BlackRock to join Uniswap, stating that she couldn't pass this opportunity to work in the next wave of innovation 'that was so critical to the future of finance'.[7] The emerging Web3 ecosystem now boasts thousands of companies, with investors pouring approximately $94 million into it between 2015 and 2022.[8]

While the history of Web3 is also full of scams and risks, the current sentiment is that Web3 has huge potential and could bring increased benefits to all players in financial services. In 2023, Larry Fink, CEO of BlackRock, appeared on CNBC, stating that crypto had 'a differentiating value versus other asset classes. But more importantly, because it's so international, it's going to transcend any one currency and currency valuation'.[9] This was in contrast to his remarks in 2018.

With regulatory frameworks becoming clear across the globe, new solutions and players will continue to emerge. Many expect we will live in a hybrid model to start with. But ultimately, both worlds will merge, similar to how our physical and digital lives exist today, resulting in seamless, more efficient and inclusive financial services.

Failing to prepare or, at a minimum, being aware of this revolutionary technology could lead to serious challenges down the road. The impact will span your career, team, product, business model and more.

My story

Having worked for the world's biggest banks and consultancy companies, I have always been at the intersection of innovation and financial services. This unique position has allowed me throughout the years to discover the power of new technologies and how they can transform drastically not only processes but also business models.

My journey in Web3 started with the infrastructure. A groundbreaking technology called blockchain instantly caught my attention, given its enormous potential to revolutionize finance. Blockchain, a shared database in which all entities have immediate access to the transaction information and status, could drastically reduce, if not eliminate, the need for reconciliations and reports. This transparency promised to drastically reduce the need for time-consuming and manual tasks that are commonplace in traditional finance.

Over the following years, my interest led me to champion and drive experiments in this space professionally and research further personally. And even though I played a bit with the investment side of this world, what really sparked my interest was Web3. Web3, still an unknown word for most, was already used by experts to describe a new vision of the internet built on the blockchain and centred around openness and decentralization. This vision would have ripple effects across all industries.

The implementation of Web3 in financial services would mean the opportunity to create a new financial system built on the blockchain, instead of legacy systems, with new forms of money in addition to fiat currency. This Web3 vision described something that was revolutionary instead of incremental like many technologies I had worked with previously.

In Web3, we have the opportunity to rethink the concept of money, ownership and financial systems. We are no longer incrementally adding new functionality to existing systems or automating parts of the process. We are creating new business models, services and offerings. This could be one of the most transformative times in financial services, and I want to look back and say I was part of it.

After many years of engaging, building and testing with founders and startups in Web3, I believe there is a real opportunity and potential in this space to transform and improve financial services. While initially Web3 and traditional finance were built as separate worlds, we are now at a turning point where both worlds are coming together.

However, to create powerful solutions, we need players from all backgrounds, both traditional and Web3 native, and skillsets (product, compliance, technology) to collaborate and work together.

And so, this book is my invitation for you to join me on the Web3 journey, an ecosystem and vision that is changing the way we think about finance. This book will demystify the buzzwords, and explain the emergent use cases and their profound implications for finance players. It will also introduce you to the pioneering companies already driving the change, offering a closer look at their innovations and the practical implications of adopting blockchain technology and Web3 concepts. After reading this book, you will not only grasp the fundamentals of Web3 but also gain unique insights into Web3 transformative potential for the financial services industry, equipping you to actively participate and shape this exciting new vision.

You may be tempted to ignore Web3 for a few more years and focus on your other priorities. But, the reality is that 'the genie is out of the bottle', and Web3 is not going back, nor will it be stopped. Its decentralized, global and open-source features allow anyone, from individual innovators to major corporations across the globe, to build and launch solutions. So, even if a specific country attempts to block it or deem it illicit, the international and interconnected nature of Web3 means that its development and use will likely continue in other regions. In fact, many startups across the world are continuously releasing new solutions.

However, it is important to recognize the challenges and the need for clear regulatory frameworks to enable sustainable growth and stability of Web3. Regulators worldwide are increasingly looking into this emerging space, working together with a variety of stakeholders to develop new regulations. Such efforts will provide not only clarity, customer protection and market integrity but also credibility to this industry. Web3 players and experts that have been building and exploring this space will now have defined rules and clarity to build on. Any company or leader who is not aware of or does not understand the potential, risks and limitations could face disruption and be left behind.

So, it is critical for all leaders, teams and individuals in financial services to understand Web3 to be able to adapt, embrace and innovate.

Why now?

As we stand on the brink of a new paradigm, Web3 cannot be overstated.

In 2023, a report by US venture capital firm a16z found that, despite the gloomy stories in the news, Web3 had a growing and thriving community of users and builders.[10] The report stated that in

2023 the number of participants with active accounts hit an all-time high of 15 million (doubling over the previous two years). Additionally, more than 700 new applications were created and almost 30,000 developers contributed to or built on existing projects, an increase of 60 per cent over the previous three years.

The last few years have also marked a turning point in how traditional financial institutions and regulators perceive and interact with this transformative technology. Many traditional institutions are now investing heavily in Web3 startups and adopting blockchain technology by testing and developing new solutions. For example, PayPal and Société Générale recently announced the launch of their own stablecoins, PayPal USD and EUR CoinVertible respectively. A number of central banks continued discussions and reviews of their own CBDCs. The European Union passed the Markets in Crypto-Assets (MiCA) Regulation, and other regulators across the globe are looking at providing clear frameworks.

Many experts in traditional companies have noted, in private and public, that they have finished with pilots and testing the technology. After many years of experiments, they are now comfortable with the benefits and want to focus instead on launching scalable solutions that provide commercial value. So, the issue is not why you should learn about Web3, but why you can no longer afford not to.

These are unprecedented times of disruption, and it is imperative that everyone in financial services recognizes the change. This book serves as a handbook for financial services organizations seeking to deepen their understanding of Web3.

Insights from experts

Throughout the book, you will see insights from leaders working at the intersection of Web3 and finance. Those experts have kindly spent some time with me sharing stories, experiments and learnings from throughout their journey. Ensuring that I represented a range of different voices and experiences was key for me as I designed and wrote this book. We all have bias, and, in such a complex set of new technologies and concepts, so much is still being built and defined and as such it is important to hear, learn and share with the community. I hope you enjoy their insights as much as I did.

Book structure

I want to invite you to read this book based on your existing knowledge and on what you want to get out of the book.

If you are a novice seeking to learn about this space, start from the beginning and follow the chapters as they are outlined.

If you already understand some of the concepts and want to bridge gaps in your knowledge, I suggest you jump to the chapters that will be most helpful to you. Use it as your guide, and feel free to dip in and out of chapters depending on what you need at the time.

This book will provide you with everything you need to know about Web3 and its potential impact on financial services.

- Part One will cover the historical context of Web3, what it is and the disruption potential in financial services. It looks at the evolution of the internet, key principles in the Web3 vision and how it could be one of the greatest disruptions for financial services.

- Part Two will cover some of the emergent use cases driving change in financial services: custody, evolution of money and payments, tokenization, lending and borrowing and digital identity. In this part we will investigate how incumbents and challengers are testing and adopting Web3 concepts and emerging technologies.

- Part Three will consider the impact on the ecosystem, going through the opportunities, challenges and implications to traditional institutions, decentralized finance (DeFi), investors and regulators.

- Part Four will close by reviewing changes needed for mainstream adoption and how the future of finance will look.

Innovation and digital transformation are not new in financial services. Throughout the years, stakeholders have had to adapt and adopt new technologies and solutions. But such transformation has, until now, been mostly incremental. In contrast, Web3 represents a more fundamental shift, with the potential to disrupt financial services at its core.

While there are still risks associated with this nascent technology and its uses, new applications continue to be launched across the globe every minute. How far these technologies will impact the industry is yet to be seen. However, the adoption is growing, leading to increased interest from incumbents, regulators and investors.

Now, more than ever, it is important for leaders and teams to understand the core features of this emerging technology, its use cases, risks and opportunities. I believe that those who do not embark on this journey will be left behind in the years to come.

Endnotes

1 S Mollman. Blockbuster 'laughed us out of the room,' recalls Netflix cofounder on trying to sell company now worth over $150 billion for $50 million, *Fortune*, 14 April 2023, fortune.com/2023/04/14/netflix-cofounder-marc-randolph-recalls-blockbuster-rejecting-chance-to-buy-it/ (archived at https://perma.cc/SX8K-3P3W)

2 F Imbert. JPMorgan CEO Jamie Dimon says bitcoin is a 'fraud' that will eventually blow up, CNBC, 12 September 2017, cnbc.com/2017/09/12/jpmorgan-ceo-jamie-dimon-raises-flag-on-trading-revenue-sees-20-percent-fall-for-the-third-quarter.html (archived at https://perma.cc/7H3U-56QD)

3 F Imbert. BlackRock CEO Larry Fink calls bitcoin an 'index of money laundering', CNBC, 13 October 2017, cnbc.com/2017/10/13/blackrock-ceo-larry-fink-calls-bitcoin-an-index-of-money-laundering.html

4 Y B Perez. Meet the 25 Banks working with distributed ledger startup R3, CoinDesk, 7 November 2015, coindesk.com/markets/2015/11/07/meet-the-25-banks-working-with-distributed-ledger-startup-r3/ (archived at https://perma.cc/E4WV-TFUK)

5 Paypal Newsroom. PayPal launches U.S. dollar stablecoin, 7 August 2023, newsroom.paypal-corp.com/2023-08-07-PayPal-Launches-U-S-Dollar-Stablecoin (archived at https://perma.cc/FDS3-7GJL)

6 Atlantic Council. Central Bank Digital Currency Tracker, www.atlanticcouncil. org/cbdctracker/ (archived at https://perma.cc/CX8L-BYCD)

7 K Rooney. As Wall Street banks embrace crypto, high-flying start-ups look to lure top finance talent, CNBC, 1 April 2022, cnbc.com/2022/04/01/as-wall-street-banks-embrace-crypto-start-ups-look-to-lure-top-finance-talent-.html (archived at https://perma.cc/YHJ7-EPE3)

8 Bain & Company. Web3 remains highly relevant for private equity, 27 February 2023, bain.com/insights/web3-remains-highly-relevant-global-private-equity-report-2023/ (archived at https://perma.cc/HW3X-Y835)

9 J Oliver. Larry Fink unpacks BlackRock's approach to crypto, saying it can 'transcend any one currency', Cryptoslate, 14 July 2023, cryptoslate.com/larry-fink-unpacks-blackrocks-approach-to-crypto-saying-it-can-transcend-any-one-currency/ (archived at https://perma.cc/Z8N6-D9D9)

10 a16z crypto. State of crypto 2023, api.a16zcrypto.com/wp-content/uploads/2023/04/State-of-Crypto.pdf (archived at https://perma.cc/6SH6-EUBL)

02

What is Web3 and why does it matter to financial services?

THE EVOLUTION OF THE WEB

The creation of the internet cannot be credited to only one person. Instead, this technological innovation was fuelled by the work of many scientists, programmers and engineers over the years. In the late 1960s, the Cold War was at its peak, with the United States and the Soviet Union working to increase their science and technology capabilities to prevent and prepare for future attacks. During this period, computers were heavy, immobile and expensive machines only used by universities and military researchers. These machines, while powerful, were limited in numbers. To access the computer, researchers had to travel to where the computers were located.[1]

Researchers started to become frustrated. They needed to access the computers, but journeys were long and time-consuming. They needed to find a way to access the computers without having to travel to their location. Focused on finding the solution, several scientists and engineers started working together to enable computer communication. The Advanced Research Projects Agency Network (ARPANET) was created and funded by the US Department of Defense.

The first significant breakthrough came in 1969 when ARPANET delivered the first message. From a computer in the research lab at UCLA to a second one at Stanford, the message 'LO' was transmitted. Student Charley Kline was trying to type 'LOGIN' but the system crashed after the first two letters were sent. The technology continued to grow throughout the 1970s, with the development of TCP/IP (Transmission Control Protocol/Internet Protocol). This communication model set the standards for transmitting data between networks. Think of it as a 'universal language' to allow different types of computers on different networks to 'talk' to each other.

Web1

In 1990, Tim Berners-Lee, a British scientist, proposed the World Wide Web (WWW) while working at CERN – which most people recognize as the internet today. This invention provided a more powerful and user-friendly interface than previous applications. This first iteration of the web (1980–2000) is often referred to as Web1. During this period, the web was primarily a static information repository in which users could search and read information but could not comment or share. For example, the sites provided digital versions of physical newspapers or documents for users to access/read.

Web2

The next paradigm shift for the internet started in the early 2000s. The second iteration of the web, Web2 (from the 2000s to the present), is characterized by being more dynamic and interactive, with users able to read and write content. The invention of smartphones, mobile internet access and social media has propelled the growth and usage of the internet. Companies like Apple introduced sleek and simple user experiences (UX), which led to quick traction and growth. Web2 tech companies like Facebook, YouTube, Google and Twitter (X) are used daily by millions of people, who consume, create and share their own content (for example, sharing videos and photos and adding comments and reactions to friends' posts). Interactivity, collaboration and knowledge sharing are some of the advantages of Web2.

However, Web2 has also presented some challenges and risks. The collection of individuals' personal data for targeted advertisement and monetization has become prevalent, raising privacy concerns. Many Web2 companies have adopted an advertising revenue model in which the product/service is free to the users, while user data is shared with advertisers. 'If something is free, you are the product' is a common phrase used to reflect this model.

Web3

In 2014, Gavin Wood, the co-founder of Ethereum and founder of Polkadot, coined the term Web3 to represent the next evolution of the internet.[2] In Web1, users were only able to read; in Web2, users were able to read and write (think social media); and in Web3, users would be able to read, write and own. As you can see, the key difference is that users in Web3 would be able to own their own data, including personal information, comments, images, digital assets and digital identity. In Web3, users would own tokens that represent ownership in these decentralized networks. This goal of returning control and data ownership back to the users reflects the next phase of the web and a response to the data privacy concerns in Web2.

While many think of data ownership when thinking about Web3, this is too reductive for what we consider as Web3. In fact, in the early days of Web3, projects and teams often focused too much on ownership, starting by issuing tokens and defining the tokenomics (i.e. 'token economics') of the project before they even found a product–market fit. Some of those projects received early exponential interest, with users looking for quick profits instead of the long-term usage and utility of the platform. Lessons have been learnt, and we are now in a cycle in which product–market fit and long-term utility are the first steps for many projects. Data ownership and tokenomics are still important but only fully built on at a later stage.

While a common set of beliefs compose this vision, Web3 is still in its early stages and is not fully materialized. The Web3 definition is evolving as concepts and models are tested and redefined. Nowadays, Web3 is more than just data ownership; it really encompasses the new version of the internet, with an ecosystem of players building new solutions on the blockchain while trying to balance decentralization, openness and ownership.

The invention of the internet has drastically changed our society, our interactions with each other and how we live our lives. In 2023, more than 5 billion users, around 64 per cent of the global population, used the internet to find the latest news, buy groceries or talk to family members based in another country.[3] We are now at another turning point in which the next iteration of the internet could upend existing business models and assumptions. This iteration will have a direct impact on financial services.

While financial services have previously been disrupted by digital technologies and new players, that disruption was mostly the digitization of existing systems and the creation of new interfaces and user experiences. Web3's vision aims to disrupt the core of financial services, from new financial rails, new forms of money and new representations of real-world assets.

More than crypto

One key distinction I would like you to take from this book is that Web3 is more than crypto. Often when speaking with leaders in traditional institutions, there is an inherent assumption that Web3 is crypto or Bitcoin. Many withdraw from discussions because the financial institution they work at has a rule of 'not touching crypto'. Although Web3 was built on the foundations of Bitcoin and is often discussed in the news as synonymous with it, it has evolved into a wider vision beyond crypto, encompassing an entire ecosystem of blockchains, applications, use cases, governance models and entities that leverage blockchain technology.

FROM BITCOIN TO WEB3 ECOSYSTEM

The inception of Web3 dates back to 2008 when an enigmatic figure using the pseudonym Satoshi Nakamoto published 'Bitcoin: A peer-to-peer electronic cash system'.[4] In this groundbreaking whitepaper, Satoshi outlined a disruptive solution: a decentralized peer-to-peer cash system. This revolutionary solution aimed to enable online payments to be sent directly from one person to another without going through an intermediary, like a bank or government. One year later, Bitcoin was officially launched (coincidentally or not, in the wake of the financial crisis), and back then this innovation was only known and discussed in a niche of internet forums and technology circles, largely unnoticed by the broader public. Only in 2013–2014 did Bitcoin start to attract mainstream media attention due to high price volatility and stories of breaches and hacks.

In 2011, a 17-year-old programmer called Vitalik Buterin was first introduced to Bitcoin and, although he initially dismissed it, he later connected with the idea. Vitalik was curious about the decentralized payment system, but as he engaged more in the ecosystem and learnt more about blockchain, he started to believe Bitcoin had limitations by being focused on only one use case: peer-to-peer payments. In 2013, Vitalik wrote the Ethereum whitepaper envisioning this alternative protocol that would power decentralized applications (DApps).[5] Unlike traditional applications, which operate and rely on a central server, DApps function autonomously on blockchain, a decentralized network. This vision was only possible due to the introduction of smart contracts, self-executing contracts on the blockchain that automatically enforce and execute the terms of a contract, based on 'if–then' rules. The innovation of smart contracts enabled the automation of complex operations and agreements, eliminating the need for intermediaries and marking a pivotal moment in the evolution of the industry. Ethereum set itself apart from Bitcoin by facilitating not just cryptocurrency trades but also an array of new use cases and applications across different industries.

In 2014, Vitalik, alongside Gavin Wood and a number of other co-founders, launched a successful crowdsourcing campaign in which they sold ETH (Ethereum native coin) in return for funding (an initial coin offering, or ICO). Ethereum officially launched in 2015 and is still one of the most popular platforms for decentralized applications. By April 2023, Ethereum had over 4,000 DApps running on its platform, including exchanges, NFT marketplaces, financing apps, gaming and social media apps.

In 2014, while working on the Ethereum project, Gavin Wood coined the term Web3. The definition of Web3 as an 'alternative vision of the Web' shifted the discussion from pure crypto and Bitcoin to a wider concept of new technologies, business models and ideas.

Throughout the following years, there has been continued expansion and development in the Web3 space, with new funding approaches and decentralized governance models being tested and a huge number of new applications being built. Between 2017 and 2018, ICOs gained significant popularity as an easy and quick way for new blockchain-based projects to raise funding; it is estimated that $4.9 billion was raised via ICOs during that period.[6] In exchange for funding, users received tokens that could be used as a medium of exchange or utility within the project's ecosystem. By 2019, the concept of decentralized autonomous organizations (DAOs) had gained prominence, offering a novel approach to decentralized governance and decision-making. DAOs are member-owned communities that operate without centralized leadership, where decisions are made collectively by their members, often using governance tokens. These tokens empower individuals to participate in decision-making, for example, by voting on proposals submitted to the DAO, replacing top-down governance structures seen in Web2 with CEOs or boards of directors. At the time of writing (January 2024), there were 9.9 million governance token holders.[7] ICOs and DAOs are examples of the new concepts and models that make up Web3, aligned with the core principle of decentralization of Web3 and emphasis on community engagement and ownership.

The early 2020s witnessed unprecedented growth in the decentralized finance (DeFi) industry, with the amount locked in DeFi protocols going from $700 million at the start of 2020 to $15 billion by December the same year.[8] The term DeFi encompasses financial services applications that are built on the blockchain ecosystem, decentralized networks, removing the need for intermediaries. This period in 2020 is often referred to as the DeFi Summer.

In 2021, non-fungible tokens (NFTs), representing ownership of digital and physical items on the blockchain, captured the world's imagination. Artists, creators, collectors and the world's biggest brands flocked to NFT marketplaces, such as OpenSea, to buy, sell and mint NFTs. Around the same time, blockchain games, integrating blockchain and digitial-asset elements into the gaming experience, made the news. One notable example is *Axie Infinity,* which pioneered a play-to-earn model, providing income to players. In the Philippines, players earned weekly incomes of $300 to $400, which was more than the average local monthly income, unlocking new economies. In 2022 and 2023, there was a new cycle of innovation, with stablecoins and tokenization use cases increasingly discussed in the mainstream news, providing confirmation of the opportunities for disruption in financial services.

Throughout the years, developers and teams have continued to work on the Web3 infrastructure with the emergence and growth of new blockchains and networks as well as privacy, scalability and interoperability technologies. Being an open-source technology, it benefits from the ongoing efforts of thousands of developers.

Demystifying Web3

Given its broad nature, Web3 can sometimes seem overwhelming or opaque. I like to think of Web3 as an umbrella term for this new online decentralized ecosystem powered by blockchain technology.

To understand the full picture, we need to consider the different blocks that make up this vision. For now, we will focus on two key building blocks: principles and foundational blocks. Throughout the book, we will discuss further these blocks with real use cases and examples, as well as adding new concepts relevant to the discussion. Right now, I just want you to be aware of the foundation.

Web3 principles

DECENTRALIZATION

In Web3, services and products are not controlled by a central entity, such as a bank, government or company. Instead, Web3 relies on decentralized networks and protocols. One well-known example is Bitcoin, which uses blockchain technology to create a decentralized and transparent ledger of transactions. Users can send peer-to-peer payments without the need for intermediaries, such as banks or payment providers.

If this decentralized vision is adopted, it could mean the disintermediation of existing companies and institutions. In this scenario, what would their new role be, if intermediaries were no longer required to provide the service, control and governance? What would this mean for their existing business models?

In practice, however, decentralization is not a binary choice and adoption needs to be considered in a spectrum across technology, economics and governance. In the example here, Bitcoin represents a high degree of technological decentralization. The blockchain technology allows for a decentralized network where transactions are processed and verified by a distributed community (called miners) instead of a central authority like a bank. However, other considerations, such as the concentration of power in a few hands (for example, the miners) and governance aspects, like the influence of core developers, can introduce a varying degree of centralization into the system.

Throughout this book, we will discuss different components, use cases and protocols and reflect on the different levels of decentralization. We should note, however, that projects can also evolve in the decentralization spectrum throughout their lifecycle. For example, many projects start with centralized governance, with a few founders and a team of developers building the project and making key decisions, and may evolve into a decentralized governance structure later.

OWNERSHIP

In Web3, ownership means that users control their assets and the data and content that they create or buy on the internet. Web3 introduced a new concept called digital assets, also known as tokens, that can represent ownership of money, art, data, real estate and much more. NFTs, for example, include proof of ownership in their metadata that details existing ownership and their history. This is a fundamental aspect that ensures the integrity, authenticity and value of NFTs in the digital economy.

Community is also essential in Web3, with protocols using tokens as a medium to ensure builders, operators and users own a piece of what they use, build and operate. In essence, these contributors own tokens that represent ownership in these decentralized networks. This ownership acts as an incentive and binds the community together. For example, in Bitcoin, in exchange for updating the ledger and keeping other actors honest, miners receive a reward in BTC (Bitcoin). Other models include receiving tokens for a service, such as providing liquidity for a trade. Sometimes, that same token can also be used to participate in the governance of the network, acting as both a utility and governance token.

IDENTITY

In Web3, users have full control and ownership over their data, which includes their identity as well as money, assets and others. Through self-management of their identity, individuals can provide, revoke or modify access to their data and digital identity. Aspects of their identity can be proven without the full identity profile being shared. Imagine users being able to prove they are over 18 years old, without having to disclose their date of birth. Or banks querying transaction data without seeing where the user was born. Both on-chain data (e.g. transactions or interactions) and off-chain data (e.g. ID or driving licence) can be added to an individual's identity, which provides a fuller picture of an individual and supports financial inclusion. For example, individuals that lack physical IDs could use on-chain data for opening bank accounts or as collateral for loans.

Web3 foundational blocks

TECHNOLOGY
Blockchain is the underlying technology enabling the Web3 ecosystem, a decentralized distributed ledger that stores data across multiple computers. The blocks in the blockchain represent data, and, as new data is validated and added to the network, a new block is created and added permanently to the chain. Every node in the blockchain has a real-time, updated copy of the ledger, which, in simple terms, provides transparency and eliminates the need for reconciliation.

AGREEMENTS/CONTRACTS
Smart contracts are computer programs that run automatically and autonomously on blockchains. In simple terms, they are digital contracts that contain a set of rules and conditions (similar to 'if–then' rules). For example, a smart contract can be programmed to distribute a payment on the 15th of each month. Because actions are performed autonomously, they eliminate the need for intermediaries or human resources, reducing costs significantly.

REPRESENTATION OF VALUE
Digital assets on the blockchain represent a broad category of assets that can either be a store of value or a medium of exchange (similar to a currency), which are recorded and managed on a blockchain

network. Digital assets include cryptocurrencies, CBDCs (issued by central banks), stablecoins, NFTs and tokenized assets.

We will deep-dive into digital assets later in this book, with a number of real use cases and examples. As you will see, digital assets are a significant innovation representing a new digitization of finance, offering improved liquidity, transparency, reduced transaction costs and improved efficiency. As with any new innovation, challenges are also applicable, such as regulatory uncertainties and security concerns currently being addressed and considered by a number of stakeholders in the financial world.

USER INTERFACE

The wallet is the entry point for users. Users can access their data and assets stored on the blockchain through the wallet. Wallets are either non-custodial or custodial. In non-custodial wallets, users have full control over their data and funds. In contrast, custodial wallets are managed and secured by a third party, which has control over the user's funds and data, providing convenience but less direct user control. Custody will be discussed in detail in Chapter 3.

Digital transformation in financial services

DIGITAL DISRUPTION RESHAPING FINANCE

In 1967, Barclays made a well-known disruption to the banking industry, still being used today, by introducing the first ATM (automated teller machine).[9] The introduction of the ATM allowed customers to access cash 24/7, no longer restricted by branch hours. The following years were fuelled by continuous innovation, and the rise of Web1, in the 1990s, prompted banks to explore digital opportunities. In 1994, Stanford Credit Union took the lead, launching the first online banking service, allowing customers to manage their finances without ever having to step into a branch. The advent of smartphones in the early 2000s changed the industry once more. Mobile banking enabled everyday banking on the go. With banking at their fingertips, consumers could receive money from their family, split dinner bills and pay for expenses whether they were at home, abroad or on the move.

However, the 2008 financial crisis served as a turning point, redirecting the focus of incumbents in financial services from innovation towards internal realignment, governance and control measures. This new climate of mistrust towards traditional banking, coupled with the rise of new technologies, paved the way for new players, including fintechs, neobanks and bigtechs. These new players approached financial services from fresh perspectives, targeting specific user segments and leveraging new technologies like automation and AI, to create tailored products and services. Freelancers and founders of small businesses, for example, were now able to keep track of invoices, payments and tax calculations. Leveraging beginner-friendly interfaces, customers were able to have a single view of all of their accounts, start investing and grow their savings.

Fast forward to the 2020s, a time marked by a global pandemic that posed unprecedented challenges to physical banking. The crisis accelerated the move to online banking and reduced the reliance on cash. Consequently, customers became more technology savvy, embracing digital banking with greater confidence and ease.

Customers' expectations of banking have shifted drastically. They now expect digital-first, quick and seamless experiences from all aspects of their life, including financial services. Trust dynamics have also evolved, with new generations of customers, who grew up surrounded by digital and technological experiences, embracing new players in the ecosystem instead of incumbents. An EY survey found that '51% of Gen Z and 49% of millennials named a fintech as their most-trusted financial brand'.[10] Given this new access and adoption of digital channels, customers have become much more open to new and alternative financial products. They are exploring access to financial products previously reserved for a limited group of industry experts.

As we have seen throughout history, the financial services industry is constantly evolving, from the adoption of new technology to adapting to societal changes and customer expectations. Visionary leaders have been quick to embrace digital transformation, recognizing its profound implications for business models and strategies. Big digitalization projects have taken place in the background for years, leveraging new technologies like automation and workflow tools. New innovation driven by fintechs, neobanks and bigtechs have focused mainly on offering new user interfaces plugged into legacy financial systems. However, the reality is that the traditional financial services ecosystem is still famously tangled in a number of legacy technology problems and intermediary complexities. This is where Web3 comes in, representing a fundamental shift aiming to address these deep-rooted challenges and inefficiencies.

Web3 impact on financial services

The internet evolution, from Web1 to Web2, enabled the innovation and adoption of new banking formats such as online and digital banking. However, the money and financial rails were still separate from the internet, perpetuating legacy challenges and complexities. With Web3, there is an opportunity to leverage internet-native rails (blockchain) for financial services and to embed funds and value transfer on it. As Circle, a Web3 native startup, puts it, Web3 aims to '[embed] money into the internet'.[11]

Web3 will fundamentally transform financial services by replacing the existing financial rails, enabling new forms of money and representations of real-world assets.

New financial rails

Historically, financial ledgers have been centralized, with institutions like banks acting as trusted intermediaries responsible for ensuring the integrity and control of financial data. Despite significant efforts and investments to modernize and improve the traditional banking infrastructure, it still faces issues with operational costs, risks and efficiency. International processes, in particular, can be slow and expensive, often hindered by fragmented systems and processes that vary across regions and players.

Web3 introduces a revolutionary alternative to traditional financial infrastructure. In Web3, the functions of handling, storing, processing, validating and authenticating financial data are all performed on blockchain – a decentralized digital ledger. This decentralization means that the role of a centralized entity could no longer be required. As an example, customers can send money to friends and family, across the globe, quickly and with lower transaction fees. While, initially, customers could mostly send cryptocurrencies, new forms of money are now part of the portfolio of payments.

Similarly, consumers are no longer restricted to lengthy approval processes from banks to obtain loans. Instead, they can get a loan from a decentralized finance (DeFi) protocol. Because the smart contract manages all aspects of the loan (from interest, repayment, liquidation and so on), no intermediaries are needed.

New digital forms of money

In contrast to other iterations of the internet, Web3 introduces a new way of thinking about money. While money and how we use it have evolved over time, for example from cash to mobile money, that evolution was always centred on existing centralized banking infrastructure. Web3 pushed the discussion of the future of money in a new direction.

As we discussed earlier, the launch of Bitcoin in 2018 established a new form of money: a decentralized blockchain-based currency, outside the remit of banks and governments. Over the following years, other decentralized cryptocurrencies emerged, used as investments or to buy and sell goods and services in this new digital world. However, the extreme price volatility of these cryptocurrencies restricted their practical use. This led to the emergence of stablecoins – a type of cryptocurrency whose value is pegged to another asset class, such as a fiat currency or gold. In recent years, central banks worldwide have also started to explore their own stable digital currencies (CBDCs), and many incumbents have also launched new forms of money, such as deposit tokens.

We will take a deep dive into the new forms of money in Chapter 4 of this book.

Representation of real-world assets

Web3 is also revolutionizing the financial landscape by bridging the physical and digital worlds. It achieves this by enabling the digital representation of real-world assets, or fractions of the assets, alongside their financial flows, ownership, rights and history. This innovation brings significant benefits, including reduction of settlement time, creation of market liquidity and enhanced transparency of previously illiquid assets. Imagine a world where any asset, from real estate to artwork, can be traded anywhere, 24/7, democratizing investment and unlocking new revenue streams and business models in financial services and beyond. We will discuss tokenization further in Chapter 5 of this book.

The next iteration of the web (Web3) has the potential to become one of the most significant disruptions for financial services, increasing speed, reducing costs, simplifying the industry, and unlocking new products and services. Web3's emphasis on decentralization represents a significant opportunity for financial inclusion, potentially bringing financial services to previously underserved communities. This disruption could lead to the disintermediation of traditional roles and business models.

Financial services players in Web3

Following the disruption and new opportunities created by Web3, a diverse array of new financial services players is emerging, embracing new innovations, concepts and models, and expanding the landscape of companies providing financial services in Web3.

DeFi emergence

Defi, or decentralized finance, represents an ecosystem of decentralized applications that provide financial services products and services (including savings, loans, trading, insurance and more). In Defi, there is no central entity providing financial services, instead, DeFi leverages Web3 technologies, like blockchain and smart contracts, to provide access to finance. If widely adopted, DeFi could disintermediate TradFi with significant impact to existing business models and strategies.

DeFi embraces the core values of the open internet, allowing access to anyone with a smartphone and internet connection, and provides control and ownership to users, often seen as lowering barriers to access, reducing costs and empowering underserved communities.

While DeFi potential is significant, as we will see throughout this book, this is still a young industry trying to find a balance between governance, control and decentralization. Additionally, DeFi applications have steep learning curves with complex user experiences restricting adoption. To fill this gap, CeFi has risen by providing an easier and more familiar point of entry to customers.

CeFi rise

CeFi, or centralized finance, represents new platforms that provide financial services on blockchain, similar to those offered by DeFi. However, in contrast to DeFi, CeFi platforms tend have a higher degree of centralization and often adhere more closely to regulatory requirements. CeFi platforms typically have central entities making decisions, running and governing the platform, similar to traditional companies. CeFi serves as a hybrid between the traditional model and new Web3 concepts and technologies.

TradFi adoption

TradFi is a term used to represent traditional finance. The existing mainstream financial system players, like banks, investment banks and fintechs, would be included in the TradFi term. As discussed earlier, most players in TradFi have adopted technology throughout the years to digitize, simplify and improve the services and products provided to their customers. Those services and products are still offered in a centralized way, and they must comply with existing regulatory requirements, which may constrain the risk and innovation they can take.

Traditional finance players' relationship with Web3 has evolved dramatically, with more companies starting to test and adopt business models and concepts from Web3. Many leading companies are experimenting with central banks, regulators, other institutions and Web3 natives to explore the technology and better understand the risks and benefits. Most experiments and products focus on institutional investors and affluent and high-net-worth (HNW) clients, given that their risk appetite is often higher than typical retail clients. Additionally, investors have shown increased interest in including crypto and digital assets in their portfolios.

Currently, regulatory frameworks are still in their early stages and will require local maturation and global cooperation for Web3 to be broadly adopted in financial services. However, as we continue to see more regulatory clarity around the world, we expect more traditional players will join new startups and companies in taking advantage of emerging technologies and concepts.

Throughout this book, you will see examples of experiments and solutions driven by all of these players. In Part Two we will deep-dive into each player and consider the opportunities and challenges for each one of them.

Web3 criticisms

Before we dive into this new world of Web3, it is important to understand some of the criticisms and concerns that have been raised. While Web3's ethos aims to democratize and empower communities, many believe it is not achieving its promises. *Is Web3 building fairer and more democratic economies?*

Many discussions get heated quickly, with proponents from both sides using several common arguments to back their positions. Some leaders in the industry say those arguments escalate quickly because money is involved. And while that may be part of the reason – after all, money always leads to contentious debate – I believe those debates are about much more than money and technology. A big component of Web3 is questioning existing political norms and societal beliefs.

For example, proponents of Web3 envision a future in which decentralized cryptocurrencies replace or compete with traditional fiat money, challenging the political and societal norms that established central banks as the sole authority in issuing and regulating money. Similarly, Web3 challenges the societal belief that corporations and governments should have broad access to personal information. Web3 even challenges traditional political structures and corporate hierarchies with the introduction of decentralized governance models. No surprise that such big topics lead to heated debates.

Now, let's consider some of the criticisms.

CRITICISM 1: WEB3 PROJECTS ARE NOT REALLY DECENTRALIZED

As we will see throughout this book, the reality is that, currently, Web3 is not as fully decentralized as originally envisioned. Instead, different components of Web3 have different levels of decentralization. However, is full decentralization something that the global population actually wants?

Full decentralization would mean, for example, that users would have to run their own servers or that they would have to secure their money and assets themselves, instead of using an intermediary like a bank, which is not something everyone wants or even can do. Many experts believe that we need to move on from a decentralization discussion. Instead, the industry is providing a spectrum of choices and options for different users. Some will want and will adopt more decentralized solutions, while others will be happy with the support of an intermediary.

CRITICISM 2: WEB3 PROJECTS ARE STILL OWNED BY A HANDFUL OF VCS, CONTRADICTING THE IDEAL OF COMMUNITY-DRIVEN DECENTRALIZATION

As we will see in Chapter 10, currently, some Web3 projects are indeed controlled by a limited group. This group mostly consists of crypto-native and technology-savvy users as well as investors. When tokens are initially distributed, those who were involved earlier on are the ones who benefit the most. This typically includes the project's founder, the core team of developers, venture capital organizations or individuals who provided initial capital and early members of the community. Such a distribution model can lead to a concentration of wealth and influence in the hands of a few individuals, often at odds with the decentralization ethos.

This situation underscores the complexity of implementing some of the foundational vision. So much of this space is still trying to find the right balance between the initial vision and the intricacies involved in the implementation. Decentralized autonomous organizations (DAOs), for example, which are designed to provide full ownership and voice to the community, have shown to be complex undertakings. While DAOs democratize governance, in practice, having a large group of people making decisions is often slow and cumbersome. Additionally, many users in the community are not actually interested or even equipped to be part of the decision process; highlighting a gap between the ideal of universal participation and the realities of community engagement and governance efficiency.

The good news is that this industry has a number of experts from all walks of life and expertise trying to solve some of these complex problems and develop solutions further. Because the technology is open source, anyone, anywhere, can be part of the solution, driving faster innovation.

CRITICISM 3: THE INDUSTRY IS FULL OF SCAMS AND BAD ACTORS, WITHOUT ANY BENEFIT OR REAL VALUE; A SOLUTION TRYING TO FIND A PROBLEM TO SOLVE

While the industry has suffered from scams and fraud stories, real value is already being delivered by this technology.

Throughout this book, we will see a variety of real-world applications of Web3. Notable examples include the use of cryptocurrencies and stablecoins in emerging markets, serving as both a store of value and medium of exchange; providing a lifeboat in complex political and economic environments. For example, migrant workers using blockchain rails to send money home in a faster and cheaper way, or founders leveraging decentralized applications to secure funding used in establishing and expanding their businesses.

The disruptive potential of Web3 highlights the need for thoughtful consideration of its implication for society, governance and the future of finance. As we explore the applications of this emerging technology in financial services, we need to also have a critical and open mindset for existing limitations and challenges.

Future outlook

While Web3 can be traced back to the days of Bitcoin, it has evolved into an ecosystem of new players and solutions that will compose the new phase of the internet. Still in its early days, Web3 has already made a mark with use cases and solutions already live and making inroads in many industries, including social media, gaming, arts and creators economy and financial services. In contrast to other phases of the web, Web3 embeds financial systems and money on the internet. This is a drastic change for an industry that has been running on legacy financial rails for decades, in which transformations mostly occurred at the user interfaces and experience level. Web3 has the potential to drastically change how financial services work and how we think about money.

Web3 will also bring benefits to incumbents. Bain & Company research suggests that 'Web3 could reduce the operational cost to deliver banking services by 15% to 25%' by enabling straight-through processing, reducing duplicative work and eliminating manual reconciliations.[12] More than making existing processes faster, cheaper and simplified, as we will see in this book, Web3 has the potential to unlock new revenue streams and business models not possible before due to technological advancement. But for incumbents to leverage those benefits they will have to rethink their products, services and processes. Many have already started to do so by engaging in experiments with central banks, regulators and other Web3-native companies.

Web3 also has the potential to open financial services to underbanked societies – an area dear to many in the fintech community. Cryptocurrencies and stablecoins are already being used as a store of value, for remittances, as aid for war refugees and for funding to launch businesses in emerging countries.

We are still far from mass adoption, as the technological, reputational and regulatory risks remain front of the mind for many in the traditional financial services industry. In this book, we will look at the solutions and experiments conducted so far, how the different players see this space, and the improvements required for mass adoption. Ultimately, I believe Web3 will represent a shift in how financial services and products are created and consumed, impacting consumers and businesses.

SUMMARY OF KEY POINTS

- Web3 is the next iteration of the internet. It is an umbrella term for a decentralized internet powered by blockchain technology. Web1 was a static web that allowed users to read; Web2 allows users to read and write content; while Web3 aims to allow users to read, write and own their data.

- Web3 encompasses more than crypto. The Web3 ecosystem includes new concepts and business models powered by emerging technology.

- Web3 has the potential to become the most significant disruption for financial services. In contrast to other iterations of the internet, Web3 involves the transfer of financial value, embedding money into the internet.

- Decentralized finance (Defi) has the potential to disintermediate traditional finance. In 2020, there was a boom in the number of use cases and applications created by Defi protocols, this period is called the DeFi Summer.

- Web3 has the potential to make financial services faster, cheaper and simpler. However, the technological, reputational and regulatory risks remain at the front of mind for many senior leaders in traditional financial services.

Endnotes

1 Science Media Museum. A short history of the internet, 3 December 2020, scienceandmediamuseum.org.uk/objects-and-stories/short-history-internet (archived at https://perma.cc/4QGH-9F64)

2 T Stackpole. What is Web3?, *Harvard Business Review*, 10 May 2022, hbr. org/2022/05/what-is-web3 (archived at https://perma.cc/XB4S-NYSD)

3 Statista. Number of internet and social media users worldwide as of April 2023, statista.com/statistics/617136/digital-population-worldwide/ (archived at https://perma.cc/FSL7-X7V4)

4 S Nakamoto. Bitcoin: A peer-to-peer electronic cash system, 21 August 2008, papers.ssrn.com/sol3/papers.cfm?abstract_id=3440802 (archived at https:// perma.cc/SMJ8-G2BK)

5 V Buterin. Ethereum: A next-generation smart contract and decentralized application platform, Etherium, 2014, ethereum.org/content/whitepaper/ whitepaper-pdf/Ethereum_Whitepaper_-_Buterin_2014.pdf (archived at https://perma.cc/PX83-H7NA)

6 H Page. 2017's ICO market grew nearly 100x from Q1 to Q4, Crunchbase, 11 January 2018, news.crunchbase.com/fintech-ecommerce/2017s-ico-market-grew-nearly-100x-q1-q4/ (archived at https://perma.cc/7TDL-75DE)

7 DeepDAO. Organizations, deepdao.io/organizations (archived at https:// perma.cc/7N2Q-63GZ)

8 R Stevens. The 2020 year in review: DeFi, Decrypt, 26 December 2020, decrypt.co/52298/the-2020-year-in-review-defi (archived at https://perma.cc/ L5VE-MRVU)

9 Barclays. From the archives: The ATM is 50, 27 June 2017, home.barclays/ news/2017/06/from-the-archives-the-atm-is-50/ (archived at https://perma.cc/77ZA-7KB2)

10 N Lele, A Udiavar and R Mannamkery. How financial institutions can win the battle for trust, EY, 11 June 2021, www.ey.com/en_us/nextwave-financial-services/how-financial-institutions-can-win-the-battle-for-trust (archived at https://perma.cc/EX7M-D8R5)

11 J Fox-Green and K Razzaghi. The convergence of money and the internet, Circle, www.circle.com/blog/blockchains-and-the-history-of-the-internet (archived at https://perma.cc/RC8P-ERBL)

12 S Erni, R Walker, C Albuquerque, T Olsen, S Soni and S Ganesh. Web3 experiments start to take hold in banking, Bain & Company, 14 December 2022, bain.com/insights/web3-experiments-start-to-take-hold-in-banking/ (archived at https://perma.cc/SR3J-TJHQ)

PART TWO

Emergent use cases driving change in traditional financial services

03

Custody

LOST BITCOINS

Stefan Thomas, a German-born programmer, was living in Switzerland in 2011 when he took a job editing a video called *What is Bitcoin?* At the time, crypto was not popular, but the company he was working for decided to pay him in Bitcoin for editing the video. He was given 7,002 bitcoins for the job.[1] He saved his Bitcoin in a self-custody wallet, wrote down the password on paper and forgot about it, until years later when the value of Bitcoin peaked.

When he went to look for the paper, he couldn't find it. Somehow over the years, Stefan lost the paper with the password. Testing his luck, Stefan tried to guess the password but was unsuccessful. In 2021, he had only had 2 guesses left out of 10; the self-custody wallet he used was designed to permanently erase its contents if someone tried 10 incorrect password guesses. At the time of writing (January 2024), Stefan is still trying to figure out the password that would unlock more than $200 million.

In a similar vein, James Howells, an IT worker living in the UK, lost around 7,500 bitcoins, which in 2023 would have a market value of nearly $217 million. In 2013, James mistakenly threw away the hard drive where he kept the bitcoins in the bin, while cleaning his flat.[2] Since then, he has been on a campaign to get access to the local garbage dump to find his lost fortune. As of the time of writing, he has had no success.

Both Stefan and James are now at peace with the loss of what would have made them millionaires.

In the early days of Bitcoin, the most secure way to store digital assets was in the form of self-custody, often through paper wallets in which investors would write down the private key on a piece of paper. However, tales like Stefan's and James's real-life experiences revealed the inherent risks in self-custody, with many investors either losing their keys or falling victim to theft by nefarious individuals.

Fast forward a few years; centralized exchanges emerged as a convenient way to buy and sell digital assets. These exchanges offered custody services as part of their platforms. However, the growing number of hacking incidents and security breaches raised concerns over the safety of the assets held by those platforms. One notorious example was the infamous hack of MT. Gox exchange in 2014. At the time, MT. Gox was one of the world's largest Bitcoin exchanges and the breach resulted in the theft of 850,000 bitcoins (BTC), now valued at almost $23 billion, from its customers.[3]

As digital assets continued to attract more investment and institutional interest, the demand for custody solutions that not only provided robust security but also complied with regulatory requirements began to surge. One response to this demand was the launch of Anchorage Digital in 2017. In a discussion with Diogo Mónica, co-founder and President of Anchorage Digital, he recounted the origins of Anchorage Digital and the role it aimed to play:

> We decided to make the jump into the digital asset industry in 2017 after a fund approached us with a unique security problem. They had lost the passphrase to a $1.5 million Bitcoin wallet and offered us 20% if we could recover the lost assets. That was a major wake up call for us—here was a very sophisticated institution, which did not have a very sophisticated approach to crypto custody.
>
> Seeing a major opportunity in safe and secure crypto custody, Nathan and I founded Anchorage Digital in 2017.

Given growing pressure from institutional clients, traditional financial institutions, including asset managers and banks, have more recently expanded their custody services to include cryptocurrencies.

The entry of established players into crypto custody is significant, given their extensive experience and market share in traditional financial assets custody. Currently, their offering is mostly still limited to institutional clients and a limited number of cryptocurrencies. However, as regulatory frameworks become clearer and technology improves, we can expect an increase in the number of cryptocurrencies and types of digital assets covered.

Custody

In simple terms, custody is the process of securing assets and the management of the same.

This concept is not something new. In the early days, individuals secured the assets themselves, a form of self-custody. Later, third parties filled this role as custodians, hired to keep assets secure and safe.

ORIGINS OF CUSTODY

Prior to the 20th century, individual investors held their own securities (i.e. stock and bond paper certificates), carrying the risk of damage or theft. However, this self-custody practice started to fade away as investors recognized the inherent risks.

Banks were the natural providers of physical safekeeping services as they already had strong vaults in which they held cash, gold, jewels and other valuables. Over time, banks expanded their services from the safekeeping of physical securities to include settlement, ensuring that the delivery and receipt of securities aligned with the agreed amount, and servicing, such as the collection of dividends and interest, tax payments or reclaims, corporate actions and others.

As paper was replaced by electronic records and new regulations were introduced, so was the custody model. Nowadays, custody is provided by various institutions, primarily brokers, commercial banks and investment banks that cater to different customer segments.[4]

Digital asset custody

In crypto or Web3, custody also means the process of storing assets securely and safely. However, instead of traditional financial assets, we are referring to digital assets and cryptocurrencies. Additionally, digital asset custodians do not technically store any of the assets since all data and transactions are held on the blockchain. Instead, they secure investors' private keys, which are the proof that investors own the assets held within their wallet.

Web3 wallets

You may have heard of crypto wallets. However, unlike a normal wallet, which can hold cash, credit cards, loyalty cards and IDs, crypto wallets don't technically hold crypto or digital assets. Instead, crypto wallets store the public and private keys required to buy, sell or interact with cryptocurrencies while the users' funds and assets live on the blockchain.

When a user performs a transaction, they are not sending crypto tokens from their mobile phone to someone else's mobile phone. Instead, the user's private key signs the transaction and broadcasts it to the blockchain network. The network then includes the transaction to reflect the updated balance in both the sender's and recipient's addresses. In short, crypto wallets are designed to securely store private keys and interact with blockchain networks.

Before we dive deeper, let's understand the concepts.

DEFINITIONS OF CRYPTOGRAPHIC KEYS AND SEED PHRASES

Public keys are used as public addresses for transactions, similar to a traditional bank account number. You need to know the public address to send assets to someone else and likewise provide it to someone else to receive funds. Some wallets have adopted QR codes to make this process easier.

Private keys are used to digitally sign a transaction, similar to a personal identification number (PIN). In other words, they are used to authorize the movement of funds. However, unlike a PIN, private keys cannot be reset. If lost or stolen, owners can lose access to their funds forever.

Seed phrase is a list of 12 randomly generated words, which act as a backup or recovery mechanism in case the user loses access to their device. Anyone with access to the seed phrase is able to get full access to the funds held in the wallet, so it is important to keep the phrase in a secure location. Many wallets advise against printing it out, taking a picture or screenshot, or even writing it down, given that the loss or theft of the phrase could lead to the investor losing all access to their funds.

The public and private keys and seed phrases are generated when a wallet is created.

While in traditional banking, all custodians are financial institutions, as required by law. In Web3, holders, both individual and institutional investors, have the opportunity to become their own custodians. A simple analogy is whether investors will keep their money and valuable items safely secured under their bed (self-custody), or if they store them at a vault secured by a third party (third-party custody).

Self-custody wallets

In self-custody wallets, the investor holds their own private keys and has higher control over their assets since they are the only one able to access them. Self-custody was created based on the Web3 ethos of decentralization and full data ownership, in which users have full control over their data and assets and do not require intermediaries for services, often referred to as 'being your own bank'.

However, self-custody wallets also have challenges. The user experience (UX), for example, is relatively complex and requires some technical know-how. In self-custody, investors are responsible for their own wallet security against hacks or other vulnerabilities. Note that security activities are often performed by large teams within banks, with high budgets, so it is a big ask for individuals to do.

Additionally, in self-custody, investors are responsible for keeping keys and seed phrases safe, which may seem simple but is hard to achieve in reality. There are a number of similar stories to Stefan and James, featured at the start of this chapter, of individuals losing or forgetting their keys. Such mistakes can even be made by experts in this industry.

STOLEN FUNDS

Ivan Bianco, a blockchain gaming YouTuber from Brazil, started Fraternidade Crypto in 2014 and has gained over 2.2 million views so far. In 2023, during a live broadcast, Ivan accidentally opened the Notepad application, with the private key and seed phrase for his Metamask wallet (a self-custody wallet).

When the influencer realized his mistake, he abruptly ended the broadcast and rushed to create a new wallet, but the money was already gone. One of the viewers was quick to access Ivan Bianco's assets and take approximately $60,000 in crypto and NFTs from his wallet, in a matter of minutes. The stolen assets included 86,600 MATIC tokens and 3.35 ETH.[5]

Being a big influencer in the blockchain space, this misstep was a reminder of how easily mistakes can be made which can impact individuals' life savings. As a last resort, Ivan filed a report with the police without much hope. But, unexpectedly, the thief reached out to Ivan Bianco after the incident, expressing remorse and returning the vast majority of the funds.

Third-party custody wallets

Third-party custody wallets emerged as an alternative for users who do not want to manage their own accounts or find it too intimidating to deal with the tech. Third-party custodians are (usually) regulated, licensed and often follow traditional Know Your Customer (KYC), anti-money laundering (AML) and other checks. They hold the custody of the private keys on behalf of their clients and are responsible for the security and safety of the investors' keys and assets. The user interface of third-party custodial wallets also tends to be much more friendly and easier to use, providing a good bridge for Web2 native users to get onboarded into Web3.

However, this type of custody also has drawbacks. Investors must trust that custodians will keep their assets safe and act in their best interest. They could run the risk of losing control over their assets if, for example, the custodian goes bankrupt, is hacked or decides to freeze the investors' assets. One example of such risk was discussed at the start of this chapter, in which investors who had entrusted their Bitcoins to MT. Gox lost their funds during the hack. Other hacks and collapses have generated similar pain to investors in the last few years. In 2022, crypto investors lost nearly $4 billion to hackers, according to Chainalysis.[6] Every time a big hack takes place, we see a movement of funds from third-party custody wallets to self-custody wallets, with investors trying to protect their funds.

Not your keys, not your crypto

Third-party custody is perceived by maximalists as going against the original ethos of Web3 of decentralization and data ownership. In the Web3 vision, investors do not require centralized parties to access funds and have full ownership over their assets. Since whoever has control of the private keys has custody over the assets, the mantra 'Not your keys, not your crypto' is often used by veterans to reflect this sentiment.

Self-custody is such a critical feature for this group of maximalists that in 2023 the announcement of 'Ledger Recover' by Ledger raised significant controversy in the industry.

LEDGER
Recovery feature backlash

Launched in 2014, in France, Ledger provides security and infrastructure solutions to digital assets, for consumers and institutional investors. Ledger sells a number of custody wallets. One of the well-known products of the company is Ledger Nano, a self-custody hardware wallet, a small USB device in which private keys are stored offline.

In 2023, Ledger (the company) announced they would be launching a new opt-in recovery feature, available for Nano X models. With this recovery feature, users who opted in would be sharing their seed phrase with a set of trusted custodians, including Legder. This way, if users lost or forgot their seed phrase, they could ask Ledger for help, prove their identity and get their access restored.

This announcement provoked criticisms from the community. In their view, this update would go against the company ethos of 'be your own bank' and created security concerns around who would be able to access their keys.

While a maximalist view of self-custody may appeal to those who prioritize autonomy and control above all else, it is important to recognize that not everyone has the technical expertise or resources to manage their digital assets safely. And so, both models of self-custody and third-party custodian should be considered, with investors adopting the one that most aligns with their risk and use case.

Often, investors and users will start with third-party custody and, as they learn more about the concepts, move into self-custody wallets. Sometimes, investors may even adopt both models, with a big portion of their wealth in self-custody wallets and a smaller portion used for daily trading in third-party custody wallets.

Digital asset custody in action

In 2023, CoinMarketCap listed 26,230 cryptocurrencies,[7] an exponential increase from the seven cryptocurrencies reported in 2013.[8] As the world of Web3 continues to expand, new types of digital assets will continue to emerge, increasing their collective value and the need for safe and secure custody.

Exchanges

Exchange wallets were one of the earliest entrants into the digital custody market, with the first few emerging around 2010 to allow investors to buy and sell Bitcoin. Exchanges have come a long way since those early days and are now much more mature, licensed and regulated by local jurisdictions worldwide. Many are now providing self-custody wallets alongside their third-party wallets, providing a bridge between Web2 and Web3.

COINBASE

Founded in 2012 by Brian Armstrong and Fred Ehrsam, Coinbase has played a pivotal role in making cryptocurrencies accessible to millions of users worldwide. At its core, Coinbase operates a centralized crypto exchange that also provides custody for investors. In simple terms, when an investor buys, sells or trades digital assets using the Coinbase.com exchange, those assets are securely stored by Coinbase.

Beyond its widely recognized exchange, Coinbase also offers the Coinbase wallet, which is a self-custody wallet in which users are in full control of their keys and assets. Challenges related to self-custody wallets (as discussed earlier) apply to this wallet. Recently, Coinbase announced changes to this wallet to make the service more streamlined and easier to use, with users able to send funds to friends or family via a simple text message.

Coinbase's mission revolves around simplifying the onboarding process into the world of Web3 and digital assets. In alignment with this vision, in 2023, Coinbase launched Wallet as a Service (WaaS). WaaS is a scalable and secure set of wallet infrastructure APIs, designed to enable companies to create and deploy fully customizable on-chain wallets for their end users. 'Wallet-as-a-service could help bring the next hundred million customers into Web3 through a seamless wallet-onboarding experience,' stated the announcement. Instead of the traditional seed phrase, WaaS is powered by multi-party computation (MPC). 'In a world where wallets are simple, companies can finally build Web3 experiences accessible to everyone regardless of technical knowledge.'[9]

Crypto-native custodians

Crypto-native custodians emerged to provide custody of cryptocurrencies to institutional clients. Many of those companies were created by founders who had previously worked in the fintech or financial services space and saw the emergence of digital assets as a new asset class. While they started with custody as the first use case, they quickly expanded to other areas of Web3.

ANCHORAGE DIGITAL

Diogo Mónica and Nathan McCauley met while working together at Square. Later, both decided to move to Docker, where they helped secure the core infrastructure used in top banks, governments and the world's three largest cloud providers. In 2017, seeing a demand for institutional-grade security solutions, they decided to take the leap and launch Anchorage Digital.

Throughout the years, the team focused on building the custody solution further and pursuing regulatory oversight. In 2021, Anchorage Digital made history when it became the first crypto bank federally chartered by the US Office of the Comptroller of the Currency (OCC). Since its launch as a custodian, it has expanded to a robust suite of additional services, such as secure trading, financing, staking and governance.

Diogo Mónica, co-founder and President of Anchorage Digital, told me about this journey:

Anchorage Digital provides safe and secure infrastructure for institutions to participate in the digital asset ecosystem. As home to the only federally chartered digital asset bank, our platform is designed to keep assets safe. But unlike a traditional bank, Anchorage Digital Bank deals primarily with digital assets.

Safe and secure digital asset custody is the basis of our institutional platform. While we started with custody in 2017, we have since scaled our platform offerings in response to growing institutional demand. Today, Anchorage Digital offers custody, settlement, staking, trading, governance, and more, similar to what you'd see as a suite of offerings at a traditional bank or financial institution, yet all focused on crypto, and tailored for institutions.

Our global client base includes a wide range of institutions, including crypto protocols, investment funds, SEC-registered investment advisers, family offices, and other financial institutions.

Diogo describes the vision for the company:

At Anchorage Digital, we believe wide-scale crypto adoption is inevitable. As the digital asset class continues to grow, our ultimate vision is to provide the infrastructure that powers a major portion of the global economy.

Traditional custodians

In recent years, traditional financial institutions and banks have expanded their custody services to include cryptocurrencies. The expansion in this market was due to growing pressure from clients and regulatory clarity in US, Europe and Asia.

FIDELITY PROVIDES CUSTODY SERVICES TO INSTITUTIONAL CLIENTS

Fidelity, the US-based asset manager, was one of the first traditional financial institutions to offer custody for institutional clients. Back in 2014, Fidelity Investments started to research blockchain and digital assets solutions and one year later created a dedicated blockchain incubator. The incubator was composed of blockchain technologists, product managers and financial and legal specialists, who continued the research, academic partnerships and experiments over the following years.

Over the same period, Fidelity noticed a demand from its institutional clients to handle cryptocurrency custody and trade execution. In 2018, it decided to launch a separate entity called Fidelity Digital Assets – the 'first step in a long-term vision to create a full-service enterprise-grade platform for digital assets,' stated the Fidelity leadership during the launch.[10] In March 2019, Fidelity began to offer bitcoin custody services, crypto trading and execution services.

Over the years, Fidelity expanded its crypto services and currently offers bitcoin and ether custody and trading. The company continues to work towards increasing its asset coverage and services provided. Fidelity's entry into the digital asset custody space signified the increased interest in cryptocurrencies by institutional investors and helped build trust in the industry. In recent years, other traditional institutions have followed suit and provided digital asset custody to institutional clients.

Opportunity for traditional custodians

Currently, traditional financial services are at different stages of their digital asset journey, but many start their journey via a custody or tokenization use case. Given that custody is the bread and butter of traditional companies, and there is increased interest in digital assets from institutional investors, there is a clear market opportunity for traditional custodians to join this space.

Traditional custodians have a lengthy experience of providing safe and secure custody of assets while complying with regulations. They have been providing custody of traditional assets for decades, and are well positioned to take the lead as new regulations emerge.

Institutional clients have also shown an appetite for solutions to be provided by traditional institutions. Many institutional investors want to increase their digital asset allocation and would be propelled to do so if they could have an integrated portfolio solution. A Celent and BNY Mellon survey suggested that '72% of institutional investors would like an integrated provider for all digital asset needs'.[11]

However, traditional financial custodians who provide digital asset custody offerings or want to do so in the future are also faced with a learning curve. For example, there is no standardization in the industry, with each protocol choosing its own governance, consensus mechanisms and smart contract languages. Custodians must understand the different concepts and risks of this new technology.

Sub-custodians

While some traditional financial services built the custody services internally, others use sub-custodian providers to build their digital asset custody offerings. Those sub-custodians have the technology and industry knowledge of digital assets, while traditional financial services have a strong client base and regulatory knowledge. The end clients (investors) interact directly with their traditional financial institution through the same interface and experience as for traditional assets.

This type of 'white label' solution is one used extensively in banking and fintech. In essence, a financial technology solution is rebranded and customized by banks or fintechs. This allows them to offer new products to their customers without having to build solutions from scratch but instead leverage existing solutions in the market. From the client's perspective, they only see and engage with the bank's or fintech's brand.

Challenges of digital asset custody

Custodians face a number of challenges in providing secure and reliable custody services for digital assets. Some key challenges to consider include security, accessibility and regulatory requirements.

Security risk

Many custodians are, in fact, no strangers to cyber-attacks and breaches. In response, custodians have prioritized risk controls and insurance options throughout the years to protect against challenges associated with safeguarding digital assets. Some exchanges, namely Binance, even created emergency reserves held to protect investors' assets. Although this is not a standard in the industry, I can clearly see these types of schemes becoming more prominent in the future, similar to compensation schemes in traditional finance, which were set up as a response to financial crises in traditional markets.

BINANCE HIT BY HACKERS' ATTACK

Back in May 2019, one of the world's largest cryptocurrency exchanges, Binance, confirmed that hackers had stolen over $40 million worth of Bitcoin.

Hackers used various attack methods to carry out the 'large-scale security breach'. The theft occurred from the company's hot wallet (which, at the time of the attack, accounted for 2 per cent of its total bitcoin).[12] Once the transactions were executed, various alarms were triggered in the Binance system, so it immediately stopped all withdrawals.

Binance noted that it would cover the event in full, and no user funds would be impacted by this attack. User losses were covered by the Secure Asset Fund for Users (SAFU), an emergency fund to protect users' funds, created by Binance in July 2018. The fund is composed of a percentage of trading fees that are committed to this fund.

Accessibility vs security

Given the new nature of digital assets and the rapid growth of this industry, digital asset custodians face unique challenges in ensuring the security of the assets and wallets of their clients. One universal challenge is finding the right balance between ease of use and security. Different investors' profiles will value one more than the other. For example, an investor who trades frequently will prioritize being able to access assets (usability) quickly. In contrast, an investor who plans to hold assets for the long term may value security above all else.

To tailor to the investors' requirements, different custodians will use a variety of methods to store the private keys, with the most common categories including hot, cold and warm wallets.

DEFINITIONS OF DIGITAL WALLET TYPES

Hot wallets are connected to the internet; the private keys are always online. Since this does not require human intervention, everything happens automatically, providing a seamless user experience. Investors can easily and quickly access and trade their digital assets. However, this connectivity to the internet also makes hot wallets more vulnerable to cyber security threats.

Cold wallets are the opposite to warm wallets. The private keys are stored offline, and human intervention is required to digitally sign each transaction, making it less convenient for the user. However, given that private keys are stored offline, the wallet's security is maximized, making it less susceptible to cyber-attacks.

Warm wallets combine some of the convenience of hot wallets with an additional level of security. Warm wallets are always connected to the internet but require human intervention to sign every transaction.

Some custodians will use a combination of storage methods and additional features to make it safer for the investor. Additional security techniques have been developed and are being applied by custodians, including multisignature, a feature that requires multiple private keys to sign the transaction. This feature provides further security, given that, even if one or a few keys are compromised, the transaction is still not completed, protecting the investor.

Regulatory compliance

The regulatory environment for digital assets is still evolving and custodians must stay up to date with changing regulations to ensure compliance. As new forms of digital assets are included in their remit, custodians face the challenge of keeping up to date with different classifications and frameworks by regulators. A complex task for custodians with a global footprint, in which interpretations and classifications of different digital assets vary: is it a security, commodity, currency or other?

Risk management, controls and segregation of duties

CELSIUS NETWORK

Founded in 2018, Celsius Network was a lending and borrowing platform aimed at disrupting traditional banking by offering exceedingly high returns, as much as 18.6 per cent at one point. Celsius Network grew quickly, attracting both retail and institutional users. By October 2021, the company claimed that it had $25 billion in assets under management.[13]

Celsius' Earn program was its main product and the one often advertised. The program allowed users to deposit crypto assets into an account held by Celsius, and receive rewards in the form of weekly interest rates.

In April 2022, Celsius introduced a custody program after it was ordered by the New Jersey Bureau of Securities to create a product that was distinguished from Celsius' Earn product. The new custody program allowed customers to continue receiving rewards for their existing Earn accounts but required them to make all future deposits into a Custody account. For unaccredited customers, residing in nine states where Celsius could not offer Custody accounts, their accounts were moved to a Withhold status.

In June 2022, amid crypto markets' decline and the bankruptcy of Terra-Luna, an algorithm stablecoin, Celsius started facing liquidity issues and announced it would be pausing all withdrawals, swaps and transfers between accounts. In simple terms, 1.7 million users who deposited money with Celsius were not able to take it out. After a month of turmoil, on 13 July 2022, Celsius filed for Chapter 11 bankruptcy protection.

Investigations, led by an independent examiner in Celsius' bankruptcy case, have since found that the custody program was launched without sufficient accounting and operational controls or technical infrastructure. 'Custody accounts did not regularly reconcile with assets held in the Custody wallet, with shortfalls in custody accounts being funded from other holdings,' stated the report.[14] Additionally, the company did not have segregation of client assets since 'no effort was made to segregate or separately identify any assets associated with the Withhold accounts', which led to uncertainty on which assets belonged to the customer at the time of the bankruptcy.

Similar to Celsius, other companies in this space have since demonstrated a lack of controls and segregation of duties – practices that are common in traditional finance and raised by many as required for this industry to grow and evolve.

Diogo Mónica noted how events in 2022 (exchange fraud and bankruptcy) highlighted the need for separation between custody and exchange functions:

> Market events from 2022 highlighted how a clear distinction between custody and exchange is a critical check-and-balance missing in crypto today. Separating custodian and exchange functions is a time-tested standard in traditional finance market structure. That is why you would never custody a security on the New York Stock Exchange.
>
> The vertical integration of crypto platforms can create potential conflicts-of-interest and undermine market stability. The industry saw this firsthand with the FTX collapse, when billions in digital assets were left stuck on a failed exchange.

As a third-party custodian, Anchorage Digital is paving a path forward for safe, secure, and regulated market structure. Drawing from the playbook of traditional finance market structure will be key to unlocking the next phase of institutional crypto adoption.

A similar view was raised by Alex Manson, CEO of SC Ventures. In a recent discussion with Alex, he described his journey in digital assets and how there was no institutional-grade infrastructure when he embarked on this journey. Led by increased interest from institutional clients, Alex looked to engage in the industry but noted that the available solutions lacked true segregation, governance and client asset-protection measures that are standard for affiliated activities such as exchange, brokerage and lending businesses in traditional institutions:

When we first started to look into digital assets, we thought we would like to test with an asset class to trade cryptocurrencies. But if you trade cryptocurrencies, you have to put them somewhere and when we looked around, we only found startups, which may be well funded but they lacked governance structures. The governance they presented would not be acceptable to a bank or institutional investors.

The problem with custody, specifically, was that it was amalgamated with exchange, wallet and payments services. In a regulated environment, such activities are segregated to mitigate the risk of fraud. The custodian is separate from the exchange, where you execute your transactions, which is again separate to the settlement. Segregation of tasks and duties is critical. Even though those startups were well funded and had good technologies, their governance and set-up were not at an institutional-grade level.

At that juncture, we parked the idea of trading the asset class, which we have dusted off since then, and started focusing on the infrastructure. We started with custody, the first step in digital assets and a necessary condition for institutional adoption, and built Zodia Custody from scratch. On the back of Zodia Custody, we built Zodia Markets, a brokerage and exchange platform, again targeted to the institutional market.

Future outlook

In traditional banking, clients have become used to a seamless experience in which they can transfer money to their friends using their mobile number, pay for groceries, shop and buy a simple coffee with their phone. Banking users are used to being onboarded and accessing new services via log-in authentication, a combination of username and password, or via biometric authentication, fingerprints or facial recognition. If they lose or forget their username or password or both, they expect the financial institution to help them regain access via email, customer support or by raising a ticket. If they lose their card or have questions about a specific transaction, the bank will quickly cancel the existing card, send a new one, and revert the transaction while investigating. There is a new expectation from users that someone will help them with access, recovery of funds and provide 24/7 support.

Given their familiarity with Web2 banking, new retail users tend to start their journey by using third-party custody wallets. Those tend to provide a closer user experience to the one in Web2, and many users feel a sense of protection from third parties. If something goes wrong, they have a number to call or an address to send an email to. As they become more comfortable, some of them eventually move to the higher control of their assets given by self-custody wallets, often led by hack or bankruptcy stories.

From the perspective of institutional investors, they rarely utilize self-custody wallets due to legal and regulatory requirements and operational complexity. In response to investors' needs and expectations, third-party custodians have emerged as a significant presence over the years. The crypto custody market was estimated to be worth $223 billion in January 2022, up from $32 billion in January 2019, according to Markets and Markets.[15]

Recent attacks and scandals, such as the Celsius incident and FTX collapse in 2022, have drawn the attention of governments and regulators worldwide. While new regulations for managing digital assets are being created and discussed, for example, in the US registered investment advisors must use 'qualified custodians', there is still no global definition and classification of digital assets or a singular global approach. We will discuss the impacts of regulation further in the following chapters.

There is a clear market opportunity for custodian services in digital assets. However, traditional custodians need to ensure they understand the nuances and differences between blockchain and traditional systems. Additionally, custodians will need to consider the unique characteristics and challenges of different digital assets.

SUMMARY OF KEY POINTS

- Custody entails the process of securing assets and management of the same. In traditional finance, custodians secure financial assets, while in Web3 they secure digital assets.

- In contrast to traditional financial markets, digital asset custodians do not store any of the assets; instead, they secure investors' private keys.

- In Web3, there are two main types of custody options: self-custody and third-party custody. Self-custody gives full control to the investors; third-party custody provides convenience to investors.

- There is a clear market opportunity for traditional financial institutions to expand their offerings in digital asset custody, given previous experience in custody and increased interest from existing institutional clients.

- Custodians in this space need to ensure they are building secure and robust solutions that comply with regulatory requirements. Each type of digital asset will have its unique characteristics and challenges that should be considered when providing custody services.

Endnotes

1 N Popper. Lost passwords lock millionaires out of their Bitcoin fortunes, *The New York Times*, 12 January 2021, nytimes.com/2021/01/12/technology/bitcoin-passwords-wallets-fortunes.html (archived at https://perma.cc/H32Z-U3XJ)

2 S Carter. Man accidentally threw away $127 million in bitcoin and officials won't allow a search, CNBC, 20 December 2017, cnbc.com/2017/12/20/man-lost-127-million-worth-of-bitcoins-and-city-wont-let-him-look.html (archived at https://perma.cc/WF48-4LZ5)

3 P Mishra. Infamously hacked crypto exchange Mt. Gox delays repayment deadline by a year, CoinDesk, 21 September 2023, coindesk.com/business/2023/09/21/mt-gox-pushes-repayments-by-a-year/ (archived at https://perma.cc/6UFT-57UN)

4 D Chan, F Fontan, S Rosati and D Russo. The securities custody industry, European Central Bank Occasional paper series, 2007, (68), www.ecb.europa.eu/pub/pdf/scpops/ecbocp68.pdf (archived at https://perma.cc/6JUK-ZPF9)

5 P Ćwik. YouTuber loses $60k in crypto after accidentally disclosing his seed phrase during a live stream, *Coinpaper*, 1 September 2023, coinpaper.com/2202/you-tuber-loses-60k-in-crypto-after-accidentally-disclosing-his-seed-phrase-during-a-live-stream (archived at https://perma.cc/5ZC7-DGGE)

6 Chainalysis team. 2022 biggest year ever for crypto hacking with $3.8 billion stolen, primarily from DeFi protocols and by North Korea-linked attackers, Chainalysis, 1 February 2023, blog.chainalysis.com/reports/2022-biggest-year-ever-for-crypto-hacking/ (archived at https://perma.cc/2AQH-3FJ4)

7 coinmarketcap.com (archived at https://perma.cc/5GET-3EK4)

8 J Howarth. How many cryptocurrencies are there in 2023?, Exploding Topics, 14 March 2023, explodingtopics.com/blog/number-of-cryptocurrencies (archived at https://perma.cc/XEB7-UGJK)

9 P McGregor. Coinbase announces Wallet as a Service. Now any company can seamlessly onboard their users to web3, Coinbase blog, 8 March 2023, www.coinbase.com/pt/blog/coinbase-announces-wallet-as-a-service-now-any-company-can-seamlessly(archived at https://perma.cc/5GET-3EK4)

10 Fidelity Investments. Fidelity launches new company, Fidelity Digital Assets, 15 October 2018, businesswire.com/news/home/20181015005732/en/Fidelity%C2%AE-Launches-New-Company-Fidelity-Digital-Assets (archived at https://perma.cc/LH6A-T8H5)

11 Celent. Institutional investing 2.0: Migration to digital assets accelerates, Celent and BNY Mellon, October 2022, media.licdn.com/dms/document/media/C4E1FAQGihvaRbpTu8g/feedshare-document-pdf-analyzed/0/1669461659673?e=1707955200&v=beta&t=DbMLGXNiSKvKfc78jsIeNVSXjbiVfJDKKdwanVElOe4(archived at https://perma.cc/5GET-3EK4)

12 A Kharpal. Hackers steal over $40 million worth of bitcoin from one of the world's largest cryptocurrency exchanges, CNBC News, 8 May 2019, cnbc.com/2019/05/08/binance-bitcoin-hack-over-40-million-of-cryptocurrency-stolen.html (archived at https://perma.cc/8VML-CTSY)

13 CNBC News. From $25 billion to $167 million: How a major crypto lender collapsed and dragged many investors down with it, 18 July 2022, cnbc. com/2022/07/17/how-the-fall-of-celsius-dragged-down-crypto-investors.html (archived at https://perma.cc/26CU-ZLWE)

14 S Pillay. Interim report of Shoba Pillay, *Examiner*, 19 November 2022, cases.stretto. com/public/x191/11749/CORRESPONDENCE/117490330235000000000004.pdf (archived at https://perma.cc/JG8T-QQQ9)

15 J Roy. Tech talk: Crypto custody, 1 May 2023, s201.q4cdn.com/666322591/ files/doc_downloads/2023/05/Tech-Talk-4-Crypto-Custody.pdf (archived at https://perma.cc/JUH9-GMK8)

04

Evolution of money and payments

consumer makes a payment for a good or service, the funds are transferred from their bank (the issuing bank) to a player like Visa (the scheme), and then Visa transfers the funds over to an acquirer (like Worldpay). The acquirer then performs what is called a 'last mile settlement', which is when the merchant actually receives the funds.

While Worldpay was already providing the option for merchants to receive the funds in either fiat or stablecoin, the other steps in the process were performed using fiat and traditional rails. With Visa now settling transactions using stablecoins over the blockchain, there is one additional step in the process that uses the new payment rail and money form. Instead of relying on payment rails that can take a couple of days, the transfer can be done instantly, accelerating the transaction time, reducing costs and improving efficiency.

This innovation by Visa is more than a technical upgrade, it is a pivotal chapter in the ongoing evolution of money and money movement.

Money has played a vital role in human history. From bartering to digital currencies, each step has made transactions faster and more convenient. Despite technological advancements in the payments system, it is still riddled with complexities, limitations and delays. Blockchain technology, as evidenced by Visa's pioneering steps, holds promise in addressing those challenges.

Evolution of money

The simplest way for individuals to exchange value is to exchange goods and services with one another, the practice of bartering.[3] In ancient societies, bartering allowed individuals to trade items they had in surplus for those they lacked. In most cases, two people would exchange goods or something of value; for example, one farmer would trade vegetables while another would provide utensils. However, this process had limitations. Individuals had to find someone who not only wanted what they offered but also had what they needed.

As societies evolved, so did the need for a more efficient trading system. Around 700 BCE, the ancient kingdom of Lydia introduced metal coins.[4] These were made from a mixture of silver and gold and had a design on one side while the other was marked with simple punches. However, carrying large quantities of silver and gold proved inconvenient and risked loss or theft. Eventually, banks started using paper banknotes for depositors and borrowers to carry around in place of metal coins. This paper money could be used to buy goods and services and taken to the bank at any time to be exchanged for their face value in metal, usually silver or gold. Gradually, governments assumed a supervisory role and later replaced paper money (i.e. promises to pay in gold or silver) with fiat paper money (i.e. dollars, pounds, yen and so on).

In modern economies, money includes the form of currency produced by a central bank (bank notes and coins) and deposits that people hold in banks. For banks, reserves held by central banks represent another form of money.[5]

Later, technological innovations improved convenience and access, with money being represented digitally. In the 1950s, credit cards were introduced, disrupting the way consumers made purchases on credit. As the internet adoption grew, online payments emerged, with the launch of Amazon, and Pizza Hut selling online pizzas in 1994. In 2001, PayPal was born, providing online payments and money transfer services.[6] The 2000s were characterized by the emergence of contactless cards and mobile payments.

In 2009, the introduction of Bitcoin disrupted money, emerging as the first decentralized digital currency – a currency that was not issued by a government or a bank and that did not run on a centralized financial system but instead on blockchain, a decentralized payment rail.

Web3 digital currencies

Bitcoin

As discussed in Chapter 2, one of the key motivations behind the Bitcoin development was enabling peer-to-peer payments. In 2010, the first exchange of Bitcoin for goods took place, and since then, other brands and stores have started to accept this means of payment.

BITCOIN PIZZA DAY

The first documented purchase of physical goods using Bitcoin occurred on 18 May 2010, when Laszlo Hanyecz, a programmer, made a post on a Bitcoin forum called Bitcointalk announcing he would pay '10,000 bitcoins for a couple of pizzas'. A couple of days later, on 22 May, Hanyecz shared on the same forum that he had successfully traded 10,000 bitcoins for two pepperoni pizzas.

At the time of the transaction, Bitcoin value was relatively insignificant; it is believed that 10,000 bitcoins were equivalent to approximately $41. Throughout the following years, however, Bitcoin had an astronomical increase in value, reaching an all-time high as values exceeded over $65,000 in November 2021.[7] This event is considered historically important to the crypto community and is still celebrated every year on 22 May as Bitcoin Pizza Day. This trivial transaction represents to many the evolution and rapid growth of the crypto space.

After the first Bitcoin payment for two pizzas, more individuals and businesses started to show interest in Bitcoin. However, Bitcoin's price saw significant volatility, attracting media attention and commentaries from financial experts worldwide.

The volatility and price uncertainty of Bitcoin restricts its use, by many, for everyday transactions. Buyers may be cautious about exchanging bitcoins for goods as they expect the value to go up, while sellers may be hesitant to accept bitcoins as a means of payment if they expect the value to go down.

Stablecoins

In 2014, the first few stablecoins were introduced by private companies, non-banks, aiming to provide a solution for users and businesses seeking price stability. This is particularly relevant since popular cryptocurrencies, like Bitcoin and Ethereum, suffer from price volatility, making them less useful as a means of exchange and more suitable as an investment or speculative form. Stablecoins were designed to maintain a stable value by being pegged to a physical commodity like gold, by algorithms or by government-issued fiat currency.

Fiat-backed stablecoins combine the benefits of decentralization and transparency of blockchain with the stability of the fiat currency. They were the perfect currency to be used by both businesses and customers for retail and services, cross-border payments and remittances.

STABLECOINS PEGGED TO THE US DOLLAR

In 2014, a startup based in Santa Monica, California, introduced the first dollar-backed digital currency. Initially coined Realcoin, it was later rebranded as Tether (USDT).[8] Tether was originally built on top of Bitcoin (blockchain) and later expanded to other blockchains, becoming an essential trading asset among crypto enthusiasts.

Throughout the years, however, Tether faced controversy, with some critics arguing that USDT stablecoin was not actually backed by real US dollars. The lack of transparency and formal audits further exacerbated sceptics' concerns regarding Tether's claim of a 1:1 peg with the US dollar. In 2023, the company claimed to be moving toward a full audit to prove it had assets to back its digital currencies.

In 2018, amid the controversy with Tether, USDC was conceived as a transparent, regulated alternative. Two of the largest cryptocurrency companies, Coinbase and Circle, joined forces to create an independent member-based consortium called Centre. Centre's mission was to provide governance and standards for the future of the digital financial ecosystem.

Later in the year, Circle launched USDC, as the sole regulated issuer under US money transmission frameworks. As the name suggests, USDC is a regulated fiat-collateralized stablecoin whose value is tied to the US dollar. For every 1 USDC in circulation, 1 dollar is held in collateral.

The creation of USDC signalled a maturation of the industry, providing users with a stable, transparent and regulated way to use US dollars on blockchains. It quickly gained traction for multiple financial applications and is one of the largest stablecoins in circulation.

In 2023, Coinbase and Circle announced that Centre would no longer exist as a stand-alone entity, with Circle remaining the issuer of USDC, holding operations and governance responsibilities in-house, holding all the smart contract keys, complying with regulations on governance of reserves and enabling USDC on new blockchains.[9]

Regarding the next chapter for USDC, Dante Disparte, Chief Strategy Officer and Head of Global Policy at Circle, explained:

> USDC is a five-year-old innovation. When we first developed USDC, many of the existing rules, for example, around stablecoins, MiCA [the EU's Markets in Crypto Assets Regulation] and any existing regimes for digital assets, did not exist. And so, the Centre Consortium was supposed to help fill the gaps where regulation and policy stopped.
>
> The role of the governance consortium was to effectively set up a set of standards around the open source roadmap, interoperability and additional open source solutions, for example, decentralised identity and other technologies, tools and approaches that might make the use of digital assets, but in particular stablecoins generalisable and accessible by as many counterparties and or people as possible.

At the time, Dante shared his reflections on being a board member at Centre:

> Everything we would do at the Centre consortium was never meant to substitute regulation. Instead, it was always intended to be supplemental to regulation.
>
> And so today with the abandonment of the centre model it is effectively an acknowledgement that there's sufficient regulatory clarity that you didn't need anything like a stablecoin self-regulatory organisation (SRO) that you could abandon it entirely.

In 2023, USDC and Tether (USDT) equated to more than 80 per cent of total market capitalization for all US-dollar-pegged stablecoins.

In late 2023, the world of stablecoins was again in the spotlight with PayPal announcing it was launching its own stablecoin, PayPal USD (PYUSD), a fully backed regulated stablecoin, issued by Paxos.

PayPal's move into stablecoins was a clear indicator of the growing integration of decentralized currencies into mainstream financial services, blurring the lines between traditional financial services and digital currency spaces. Given the scale and role of PayPal in traditional financial services, many believed this could be the catalyst to onboard many users into Web3 and accelerate the adoption of this new form of money in everyday commerce. Similarly, it created a new debate about how many stablecoins we would have in the future. *Will every financial institution have its own stablecoin?*

Another inflection point came in 2019 with the announcement of Libra, later renamed Diem, by Facebook. Facebook initially pitched Libra as a mainstream cryptocurrency that could be spent online or offline, much like the dollar. It was meant to make digitally transferring money quicker and easier than it is today, and companies like Facebook would be able to offer financial services around it.

While there was a lot of development in the crypto industry, it was still seen to be outside the mainstream economy. However, Facebook's scale and access to Web2 users meant a real threat to the traditional government-run financial system. The announcement from Facebook quickly raised alarm bells, and although the company tried to reduce its remit, the project was later closed down due to various setbacks and regulatory pressure. It is against this backdrop that central banks around the world have ramped up interest in CBDCs.

Central bank digital currency

According to the Atlantic Council Geoeconomics Center's CBDC tracker, in 2023, 130 countries were exploring central bank digital currency (CBDC), representing 98 per cent of global GDP, an increase from only 25 countries in 2020.[10]

CBDCs are, in simple terms, a digital version of fiat currency backed by a government. There are two types of CBDCs being explored: retail and wholesale. The key distinction between the designs is to whom central banks are issuing the currency. Retail CBDCs are provided to the general public, for all payments of goods and services, similar to cash but in digital form. Wholesale CBDC is issued only to financial institutions for transactions and settlements.

While central banks' motivations behind issuing a CDBC varies, a BIS survey noted that financial inclusion and monetary policy are among the top considerations for retail CBDCs. The same survey pointed out that the work on wholesale CBDC is driven mainly by the desire to enhance cross-border payments.[11]

DIGITAL EURO AND POUND

In October 2021, the European Central Bank (ECB) started working with euro-area national banks to explore the introduction of a digital euro, its design and its potential impact on the market. After the design, it will take three years to build before it goes live, so a digital euro is not expected before 2026. With Europeans relying increasingly on digital payment methods, the ECB wants to ensure a safe, smooth and inclusive transition to cashless payments, with card payments increasing from 39 per cent to 41 per cent in terms of value.[12]

The ECB foresees that a digital euro would support the digitalization of payments, fostering a competitive environment and preserving the European economy. However, the same could also pose challenges around cyber security and privacy.

Similarly, the Bank of England and HM Treasury are also exploring a digital pound. In February 2023, they published a digital pound consultation paper asking for feedback on initial policy and technical work. The digital pound would be a new form of money issued by the Bank of England and used by households on everyday payments. Currently in the second phase, the work performed over the next two to three years will inform the decision to launch.

While there is an increased number of pilots and experiments globally, only 11 countries have launched their own CDBC. The launch of a new currency still has a few challenges that central banks must consider before progressing further, including privacy, consumer protection and anti-money laundering standards.

Consumers may be sceptical of CBDCs since they may assume it could mean central bank surveillance. For central banks considering retail CBDCs, it is vital to educate users on the benefits and demonstrate that their privacy will be protected. Many new encryption and other techniques are available in the market that help ensure individuals' privacy while still maintaining enough oversight to prevent fraud.

Tokenized deposits

Tokens are sometimes referred as the response from banks to maintain the traditional two tier-system. They are digital representations of deposits held at a financial institution, converted into easily transferable and accessible blockchain tokens, and often used to move money between clients of a bank.

Bitcoin, stablecoins, CBDCs and tokens are examples of the new forms of money that are emerging in this new industry. Each has its own risks and benefits, and it is hard to know at this instance which one will prevail. Most likely, all of them will coexist in the same way that today we have different forms of money (central bank notes and deposits held by commercial banks). And, similarly to today, they will play different roles.

What's wrong with TradFi payments?

The movement of money (i.e. payments) has drastically changed in the last few decades. Recently, we have seen a dramatic decrease from the physical exchange of cash to the adoption of online and mobile payments. A report from Statista predicts that the number of active online banking users will reach 2.5 billion by 2024.[13]

While innovation in the payments industry has had a positive impact on the user experience, the infrastructure and processes still face some challenges and drawbacks, hindering their efficiency and effectiveness.

Complex and fragmented systems

Traditional payment systems are complex and fragmented and require input from a number of intermediaries, making them often expensive, slow and opaque. Cross-border transactions, for example, are still highly complex and require a multitude of intermediaries from the different countries. Each intermediary has processing times and requirements to comply with, leading to long settlement times. Due to the lack of transparency and real-time information, financial institutions spend millions on reconciling payments and information.

High costs of international transfers

While fintech companies, such as Wise, have revolutionized international money transfers, reducing costs to some extent, these transactions remain expensive for many consumers. According to World Bank data, the average remittance fee stood at 5.7 per cent in 2020.[14] An efficient and inexpensive international payment transfer system is especially important in emerging markets, in which individuals often send money home to their families to help with expenses and other financial needs.

Delays in bank debits and transfers

Bank debits and transfers still take a few business days to be settled; for example, BACS (Bankers' Automated Clearing System) used in the UK by businesses to transfer funds to their employees, for payroll for example, still takes three to six business days on average. In urgent situations, such a timeline can be frustrating and difficult for employees and businesses. Note that, in most cases, this timeline is a feature built into the process to allow for checks to take place before funds are settled.

Cost burdens of digital payments

Digital payments are also costly, on top of other charges. Payment fees and costs can impact businesses' bottom line. For example, businesses accepting card payments must pay fees of around 1.5 per cent to 3.5 per cent per transaction. This challenge is faced by both small and big businesses, as seen in 2021 when Amazon threatened to stop accepting credit cards.

AMAZON THREATS TO STOP ACCEPTING CREDIT CARDS

In 2021, Amazon sent an email to its UK customers announcing that, from January 2022, it would no longer accept Visa credit cards issued in the UK. In a statement, Amazon's spokesperson noted that the cost of accepting card payments was still an obstacle for businesses. While the company expected costs to go down given technological advancements, that was not what it was facing, with costs still high.[15]

In January 2022, Amazon announced that it was working with Visa on potential solutions for its customers and that the expected change would no longer take place.[16] One month later, the companies reached a global agreement stating they would continue to collaborate on new product and technology initiatives to provide innovative payment experiences to their customers.[17]

Web3 alternative payment rails

The introduction of blockchain technology has created a potential alternative to existing payment rails. This technology is poised to redefine transactions with its promise of speed, transparency and cost efficiency for consumers and businesses.

While traditional payment systems rely on intermediaries working together to record, review and transfer the flow of money, blockchain allows for direct peer-to-peer transactions. This feature reduces the need for intermediaries, leading to lower transaction fees, almost instant settlement and faster end-to-end processes. Additionally, costs related to reconciliation and liquidity buffer could be reduced significantly. For example, foreign-exchange costs could be reduced due to greater transparency and real-time information on foreign exchange margins.[18]

Given blockchain's transparent nature, all payments are recorded on an immutable ledger, enabling financial institutions and regulators to conduct real-time audits. This real-time transaction transparency reduces and eliminates manual reconciliation processes.

Web3 payments in action

Commerce

Spurred by consumer demand, many companies and retailers have started to accept digital currency as a form of payment in the last few years. Crypto.com reported in late 2021 that approximately 75 per cent of its clients would have paid in crypto for goods and services if they had that option.[19] Businesses across many industries, from transportation, fashion, electronics, food and beverage, now see the adoption of digital currencies as a competitive advantage. According to a Deloitte survey conducted in 2022, nearly 75 per cent of retailers planned to accept either cryptocurrency or stablecoin payments in the following two years.[20]

Businesses can either accept on-chain payments or partner with third-party payment providers. BitPay, a Bitcoin payment provider, has announced partnerships with over 250 companies and stores globally on its site. Traditional payment service providers have also started to embrace this innovation. In July 2021, Visa announced it would partner with 50 crypto companies to allow clients to spend digital currencies.[21]

EVERYDAY PAYMENTS

Lush, a vegetarian and cruelty-free skincare company, was one of the first global companies to embrace cryptocurrencies. In 2017, Lush announced that it would start accepting Bitcoin payments for orders on its websites via a partnership with BitPay.

Starbucks also opted to work with a third party to accept digital currency payments. In 2021, Starbucks announced it would start accepting digital currency via Bakk's digital wallet.

Crypto has also penetrated fashion, with Gucci in 2022 starting to accept digital currency payments. The in-store payments were initially performed via a QR code, accepting more than 10 currencies.

Retail cross-border payments: remittances

Cross-border remittances play an important role in the global economy, especially in developing countries. For example, in the Philippines, 60 per cent of the population relies on funds sent home, and remittances account for 10 per cent of the country's GDP.[22] However, traditional remittances are often slow, expensive and fraught with inefficiencies, particularly when involving multiple currencies. Many fintechs and Web3 native companies have leveraged blockchain to provide faster, cheaper and more efficient methods to send money across countries.

SENDING REMITTANCES ACROSS ASIA

In 2008, a Malaysian entrepreneur saw a huge demand for mobile top-ups. Migrants were then buying the top-up cards abroad and sending them back home for their families. Having noticed a need for seamless cross-border payments, Tranglo was born.

Tranglo expanded over the years to be one of Asia's leading cross-border payment companies, with a global network of over 150 countries. In 2012, Tranglo launched its first live crypto-enabled service in the Philippines, allowing Filipino migrants to send remittances across Asia. This service is provided by leveraging Ripple's blockchain payment solution and XRP, the native digital currency of the XRP ledger, and offers all of the benefits of crypto-enabled payments, including speed, convenience, flexibility and cost savings, all while remaining compliant with local regulations.[23]

Ripple is a leading provider of crypto-enabled solutions for businesses. Its payments solution has hundreds of customers in over 55 countries and six continents, with payout capabilities in 70 countries. Ripple has processed nearly $50 billion worth of volume and 27 million transactions since RippleNet was first launched.[24]

Wholesale cross-border payments: intra-bank payments

Current cross-border payment processes are still not scalable and seamless across countries, currencies and systems. Unlike domestic payments, where banks can use one national payment platform to pay each other, there is no unified platform for making international payments between countries.

According to a J.P. Morgan survey, multinational corporations name high transaction costs ($27 average transaction fee), long settlement times (two to three days) and the lack of transparency as the key issues with the current processes.[25]

Blockchain is being considered as a potential solution for cross-border payments, providing an alternative to the traditional banking model, whereby cross-border payments can be settled peer-to-peer using CBDCs. Commercial banks, Web3 native companies and central banks are currently working together to test hypotheses and create prototypes for this alternative model.

PROJECT DUNBAR

Project Dunbar aimed to test the use of CBDCs for international payments. This project was a collaboration between the Bank of International Settlement (BIS) and the central banks of Australia, Malaysia, Singapore and South Africa.

In September 2021, the joint CBDC pilot was announced, with the results released in May 2022. Project Dunbar developed two prototypes for a shared platform that could enable international settlements using multiple CBDCs. The experiment proved that financial institutions could use CBDCs, issued by participating central banks, to transact directly with each other on the shared platform, with the potential to reduce time and costs taken to process cross-border transactions.

Even though Project Dunbar's vision was to create one single global platform that connected all central banks and commercial banks, the complexities and unique requirements of each jurisdiction make this goal harder. The next steps include the development and testing of regional CBDC platforms. Once those regional CBDC projects have been established, the focus will shift to creating interconnectivity mechanisms. This process will involve addressing not only technical requirements but also governance and policy-related questions.[26]

Emerging markets

There are still 1.4 billion people in the world without access to financial services, often due to a lack of government-issued identity documentation; some live in remote areas with limited access to banking infrastructure or are unable to afford high transaction costs.

Crypto's ethos is centred around financial inclusion. This new industry core has always been focused on providing access to underserved and underrepresented communities. Since, in its current form, no personal information is required to open an account, anyone with a device and an internet connection can, in theory, join the financial system. Peer-to-peer settlement and remittances are also cheaper and faster than traditional rails.

While all of this seems to lead to a more inclusive financial environment, adopting crypto in emerging markets may be slower than expected. Crypto data usage and adoption statistics are hard to obtain, but studies have found that adoption is still limited.

El Salvador, for example, made Bitcoin a legal tender in 2021, requiring all businesses to accept the cryptocurrency. To incentivize adoption, the government released a custodial digital wallet with \$30 of free Bitcoin and subsidized transaction fees. Despite such incentives, only 4.9 per cent of all sales in El Salvador are conducted in Bitcoin, and 88 per cent of businesses exchange Bitcoin revenue for fiat currency.[27]

So, what is stopping adoption in markets in need of a financial alternative? There are two components to this question. The first one is that we need to consider the economic and political environments of the different countries.

In countries with volatile local currencies, cryptocurrencies will be primarily used as a refuge to store value. Countries such as Venezuela, Zimbabwe and Argentina have suffered previously from rapid currency devaluations, hurting residents' ability to save and perform basic day-to-day commerce activities. So, in those emerging countries, cryptocurrency is used as a safety net against local currency volatility, with residents holding it and only converting to local currency when needed (called 'off-ramp' in the crypto world). When considering the data for those countries, we should look at volume acquired or held as an investment, instead of movement or payments.

ARGENTINA

For many years, Argentina has faced economic challenges, marked by high inflation and currency devaluation, impacting residents' ability to save and make everyday financial transactions. In July 2023, the peso (Argentina's currency) fell approximately 51.6 per cent in value, and in November of the same year inflation topped 140 per cent.

In order to reduce US dollar circulation, the government imposed strict capital controls, resulting in a thriving black market. Locals often use *cuevas* to swap out ever-growing wads of pesos for US dollars. *cuevas* are rooms in ordinary houses in which pesos can be swapped to other currency, like dollars, euros and so on. Imagine your living room full of stack of dollars, from the floor to the wall, that's what a *cueva* looks like.

With this backdrop, it is of no surprise that many Argentinians started to look for cryptocurrencies as an alternative. Stablecoins tend to be the choice, given they are more stable than Bitcoin and Ethereum and, as such, are a more secure form for savings. 'We have really high inflation, and there are lots of restrictions against buying foreign currencies. That makes crypto a valuable option for saving,' Martel Seward, Head of Compliance and AML, told Chainalysis. He indicated that stablecoins were popular for this use case and provided a new way of meeting long-standing local demand for the US dollar. 'As crypto adoption has grown, lots of people here will now get their paycheck and immediately put it into USDT or USDC.'[28]

Argentina's economic conditions don't just make it difficult for citizens to save but also to do day-to-day shopping. While previously prices used to change once a month, now it is once a week or even twice a week. Some supermarkets and restaurants change their prices as frequently as twice a day. To support day-to-day financial transactions, companies like Binance, Mastercard and Lemon Cash created debit cards to enable Argentinians to spend their cryptocurrency in local businesses.

However, the adoption and movement of cryptocurrencies are still limited in the country and are mostly done by younger individuals with high financial literacy. An interesting development, however, is the fact that *cuevas* are starting to use crypto. Instead of having to hold big stacks of money, the movement of cryptocurrencies is safer and more efficient. Often, instead of interacting with blockchain and self-custody wallets, individuals will go to a *cueva*, which does the transaction for them. Many don't even realize that the *cueva* is using crypto behind the scenes.

This reality is quite different from the vision of the future that many Web3 advocates imagine. Proponents of Web3 visualize a world in which individuals use self-custody wallets and control their own money. Instead, Argentinians are using intermediaries and centralized apps to use this new form of money.

In 2023, in an unexpected development, candidate Javier Milei won the presidential election. This outcome signalled a shift in Argentina's political dynamics. Milei is known for his vocal opposition to the country's central bank as well as his support of cryptocurrencies as a transformative solution. Although at the time of writing he had not explicitly proposed making Bitcoin or other cryptocurrency legal tender in Argentina, he was exploring the option of dollarization.

The second component impacting emerging markets, adoption is the fact that this industry is still relatively nascent, with a poor and complex user experience and a lack of some of the building blocks. While one may be able to buy crypto in emerging markets, the off-ramps are still complex and often not available, such as the ability to convert funds from cryptocurrencies to fiat. Additionally, not all merchants accept payments in cryptocurrency yet.

In a discussion with Nitin Gaur, Global Head of Digital Assets and Technology Design at State Street, he explained the technical and economic barriers to crypto adoption in emerging markets:

> Money can have three properties: a store of value, unit of account, and medium of exchange. When we talk about payments, we consider the medium of exchange property.
>
> In countries like Turkey and Argentina, where there is an inflation problem, 33% inflation and 75% inflation, respectively, in addition to a medium of exchange people need to ensure they preserve the value of their savings, i.e. a durable store of value.

In South Africa and El Salvador, there is a different phenomenon, in those countries, they need a medium of exchange. In reality, crypto payments are already taking place, but they don't have the data to prove it. For example, in El Salvador, they have a project called 'Bitcoin Beach', a place where anyone can pay for anything from groceries to electricity bills with cryptocurrency.

However, there are technical barriers that restrict further adoption. User experience is still poor and complex, with users having to consider key management. Instead, they want simple interfaces and experiences, like sending money using a phone number, as they do with M-Pesa in Africa.

On top of that, there are crypto economic challenges that are slowing the industry from becoming more resilient and scalable. Ethereum cost, for example, is too expensive to make payments at scale.

The final consideration is market depth. The U.S. dollar is successful because you can rely on trillions and trillions of payments measured in U.S. dollars. However, the Bitcoin market cap is half a billion, Ethereum is 300 billion (at the time of the discussion), and the world is 8 billion people. There's not enough of it to serve everybody's needs without inflating the cost structure of these currencies. These currencies do not have enough market depth to serve all needs from a payment perspective.

Future outlook

The growth of Web3 is not just transforming the way we pay but also traditional concepts of money.

When people think about money, they picture either bank notes (physical) or paying via mobile (digital). However, money includes a combination of public (for example, cash issued by the state) and private (for example, deposits provided by commercial banks).

The deputy governor of the Bank of England, Jon Cunliffe, noted in his speech 'Do we need money?' in 2021 that the general public was probably unaware of this distinction. But the reality was that most of the money held and used by people in the UK was not public money but mostly private money. Around 95 per cent of the funds held for everyday payments were bank deposits instead of cash.[29]

We are now at a turning point where new forms of money and infrastructure are being tested. Stablecoins and CBDCs are, in fact, private and public forms of money respectively. One of the fundamental changes to the traditional ecosystem is that this new form of private money (stablecoins) is not issued by commercial banks but instead by technology and Web3 companies. Those same companies have also introduced new payment rails and processes, which are available globally and 24/7, just like the internet.

So, one has to ask the question: What does it mean for the future of traditional payments and traditional ecosystem players?

Many traditional players, such as banks, payment providers and central banks, have embraced this innovation. They are joining experiments and consortiums to understand how to use the new infrastructure and new forms of money. Some have gone one step further and have even created a new form of private money, for example J.P. Morgan launched deposit tokens and Paypal launched their own stablecoin. Collaborations between players will be key to driving the adoption of these new payment rails and new forms of money. The evolving regulatory landscape will also provide credibility to the industry.

SUMMARY OF KEY POINTS

- Stablecoins were designed to provide a solution for users and businesses seeking price stability. They combine the benefits of decentralization and transparency of blockchain with the stability of fiat currency.

- The rise of interest and activity in cryptocurrencies and stablecoins spurred central banks to accelerate their CBDCs initiatives.

- Payments have become increasingly cashless. There has been a drastic decrease from the physical exchange of cash to the adoption of online and mobile payments.

- While there has been significant innovation in the payments from an end-user perspective, the back-end infrastructure still faces challenges: it is costly, slow and lacks transparency.

- Blockchain-powered payment solutions could lead to faster transactions, higher transparency and lower costs.

- Many traditional players have joined experiments and consortiums to understand how to use the new infrastructure and new forms of money. Some have even launched their own stablecoin and tokenized deposits.

Endnotes

1 Visa. By settling in USDC, Crypto.com is setting a new course, 2023, usa.visa.com/content/dam/VCOM/regional/na/us/Solutions/documents/visa-crypto.com-usdc-case-study.pdf (archived at https://perma.cc/88CH-MJTP)

2 K Sandor. Visa taps Solana and USDC Stablecoin to boost cross-border payments, CoinDesk, 5 September 2023, coindesk.com/business/2023/09/05/visa-taps-solana-and-usdc-stablecoin-to-boost-cross-border-payments/ (archived at https://perma.cc/4RMF-7CZY)

3 C Dehner. The history of money: How our currency evolved from pelts to money, 17 February 2022, mint.intuit.com/blog/investments/the-history-of-money/ (archived at https://perma.cc/YEV5-77QC)

4 Bank of England. How has money changed over time, 23 March 2018, www.bankofengland.co.uk/explainers/how-has-money-changed-over-time (archived at https://perma.cc/U2WN-BZAX)

5 Bank of England. Money in the modern economy: An introduction, Quarterly Bulletin, 2014, (1), www.bankofengland.co.uk/-/media/boe/files/quarterly-bulletin/2014/money-in-the-modern-economy-an-introduction.pdf (archived at https://perma.cc/NP5S-M247)

6 BNP Paribas. 18 dates that made the history of payments, 28 December 2022, histoire.bnpparibas/en/18-dates-that-made-the-history-of-payments/ (archived at https://perma.cc/N4L7-QWTJ)

7 Statista, Bitcoin (BTC) price per day from Apr 2013–Jul 24, 2023, statista.com/statistics/326707/bitcoin-price-index/ (archived at https://perma.cc/TVB5-MV32)

8 M J Casey. Dollar-backed digital currency aims to fix Bitcoin's volatility dilemma, *The Wall Street Journal*, 8 July 2014, www.wsj.com/articles/BL-MBB-23780 (archived at https://perma.cc/T2AJ-FVCT)

9 J Allaire and B Armstrong. Ushering in the next chapter for USDC, Circle blog, 21 August 2023, www.circle.com/blog/ushering-in-the-next-chapter-for-usdc (archived at https://perma.cc/A7LG-S9ZQ)

10 Atlantic Council. Central bank digital currency tracker, www.atlanticcouncil. org/cbdctracker/ (archived at https://perma.cc/5KES-YPZY)

11 A Kosse and I Mattei. Making headway – Results of the 2022 BIS survey on central bank digital currencies and crypto, BIS Paper No 136, Bank for International Settlements, July 2022.

12 F Panetta. Keynote speech: A new horizon for pan-European payments and digital euro, 22 October 2020, www.ecb.europa.eu/press/key/date/2020/html/ ecb.sp201022~d66111be97.en.html (archived at https://perma.cc/ET87-AVUP)

13 Statista. Number of active online banking users worldwide in 2020 with forecasts from 2021 to 2024, by region, 2023, statista.com/statistics/1228757/ online-banking-users-worldwide/ (archived at https://perma.cc/5WJ7-8S97)

14 T Beck. What explains international remittance fees?, 3 May 2022, fbf.eui.eu/ what-explains-international-remittance-fees/ (archived at https://perma.cc/ GM5P-PDP9)

15 M Moon. Amazon says it will stop accepting UK-issued VISA credit cards on January 19th, 17 November 2021, techcrunch.com/2021/11/17/amazon-says-it-will-stop-accepting-uk-issued-visa-credit-cards-on-january-19th/ (archived at https://perma.cc/6JV9-55BR)

16 N Lomas. Amazon rows back on threat to stop accepting UK-issued Visa cards, 17 January 2022, techcrunch.com/2022/01/17/amazon-ends-threat-to-not-accept-uk-visa-payments/ (archived at https://perma.cc/3C5W-9KCL)

17 BBC News. Amazon strikes global deal to accept Visa credit cards, 17 February 2022, bbc.co.uk/news/business-60413957 (archived at https://perma.cc/C7BB-945T)

18 G Williams. Distributed ledgers in payments: Beyond the Bitcoin hype, Bain & Company, 12 June 2016, bain.com/insights/distributed-ledgers-in-payments-beyond-bitcoin-hype/ (archived at https://perma.cc/QC2U-K53V)

19 Cointelegraph research. How businesses can accept cryptocurrency payments, 2022, research-backend.cointelegraph.com/uploads/attachments/ cl5h0ukbj0k30rwqne8cfd4zf-how-businesses-can-accept-cryptocurrency-payments-0-13.pdf

20 Deloitte. Merchants getting ready for crypto, 2022, www2.deloitte.com/ content/dam/Deloitte/us/Documents/technology/us-cons-merchant-getting-ready-for-crypto.pdf (archived at https://perma.cc/7L25-E24X)

21 I Lee. Visa is partnering with over 50 crypto companies to allow clients to spend and convert digital currencies, Markets Insider, 7 July 2021, markets. businessinsider.com/news/cryptocurrencies/cryptocurreny-payments-visa-partnership-clients-spend-convert-digital-currencies-2021-7 (archived at https://perma.cc/Q6US-MMUZ)

22 Ripple. Payments by the numbers: A quick guide to crypto-forward payments solutions, 2022, ripple.com/reports/Ripple-Payments-by-the-Numbers-Guide. pdf (archived at https://perma.cc/J8QK-F55X)

23 Ripple. Payments by the numbers: A quick guide to crypto-forward payments solutions, 2022, ripple.com/reports/Ripple-Payments-by-the-Numbers-Guide. pdf (archived at https://perma.cc/J8QK-F55X)

24 Ripple. *Q4 2022 XRP Markets Report*, 30 January 2023, ripple.com/insights/ q4-2022-xrp-markets-report (archived at https://perma.cc/CX9N-BA99).

25 O Wyman and JP Morgan. *Unlocking 120 billion value in cross border payments*, JP Morgan, 2021, jpmorgan.com/onyx/documents/mCBDCs-Unlocking-120-billion-value-in-cross-border-payments.pdf (archived at https:// perma.cc/Y5X3-WWVD)

26 BIS. *Project Dunbar: International settlements using multi-CBDCs*, Bank for International Settlements, March 2022, bis.org/publ/othp47.pdf (archived at https://perma.cc/8MGE-5NTV)

27 J Levin. El Salvador struggles to adopt Bitcoin despite government push, *The Defiant*, 1 June 2022, thedefiant.io/bitcoin-adoption-americas (archived at https://perma.cc/FRY7-RBUT)

28 Chainalysis. Latin America: Venezuela and Argentina stand out as examples of crypto's unique utility, 11 October 2023, www.chainalysis.com/blog/latin-america-cryptocurrency-adoption/ (archived at https://perma.cc/99TS-LLKE)

29 J Cunliffe. Do we need 'public money'? – speech by Jon Cunliffe, Bank of England, 13 May 2021, www.bankofengland.co.uk/speech/2021/may/jon-cunliffe-omfif-digital-monetary-institute-meeting (archived at https://perma.cc/W6RZ-E5XL)

05

Tokenization

A BUSTLING MARKETPLACE

Imagine for a moment that we are in 2030. It's a beautiful sunny Saturday morning; you grab your coffee and go shopping. As you enter the marketplace, you are amazed at the multitude of different offerings. You notice that investors and consumers are no longer buying entire assets. Instead, they are buying fragments of the assets.

To your right, an investor purchases a fraction of a vintage sports car, a digital representation of 5 per cent ownership. To your left, a couple is buying 2 per cent of a beachfront property in Miami, dreaming of the returns or experience they will get in the following summers.

When I told this story to a friend, they looked perplexed and said, 'Whoa, that's never going to happen.' To which I replied, 'Well, it is already happening, even if at a smaller scale.'

Many Web3 digital investment platforms have emerged in the last few years with the goal of democratizing access to private markets. In those platforms, investors can buy and sell fractions of assets that until recently were considered illiquid. Nowadays, those platforms are still small, offering only a trivial set of investment opportunities and have restricted user access based on local regulations. But, as the tokenized asset market expands, more liquidity will go into those markets, and the end state will be as just described.

Tokenization has the potential to democratize access of previously exclusive investment opportunities (like fine art and expensive cars) and increase the liquidity of less accessible and traditionally illiquid assets (like real estate). Additionally, tokenization will allow for 24/7 global trading, instant settlement, and the reduction of operational costs and efficiencies.

This revolutionary disruption has not gone unnoticed by traditional financial institutions. In fact, many financial leaders are testing this use case and have voiced their support. In 2022, BlackRock's CEO argued that 'the next generation for markets… will be tokenization of securities',[1] and a BCG report estimated that the tokenization of global illiquid assets amounted to a $16 trillion business opportunity.[2] One year later, a Citigroup report dubbed tokenization the 'killer use case' that will drive blockchain mainstream.[3]

For some traditional financial institutions, tokenization is also seen as a less risky way to start their journey into the blockchain world since there is no (direct) exposure to crypto. Often, such companies will start by tokenizing one or two assets in internal environments, with results being presented to the board. Previous positive results have led to further discussions around creating tokenization as a service, sold as a new solution to their clients, or an opportunity to tokenize an asset class, typically a vanilla one. However, as we will see during this chapter, tokenization is only one piece of the puzzle, which will only provide exponential benefits if all of the other pieces are reimagined.

What is tokenization?

DEFINITION

Tokenization, in blockchain, is the process of creating a token on a blockchain that represents an asset. The asset can be either digital or physical, tangible or intangible. Tokens are issued, transacted and settled on a blockchain using smart contracts.

Digitalization and ownership

Reading that description, you may think that tokenization is the same as digitalization, and digitalization is not something new. In fact, we have been digitizing processes and documents for years. We just need to look at our phones to see a myriad of digital information and documentation used daily.

However, tokenization encompasses a few more concepts, going beyond digitalization. With digitalization, records and processes are created digitally. But the ownership, rights and history either remain on paper or are digitized in separate platforms and formats. In contrast, in tokenization, ownership, rights and history are all included in the same digital token metadata. In short, with tokenization, the asset and all relevant information are digitally represented in a token on the blockchain.

Let's look at an example. Imagine you own a house in the city that you no longer use, and you decide to give it to your daughter, who is about to start her new job.

Nowadays, to transfer the house to your daughter, you would need a myriad of paperwork to confirm your ownership, such as a deed, purchase rights, tax records and others. Even with electronic forms, digital signatures and online verifications, you would likely need support from a few intermediaries, like a notary or lawyer, and the whole process may take several days.

In tokenization, you only need to transfer the digital token, since the house's rights, ownership and history are all included in the digital token metadata. This process enables a more secure and seamless transfer to your kids. Additionally, because the process is done on the blockchain without the need for intermediaries, the transfer is (almost) immediate.

Fractionalization

What is even more exciting is that tokenization also encapsulates the fractionalization of traditionally indivisible assets. Fractionalization means the creation of smaller fractions of the same asset, which reduces the amount needed to participate in the market. This way, fractionalization opens the market to a larger base of investors while providing more liquidity to issuers.

Let's go back to our example. Imagine that you realize you need some money. You could sell the house for funding, but your daughter wouldn't have a place to live, and she is starting her job soon. So, instead, you choose to give her a portion of the house and monetize another fraction while keeping some of the ownership yourself.

Through tokenization, the house's ownership is easily fractionalized. By representing the house as a digital token on the blockchain, you can transfer a specific fraction to your daughter and sell portions of the remaining asset to interested parties. This way, your daughter has a place to live, you get the funds you need and still retain some of the house's ownership. You can always buy back the fractions or sell more as your needs change.

Fractionalization, the process of dividing a single asset into smaller traded units, is not new. Robinhood, for example, allows investors to buy fractional shares in a traditional centralized system. Many crowdfunding platforms, like Seedrs, also allow investors to make small investments in startups in return for a small portion of the business. The difference in Web3 tokenization is that fractionalization is done on a digital asset owned, stored and transferred on a decentralized infrastructure.

Programmability (smart contracts)

Tokenized assets are governed by smart contracts, which can be programmed to automatically perform an action once predetermined conditions are met. In simple terms, we often say smart contracts are like 'if–then' rules. If 'X' takes place, then the smart contract performs 'Y' automatically, without human intervention.

Again, let's look back at our example. Imagine you want to transfer the full ownership of your house to your daughter when she turns 30 years old. The smart contract will be programmed to automatically transfer the token to your daughter when she turns 30. Likewise, if you had the house rented, the smart contract could be programmed to end the rental agreement if your tenants did not pay their rent on time.

Both of those actions, the transfer of the token when your daughter turns 30 and ending the rental agreement if the tenants did not pay the rent, would happen automatically without human intervention, eliminating the need for intermediaries.

Smart contracts can also allow for what is called 'atomic settlement'. Rather than trust that each party will separately carry out their part of the transaction, smart contracts can combine two or more legs of a transaction into a single unified 'atomic' action. In financial services, this could be a robust way to achieve delivery-versus-payment (DVP) and payment-versus-payment (PVP) functionality. Such functionality mitigates settlement and counterparty credit risks, ensuring that the buyer will not pay if the seller does not deliver, and vice versa.

In our example, let's imagine that, instead of transferring the house to your daughter, you decide to keep it and rent it out. Your daughter has some savings that she wants to use towards a house of her own. After finding a house of her liking, she is ready to proceed with the acquisition. However, instead of paying upfront and relying on the house ownership to be transferred later, she buys the house using a marketplace that uses blockchain technology and smart contracts. Smart contracts will combine both steps, payment and ownership, and automatically transfer the ownership of the house when the payment is made, reducing the risk of fraud.

It should be noted, however, that the use of smart contracts and atomic settlements also involves risks, for example hackers and other bad actors may take advantage of bugs or cyber vulnerabilities and transfer funds that cannot be later recovered.

If you consider the different components – digitalization, decentralization, fractionalization and programmability – in isolation, you may not see something new or innovative. Now, the transformative potential is when they are considered together under the tokenization opportunity and seeing the benefits they bring across the asset lifecycle and value chain.

Why tokenize assets?

In 1997, a US survey identified that 56 per cent of assets held by taxpayers, with a net worth between $600,000 to $1 million, were illiquid.[4] Now, imagine that 50 per cent of your assets cannot be quickly or easily converted into cash. Unfortunately, you do not need to imagine because we still have that exact problem. In 2022 a BCG report noted that we still have 'a large chunk of the world's wealth' locked in illiquid assets.[5]

This a problem that affects all communities, from individuals who live from payday to payday, founders and SMEs (small and medium-sized enterprises) that need to raise money, to the end of the spectrum with wealthy clients having considerable portions of their wealth in assets that are not easily transformed into liquidity.

Liquidity

One of the key benefits of tokenization is this notion of transforming illiquid assets into liquidity. Tokenization provides the opportunity to monetize illiquid assets, such as art, real estate, intellectual property, patents and others. This is a game changer for token owners, who may need money and liquidity in the short term.

For example, if you have a property worth a few million, buying and selling the house can take a long time because there are only so many people who can afford it. As we have seen in the example earlier, with tokenization and fractionalization, house ownership can be split into tiny fractions, reducing the amount needed to participate. By lowering the ticket size, more investors worldwide will be able to participate in the sale of the house, increasing the speed at which assets can be sold and purchased.

Similarly, tokenization will allow startups, SMEs (small and medium-sized enterprises) and charities better access to capital. Nowadays, founders and SMEs have two main routes for funding. They either get a loan from a bank or raise money from angel investors or venture capital (VC). Getting a loan from a bank can be a time-consuming activity, with banks' due diligence activities taking months before a final decision is given to the company. After months of waiting, some companies do not have their loan approved for multiple reasons. Raising money from angels and VCs can also be challenging if the company is too small, doesn't have traction yet or the founders do not have the connections needed. With tokenization, shares can be split into small fractions and sold to a number of smaller participants. Additionally, often companies have other traditionally illiquid assets, such as their patents, IP and even the office (real estate), that can be tokenized and monetized instead of selling shares, opening up the possibilities for new forms of funds.

Both of these examples are new products that financial institutions could provide to existing and new clients, generating commercial value. Some Web3 companies have already jumped on this opportunity and provide platforms in which such tokenized assets are sold.

Democratization and financial inclusion

You may have already noticed, with the examples discussed, that tokenization is opening financial markets to retail investors, who previously could not participate due to financial constraints. In 2020, HSBC analysis found that '84% of the world's population would need to save for more than two years to be able to afford a share in each of the top five companies'.[6] Existing traditional markets restrict individuals from generating further wealth and progressing into the next social bracket. With tokenization and fractionalization, the initial ticket size is smaller, lowering the barrier to entry and also providing opportunities for portfolio diversification.

Individuals will also have the opportunity to invest and benefit from causes closer to their hearts. For example, imagine that the local community is building a new school or church. Tokenization would allow such projects to be broken down into smaller, more affordable units. Individuals would be able to buy the tokens representing their fraction of the project. Once the building is finalized, revenues can be redistributed to the token holders in perpetuity. For example, a percentage of the school tuition or donations to the church can be automatically distributed to token holders via a smart contract.

Such models can impact traditional funding models in financial services with a shift towards more decentralized, accessible and inclusive forms of investment. A focus on inclusive and socially responsible investments has been an ongoing trend, with many institutions including new ESG (environmental, social and governance) funds into their portfolio due to increased investors' demand. With tokenization, such funds could be expanded to other causes.

Operational efficiencies

For incumbents in the financial markets, tokenization can resolve inherent inefficiencies in legacy systems and processes. The programmability of smart contracts enables the automation of previously highly manual and error-prone processes, reducing operational and servicing costs. It also allows for 24/7 trading and faster settlement times (reduced from the current T+2 settlement to real time).

Some of the recent published data confirms that the expected savings are indeed achieved via tokenization. For example, Vanguard is leveraging R3's Corda through Grow Inc to achieve straight-through processing, saving 100 hours a week in labour, and J.P. Morgan's Onyx Digital Assets is projecting $20 million in savings on an expected $1 trillion in tokenized repo volume by the end of 2023.[7]

DEFINITION

Repo or repurchase agreement – a short-term agreement to sell securities and buy them back at a slightly higher price, often used for short-term funding needs.

Besides efficiency, tokenization can also bring transparency and reduce information asymmetry and cost savings at a portfolio level. Currently, different products are created in different stacks due to legacy processes and available technologies. However, with tokenization, all types of products can be created using one platform. Rates, coupons, rules and all token components are added to the smart contract and can be changed individually, when needed, without having to change the platform's rules. Since there is only one stack, processes can be streamlined with lower costs and fewer resources.

Different ecosystem players will use a shared 'golden-source' infrastructure and be able to see their assets at a portfolio level.

New products and features

Ultimately, tokenization will serve as a catalyst for unprecedented innovation in financial products and features. For example, currently, interest payments or coupons for traditional corporate bonds are paid every six months due to manual processes and operational costs. With tokenization, smart contracts can be programmed to automatically pay coupons daily, hourly or even in by-the-minute cash flows. Additionally, it will allow for live ESG tracking and dynamic portfolio reallocation, adapting investments to market conditions and investors' preferences.

Tokenization in action

The opportunity for tokenization seems endless. Since almost any asset can be tokenized, the myriad of ongoing experiments include the tokenization of art, gold, bonds, equity and real estate. Real estate and equity are currently the predominant forms of tokenized assets, according to a report from Digital Assets Research. The research identified 41 centralized financial entities engaging in tokenization; 26 have their own tokenized marketplace and 30 support the fractionalization of assets.[8] While these numbers will continue to evolve, there is already a clear interest and demand from institutions to explore tokenization.

Experiments led by traditional financial institutions are primarily focused on more conservative instruments or instruments closer to their existing BAU (business as usual), like bonds and private equity, and are unlikely to expand beyond these areas, at least for the time being. On the other hand, Web3 native companies are adventuring into new business models and underdeveloped markets, like tokenizing art and real estate. This is a common trend. When adopting new technologies, incumbents tend to start by exploring more conservative and familiar products and processes. In contrast, new companies will explore new markets and products. In tokenization, in particular, the market is still underdeveloped for less illiquid assets, like real estate, and there is a lack of legal and regulatory clarity that may keep some more traditional players at bay (at least for now).

Let's look at a few real use cases.

Collective arts

In 2018, the first piece of art was tokenized and sold in an online auction, potentially changing the dynamics in the industry.

---

14 SMALL ELECTRIC CHAIRS

In 2018, a London gallery launched the first cryptocurrency art auction. A 2-metre-high painting called *14 Small Electric Chairs*, by Andy Warhol, was tokenized, fractionalized and auctioned through Maecenas (a blockchain art investment platform).

Maecenas initially announced that up to 49 per cent of ownership was on offer. Buyers could use Bitcoin, Ether or Maecenas' own ART tokens to buy a fraction of the painting and were required to comply with KYC and AML regulations and procedures. Buyers would be acquiring a share of ownership, which meant they wouldn't own the full painting or have true autonomy over where the painting was located, but would receive payments if the painting was ever sold again.

Approximately $1.7 million was raised in the cryptocurrency auction for a 31.5 per cent stake in the artwork, whose total valuation was $5.6 million.[9]

Real estate

ELEVATED RETURNS

In 2018, a New York-based asset management company, called Elevated Returns, made history. Elevated Returns successfully structured, implemented and executed the tokenization of St Regis Resort, Aspen, raising $18 million for a stake of almost one-fifth of the resort.[10]

The St Regis Aspen is an internationally recognized resort with a 179-room luxury hotel, four onsite food and beverage outlets and 29,000 square feet of indoor and outdoor conference and banquet venues with views of the Rocky Mountains.

Elevated Returns decided to pursue selling shares of the hotel via blockchain after plans to use the St Regis Aspen as the first single-asset real estate equity-stake sale in the US fell through. 'The fees charged by intermediaries amounted to the same as doing a major listing, and we also looked at our distribution and realised we were effectively placing shares with professional investors,' Stephane de Baets, founder of Elevated Returns said at the time. 'It was basically a private placement disguised as a public offering. The worst of both worlds.'[11]

In 2019, Elevated Returns expanded to South East Asia, where it continues to explore tokenization of real estate.

Other similar initiatives have followed across the world. Binaryx is a live marketplace where investors can own fractional tokenized properties and earn rental income. For example, a Bali apartment has been transformed into tokens and is currently available for investors to acquire, with as little as $50.[12] The apartments are often rented, with the monthly rent paid directly to the token holders, giving a secure monthly income.

Mizuho Trust, Japan's third-biggest banking group, announced its plans to tokenize real estate assets in 2022. The company joined MUFG and Mitsui Trust, Japan's two most prominent banking groups, which were involved in real estate tokenization in 2021. Such initiatives were possible due to changes in regulation in 2020 regarding the use of security tokens.[13]

Financial markets

For decades, the bond market has been a popular investment for individuals and institutions, considered a safe and stable investment. In the early days, bond trading was done through the physical exchange of paper certificates, but it was later digitized into electronic entries on databases. However, there are still inefficiencies if we consider the entire lifecycle of a bond from issuance to settlement, with multiple intermediaries required from issuers, registrars, custodians and others. The opportunity to simplify the end-to-end process, reduce transaction time and costs makes bonds a great use case for tokenization and the reason why so many traditional institutions have been testing the tokenization of bonds.

TOKENIZATION OF BONDS

In 2017, the first-ever cryptocurrency bond was fully settled on a blockchain. Under the UK Financial Conduct Authority's (FCA) regulatory sandbox, the Experimental Bond was also issued by LuxDeco (a buying and selling platform for luxury home goods) through Nivaura's platform (a UK-based fintech company). Investors simply transferred ETH (Ethereum native cryptocurrency) to LuxDeco, which then transferred the bonds to investors. This transaction was time-stamped and included on the Ethereum blockchain.[14]

In 2019, Santander went one step further, issuing a $20 million bond on the Ethereum blockchain. The cash used to complete the investment and the quarterly coupons were also tokenized. John Whelan explained in a tweet that Santander used a 'whitelisting smart contract allowing only entities properly KYC'd and onboarded to hold tokens (bonds or cash)'. The announcement from Santander stated: 'Thanks to this automation, the one-year maturity bond has reduced the number of intermediaries required in the process, making the transaction faster, more efficient and simpler'.[15]

Experiments have significantly increased, especially in the last couple of years, with many financial institutions testing the tokenization of bonds on various private and public blockchain platforms. S&P Ratings estimates that 'Digital bond issuance totalled about $1.5 billion in 2022, up from almost nothing a year earlier'.[16] A few examples worth noting include UBS issuing a CHF375 million digital bond using Six Digital Exchange (SDX) in 2022. In 2023, Hong Kong issued its first tokenized green bond, supported by Goldman Sachs (which uses Canton, a private blockchain). The same year, Siemens (German manufacturing giant) issued its first digital bond on Polygon Blockchain, and, although the bond was issued on-chain, proceeds from investors were collected via traditional banking channels.

Besides bonds, traditional institutions are also testing the tokenization of other assets, including gold, private equity and others. For example, in 2023, HSBC expanded its offering from tokenized bonds to tokenized physical gold, using its blockchain platform called Orion.

What's holding it back?

Tokenization is 'the' use case that all financial experts agree on. They see it as a pivotal use case in the industry, with the potential to unlock liquidity, address legacy inefficiencies, and create new innovative products and features.

Despite its promise, the adoption of tokenization is still relatively slow. So why is that?

Liquidity and interoperability

Until now, many traditional institutions have concentrated their efforts on testing the infrastructure and the issuance of tokens. Key market features are missing, however, such as enabling secondary markets for digital issuance, which are essential for asset liquidity. While single events can happen without a secondary market, as long as there are two willing parties to trade, real traction will not occur unless there are big enough markets with liquidity at both primary and secondary levels. Liquidity is one of the requirements for mass adoption. Liquidity goes hand in hand with interoperability, allowing assets and events to go across platforms in a seamless way.

In 2023, many new solutions were focused on creating marketplaces aiming to solve liquidity and interoperability issues. For example, London Stock Exchange Group (LSEG) announced plans to launch a blockchain-based exchange to target private markets. This was aimed at creating a global marketplace platform that would allow 'participants in all jurisdictions to be able to interact with people in other jurisdictions completely abiding by rules, laws and regulations, potentially multiple jurisdictions simultaneously,' stated Murray

Roos, the group director of capital markets at LSEG, during the announcement.[17]

Likewise, Digital Asset announced the creation of the Canton Network. With an initial partner group of 30 institutions, the Canton Network was created to be 'the first open blockchain network designed with the control and interoperability needed to power synchronized markets, making it uniquely suited for financial services'.[18] Early participants included Goldman Sachs, BNP Paribas, Paxos and Microsoft. However, the industry has not yet been able to solve interoperability.

In a discussion with Tyrone Lobban, Managing Director at J.P. Morgan and head of Blockchain & Onyx Digital Assets, he told me about the latest phase of Project Guardian, a collaborative effort spearheaded by the Monetary Authority of Singapore (MAS), and how it has explored interoperability:

> This latest phase of Project Guardian is an expansion of what we have already done. To date, using Onyx Digital Assets, we tokenise US Treasuries to enable intraday repo transactions for bank and broker-dealer clients. We also tokenise money market fund shares in order that they can be posted as collateral by both buy-side and sell-side firms. And now, with this new phase of Project Guardian, the goal is to streamline and simplify the back-end processing for traditional and alternative funds across the wealth management industry. For this initiative we collaborated with Apollo, WisdomTree and J.P. Morgan Private Bank as part of the initial test.
>
> We recognise that we will not be the only ones in this space. And so that's why we set out to prove that we can interoperate with other platforms. If fund managers are going to issue their funds on different blockchains, we can provide access to those assets for wealth managers through this interoperability solution.
>
> Interoperability will be essential not just to enhance liquidity but also to improve user experiences. Wealth managers don't care that assets have been tokenised or that blockchain is being used. Instead, their priority is to provide their clients with optimal access to the best assets, enabling the best returns. If the user experience is poor and there

is poor liquidity in these markets, wealth managers will not adopt new solutions.

For Tyrone Lobban, interoperability is more than a technical issue:

> Addressing interoperability is not just a technical challenge, it also involves establishing global legal and regulatory frameworks and defining industry standards. The true birth of the Internet was really when TCP/IP was adopted: the standard that allowed for seamless communication. I don't think we've had the TCP/IP moment yet for blockchain, and it probably needs to happen to enable this connectivity.

Morgan McKenney, former CEO of Provenance Blockchain Foundation, discussed with me a number of other barriers to the adoption of tokenization, highlighting that tokenization is just the first step, with the real value coming from building the full 'assembly line' of financial services on blockchain:

> Creating financial assets natively on-chain is relatively straightforward, but blockchain's power is when the whole assembly line is on-chain. Once you have tokenised the asset, you can more efficiently distribute the risk of that asset, for example.
>
> Figure is an example of a company that has done this very successfully. Figure has issued more than $300 million per month of home equity lines of credit to real-world customers. Customers that want to take advantage of the appreciation of their house, that want to send their kids to college, etc.
>
> After approving the credit, Figure creates a 'digital fingerprint' of the loan on blockchain that reflects its key attributes without making sensitive personal information public on the blockchain. Access to the underlying loan information can then be shared with other institutions like banks and credit unions privately off chain to enable them to purchase the loans onto their balance sheet.
>
> By putting the loan on blockchain, Figure enables much more efficient asset distribution to buyers. The buyers can verify and validate the loan details through the immutable token record. This is more efficient than physically shipping loan files and documentation to debt purchasers.

Product maturity is early for institutional use cases

However, Morgan believes that blockchain technology has not matured yet in terms of its user interface for institutions, hampering adoption:

> Blockchains have not yet been fully productised into easy-to-use tools for institutions. More work is needed to package the technology into tested, compliant products for banks for example.
>
> Figure, for example, has productised Provenance for mortgages, home equity lines of credit, private market securities and private funds. However, there aren't yet a large number of other firms that have products across the breadth of financial services asset classes.

Additionally, even with tokenized assets, downstream functions aren't yet entirely reengineered and developed on blockchain. Morgan continues:

> For example, by putting private equity funds (inherently illiquid assets, meaning they're non-price discoverable) on-chain, you can easily open up access to that asset so that more investors can join over time.
>
> However, the liquidity venues and connectivity between supply and demand still need to be built. How is somebody in Asia from a private bank platform going to find and decide to buy that asset?
>
> So, the discovery process needs to be reimagined, and various wealth platforms will need to be connected into blockchains to be able to discover those tokenized assets.
>
> Simply putting an asset on a blockchain doesn't fully solve the problem of asset discovery, particularly for potential investors who are geographically distant or on different platforms.

Regulatory barriers

Morgan notes how lack of regulatory clarity in many parts of the world has also hampered adoption:

> High-profile challenges in the crypto token trading market has made many regulators extremely cautious of the entire space, including blockchain as a technology to make regulated financial services more

efficient. It will take significant time to help get regulators comfortable with risk mitigation in blockchain ecosystems sufficiently to support wide and broad use of blockchain across institutional finance.

Lack of digital money

Finally, Morgan believes that the inclusion of digital fiat currencies is a key component for further adoption and materialization of benefits:

> Most financial assets are either providing cash flows or requesting cash flows. To fully automate cash flows related to tokenised assets, digital fiat money on-chain is needed from credible and regulated providers.
>
> Then you can start really automating finance: automating the coupon payments, dividends, the capital distributions, the capital calls, loan repayments etc.

Exponential opportunities

If the industry is able to solve the tokenization challenges, the use cases and impact will be unprecedented. The fact that we will be able to tokenize almost anything will ultimately unlock opportunities for broader individuals' financial wealth and services.

In 2022, the gaming industry had more than three billion users. Many games now enable players to buy unique virtual items, like new skins for avatars, weapons or other accessories. When tokenized and placed on a blockchain, these digital assets could gain real-world value and transferability. Imagine a world where such on-chain assets can be sold or traded with friends inside or outside the game. Teenagers' digital wallets contain those assets, and their identity is a blend of both physical and digital tokens. As these young gamers transition into their student years, the scope of these digital assets' utility broadens. They could potentially use them as collateral for their student loans, or even as collateral for their first house.

Similar examples can be noted for other stages of individuals' lives. Imagine, a busy professional opts for a home exercise bike, earning reward tokens as an incentive for being active. These tokens aren't merely symbolic, they can be used for practical purposes like online purchases of gym attire.

In short, tokenization could be a paradigm shift, creating a seamless blend of digital and physical worlds. It unlocks the creation of innovative financial solutions, lifestyle incentives and brand engagement strategies, reshaping how we perceive and interact with assets across various life stages and industries.

Such opportunities aren't as far-fetched as one may think. Many luxury and big brands are already tokenizing their goods to prevent fraud, provide ownership to users and expand loyalty programmes. For example, in 2023, Nike launched a public presale for its new RTFKT Dunk Genesis trainers. Those trainers have an embedded near-field communication (NFC) chip, called the RTFKT World Merging chip. The client can obtain a digital collectable, similar to an NFT, and connect the physical trainer with the digital token. While those trainers are still expensive for the regular client, they showcase a future in which users have ownership over their data and physical assets and can use those for their financial needs.

A note on cash tokenization

Often in discussions, the tokenization of cash is included under 'tokenization'. By tokenization of cash, I am referring to stablecoins, CBDCs and deposits tokens. However, for simplicity, I have kept this chapter focused only on asset use cases, while cash tokenization is covered in the previous chapter on payments.

Cash and money are, of course, core to tokenization. For tokenization to be able to achieve a faster settlement, instant settlement of cash needs to take place. But currently, there is no cross-bank solution at scale. While some platforms use stablecoins for tokenization use cases, they still lack the regulatory clarity needed for mass adoption.

Future outlook

Back in 2017, the first tokenization took place. Six years later, the revolutionary disruption of tokenization seems, to some, still mostly on paper. Critics argue that tokenization has gained limited traction and dismiss it as mere hype. The reality, however, is more nuanced. Many experts in the industry still believe in the potential for tokenization, recognizing that implementation is far more complex.

A fragmented legal and regulatory framework across various jurisdictions and a lack of agreed taxonomy across the globe, for example the classification of tokens, are holding back the ability to scale, going against the borderless nature of blockchain's benefits. Live use cases are taking place across a multitude of private and public blockchains, leading to a lack of interoperability and liquidity between protocols. Establishing connectivity and interoperability between platforms will result in significant benefits, allowing users to easily transfer and move assets across platforms and use cases, ultimately increasing liquidity and adoption and driving network effects.

Experiments driven by traditional institutions are still small and restricted in scope. For example, many will do one or two experiments in isolation, others tokenize the asset, but the payment is still made offline, or tokenize the asset but do not incorporate the cash flows and liabilities. Underlying cash flows and liabilities need to be not only digitized but transformed into a machine-readable and executable form. Moving contracts into digital forms by attaching PDFs that still require a human to read and interpret the document 'will not be enough,' says Ralf Kubli, board member of the Casper Association.[19] Financial contracts need to be standardized at the industry level, akin to creating a universal language.

Ultimately, the full lifecycle of the asset, the end-to-end process, will need to be streamlined and moved on-chain for the exponential benefit of tokenization to materialize. But that's a big task. So, in the next few years, the focus will be on scaling solutions that provide commercial value. As those solutions are scaled, liquidity will flow into the markets, creating more interesting propositions.

SUMMARY OF KEY POINTS

- Tokenization, in blockchain, is the process of creating a token on a blockchain that represents an asset. The asset can be either digital or physical, tangible or intangible.

- Tokenization is one of the biggest opportunities in Web3, often labelled the 'killer use case' for mainstream adoption. Traditional financial institutions have indeed seen the benefits it can bring and are working on solutions to be deployed.

- Tokenization has the potential to democratize access of previously exclusive investment opportunities (like fine art and expensive cars) and increase the liquidity of less accessible and traditionally illiquid assets (like real estate). Additionally, tokenization will allow for 24/7 global trading, instant settlement, and the reduction of operational costs and efficiencies.

- For real traction, the industry will need to build big enough markets with primary and secondary markets.

- Tokenizing an asset is just the first step, but the real value is achieved once the full 'assembly line' of financial services is reimagined and built on blockchain. Until then, tokenization will not be able to achieve its full potential.

Endnotes

1 W McCurdy. BlackRock CEO says next generation for markets is tokenization, Decrypt, 1 December 2022, decrypt.co/116145/blackrock-ceo-says-next-generationmarkets-is-tokenization (archived at https://perma.cc/TAG6-F594)

2 S Kumar, R Suresh, D Liu, B Kronfellner and A Kaul. Relevance of on-chain asset tokenisation in 'crypto winter', Boston Consulting Group, 2022, web-assets.bcg.com/1e/a2/5b5f2b7e42dfad2cb3113a291222/on-chain-asset-tokenization.pdf (archived at https://perma.cc/GX59-HKM6)

3 Citigroup. Money, tokens and games: Blockchain's next billion users and trillions in value, 30 March 2023, http://citigroup.com/global/insights/citigps/money-tokens-and-games (archived at https://perma.cc/5DNX-V2ZE)

4 F P Gabriel Jr. More than 50% of wealthy's money is in illiquid assets, *InvestmentNews*,16 April 2021, investmentnews.com/more-than-50-of-wealthys-money-is-in-illiquid-assets-4114 (archived at https://perma.cc/K82L-WTUF)

5 S Kumar, R Suresh, D Liu, B Kronfellner and A Kaul (2022) Relevance of on-chain asset tokenisation in 'Crypto Winter', Boston Consulting Group, 2022, web-assets.bcg.com/1e/a2/5b5f2b7e42dfad2cb3113a291222/on-chain-asset-tokenization.pdf (archived at https://perma.cc/GX59-HKM6)

6 R Tummala and X Y Tan. The 10x potential for tokenisation, HSBC Global Banking and Markets, 20 August 2020, www.gbm.hsbc.com/en-gb/feed/innovation/potential-of-tokenisation (archived at https://perma.cc/HW27-WQ5M)

7 P Gaffney. Tokenization and real-world assets take center stage, Coindesk, 22 November 2023, coindesk.com/business/2023/11/22/tokenization-and-real-world-assets-take-center-stage/ (archived at https://perma.cc/78DX-UWBK)

8 Digital Asset. RWA tokenization report, Digital Asset Research, 12 July 2023, www.digitalassetresearch.com/real-world-assets-rwas-tokenization-report-june-2023-recap/ (archived at https://perma.cc/XVU8-RUH8)

9 A Savenko. Warhol's 14 small electric chairs sold through blockchain, 6 September 2018, ihodl.com/topnews/2018-09-06/warhols-14-small-electric-chairs-sold-through-blockchain/ (archived at https://perma.cc/V3S6-PZCP)

10 P Convery. How tokenizing real estate can turn the 'rules' on their head – by mastering them first, Yahoo Finance, 18 February 2023, finance.yahoo.com/news/tokenizing-real-estate-turn-rules-043500291.html (archived at https://perma.cc/87KP-T3EK)

11 E Mest. Blockchain technology meets real estate investment at the St. Regis Aspen, Hotel Management, 7 September 2018, hotelmanagement.net/tech/blockchain-technology-meets-real-estate-investment-at-st-regis-aspen (archived at https://perma.cc/5XFY-YB5L)

12 app.binaryx.com (archived at https://perma.cc/6HRU-EJRH)

13 Ledger Insights. Mizuho Trust to issue real estate security tokens, 25 April 2022, ledgerinsights.com/mizuho-trust-to-issue-real-estate-security-tokens/ (archived at https://perma.cc/LWV5-QZLN)

14 R Cohen, P Smith, V Arulchandran and A Sehra. *Automation and blockchain in securities issuances*, 2018, allenovery.com/global/-/media/allenovery/2_documents/news_and_insights/campaigns/blockchain/cohen_smith_automation_blockchain.pdf (archived at https://perma.cc/SG25-2NH6)

15 Santander. Santander launches the first end-to-end blockchain bond, 12 September 2019, santander.com/en/press-room/press-releases/santander-launches-the-first-end-to-end-blockchain-bond (archived at https://perma.cc/X47S-FEDK)

16 P Whitfield. Digital bonds: The disruption is underway, S&P Ratings, 27 February 2023, spglobal.com/ratings/en/research/articles/230227-digital-bonds-the-disruption-is-underway-12651017 (archived at https://perma.cc/G39Z-D5CG)

17 L Noonan and P Stafford. LSE Group draws up plans for blockchain-based digital assets business, *Financial Times*, 4 September 2023, ft.com/content/ce177de8-2828-4fe2-827f-1c25dcbc99ff (archived at https://perma.cc/PA2W-WJNN)

18 Digital Asset. The Canton Network: Creating powerful connections, changing how financial markets operate, 16 June 2023, blog.digitalasset.com/blog/creating-powerful-connections-changing-how-financial-markets-operate (archived at https://perma.cc/59DY-C6WM)

19 R Kubli. How crypto tokenization can go wrong (and how to make it right), Coindesk, 10 August 2023, coindesk.com/consensus-magazine/2023/08/10/how-crypto-tokenization-can-go-wrong-and-how-to-make-it-right/ (archived at https://perma.cc/P9C6-WHYD)

06

Lending and borrowing

MEET COMPOUND

'As an enthusiastic blockchain investor, I'm often asked what to do after purchasing cryptocurrencies. As it currently stands, just about the only thing you can do is move your assets off exchanges and into your own control. And then… wait until you're ready to sell,' Robert Leshner wrote in a blog back in 2017.[1]

This frustration led crypto pioneer Leshner to start a new company called Compound, alongside a team of engineers and blockchain enthusiasts. Compound was a decentralized protocol that would address the flaws within existing borrowing platforms. Instead of peer-to-peer lending, lenders would earn interest by providing money to a pool, and borrowers could take instantaneous loans using the same pools. In a liquidity pool, the money would be immediately available, and the pool would never be empty. The key was to set dynamic automatic interest rates based on supply and demand. When there is a large pool of crypto locked, interest rates are low. When there is a lack of liquidity in the pool (i.e. a small amount of crypto has been locked), rates would increase to attract more lenders.

In May 2018, Compound raised $8.2 million in seed funding led by big names, including Bain Capital Ventures, a16z and Polychain Capital.[2] Later in September 2018, Compound launched, allowing institutions and individuals to lend and borrow cryptocurrencies. Although the company initially only accepted four cryptocurrencies, the need to include a stablecoin in the protocol was quickly noted. Later the same year, after a community vote, DAI – a stablecoin created by MakerDAO protocol – was added to the platform.

This initial community vote demonstrated Leshner's vision to include the community's voice in strategic decisions and decentralize the project over time. In 2020, Compound initiated this journey by distributing governance tokens, COMP, to its users. Nowadays, COMP is distributed as rewards to users who interact with the protocol by lending or borrowing. COMP holders have the power to participate in governance decisions, from setting interest rates to directing treasury funds. Leshner stepped back, letting the community take the wheel through on-chain votes. As a fully decentralized autonomous organization (DAO), Compound continues to innovate and has delivered billions in loans.

Compound, Aave and MakerDAO (discussed in more detail later in the chapter) are some of the most prominent platforms for DeFi lending. Each allows users to lock their funds in the platform, and smart contracts govern how they work without centralized intermediation. As of January 2024, the total value locked (TVL) in these three lending protocols exceeds $16 billion. While the market may be still small, players in the DeFi lending and borrowing space have disrupted traditional models and beliefs. Initially used mostly for trading, new use cases have emerged, driven by the protocol's evolution.

Revolutionizing traditional lending and borrowing

Banks act as the trusted intermediary between lenders and borrowers in traditional finance. When individuals or organizations need capital – for example, to buy a house or expand their business into a new country – they approach a bank and submit a loan application. The bank assesses the applicants' creditworthiness and, if approved, determines the loan's terms and conditions. Conversely, individuals or institutions looking to earn interest on their funds, deposit them in the bank. These funds are typically pooled together and lent out to borrowers. Banks profit from the spread between the interest rates charged to the borrower and the ones paid to the lenders.

However, the traditional process has a few inefficiencies. Not everyone has access to the financial market. Underserved and underrepresented communities often struggle to meet the required credit checks and documentation. Even for those with access, the loan approval process can be lengthy, stretching over weeks if not months. Additionally, with rates at historical lows in recent years, very little interest was returned to depositors.

Having understood the limitations and the gap in the market, fintechs created a new solution called peer-to-peer (P2P) platforms, connecting borrowers and lenders. The concept began to gain traction in the mid-2000s, with fintechs offering loans to individuals and businesses that found it difficult to secure financing from traditional sources. While this new concept disintermediates access to capital, it still requires a centralized entity that performs the credit checks and identity verifications and takes a fee in return for these services.

In Web3, there is a groundbreaking shift in lending and borrowing. Banks' and fintechs' role as custodians, central ledgers and credit decision engines is being truly disintermediated. Because there are no intermediates, the new lending platforms can offer more attractive interest rates to borrowers and provide sizable returns to lenders. Since many protocols do not require credit checks and background information, the process is much faster and available to even underserved communities.

Decentralized lending and borrowing

In Web3, individuals and organizations in need of capital (borrowers) can do so by taking a loan via protocols instead of a physical or virtual bank. On the lender side (often called liquidity providers), individuals or organizations can provide funds to a lending pool and receive interest on their contributions, similar to an interest or savings account. Unlike peer-to-peer lending, in DeFi, funds are added to liquidity pools in a way that a lender may lend to a number of borrowers and vice versa. Liquidity pools are an innovation of the DeFi industry with no equivalent in traditional finance.

Smart contracts play a vital role in lending and borrowing proto-cols. They serve as the automated backbone that facilitates and governs transactions, effectively replacing the role traditionally played by centralized entities. All terms and conditions, including interest rate, loan-to-value ratio and liquidation threshold, are prede-termined by smart contracts logic.

As we have mentioned, Compound, Aave and MakerDAO are all examples of decentralized lending protocols.

Over-collateralization

In traditional banking, there are two main types of loans. The first type is collateralized loans, in which the borrower provides an asset or security as collateral. Lenders use it as a form of security, ensuring that, if the borrower fails to fulfil their obligations, the lenders can seize and sell the collateral to recover the losses. Those loans tend to be long-term loans for substantial amounts, for example to buy a car or a house. The second type of loan is unsecured or uncollateralized in which the borrower does not provide collateral to secure the loan. Instead, the lenders provide credit based solely on their creditworthi-ness, financial history, income and other factors. Those tend to be short-term loans, for example credit cards and personal loans.

In decentralized lending and borrowing, many protocols do not require identity or associated credit scores to take out a loan. Instead, decentralized lending is collateral-based, i.e. borrowers need to provide collateral as a security for the loan. In order to ensure the stability and security of the platforms, early projects adopted over-collateralization as a common practice. In essence, borrowers have to deposit more crypto collateral than the value of the loan they are taking, ensuring that, even if the collateral value drops signifi-cantly, the collateral can be liquidated to make lenders whole (i.e. ensure solvency).

Let's look at an example. Imagine that a protocol has a collateral factor of 75 per cent for USDC, a stablecoin pegged to the US dollar. Then the user who supplies $100 worth of Ethereum (ETH) as collat-eral can borrow $75 worth of USDC.

At regular intervals, protocols use oracles to verify the value of the collateral deposited. Oracles are third-party services that connect the on-chain (data on the blockchain) and off-chain environments (real-world data). Oracles are pivotal when smart contract outcomes are based on off-chain data – for example, in scenarios in which insurance payments are connected with weather information or when supply chain payments require delivery data based on IoT (Internet of Things) sensor data. In lending protocols, the accuracy and reliability of these off-chain inputs are crucial, and so protocols will often use more than one oracle to reduce the risk of incorrect data.

If at any point the value of the collateral, in this case ETH, falls below a given threshold, the collateral is liquidated. In decentralized finance, instead of liquidation happening centrally, smart contracts automatically sell borrowers' collateralized assets at discounted prices to liquidators, using the proceeds to repay borrowers' debt.

In our example, if the Ethereum price suddenly drops from $100 to $60, the collateral value is no longer fulfilling the 75 per cent collateral factor. In that instance, the protocol will offer liquidators, often other users, a chance to buy all or a portion of the collateral for $0.80 instead of $1. Note that is an illustrative example, with each protocol having its own mechanism.

For a long time, over-collateralization provided a great model for lending protocols to cover their positions and minimize the inherent risk of crypto prices decreasing significantly. This model also aligned with DeFi's vision of decentralization as trustless (a trusted third party is not required) and open access (given that anyone with an internet connection can participate). Even if borrowers defaulted, the automatic programmability of the smart contracts would ensure lenders were insured and paid using the collateral.

However, this concept is highly inefficient. Borrowers must put more money into the system than they borrow, with some assets sitting unused. Also, it discriminates against borrowers who cannot meet the collateralization thresholds, often the ones that would benefit the most; going against the ethos of equality and access to all.

New forms of collateral: tokenized assets

In an attempt to improve capital efficiency and reach underserved communities, some protocols have revaluated or expanded existing collateralization requirements.

Whereas previously, protocols would mostly accept crypto as collateral, now they also accept tokenized assets as collateral. This new paradigm reduces the need to have significant amounts of crypto at hand and, because almost anything, from gold and real estate to bonds and carbon credits, can be tokenized, it unlocks opportunities for most businesses and institutions. Arf, Goldfinch and Maple Finance are some of the most notable examples of new protocols in this space.

While this new approach is gaining traction in the industry, some processes and requirements still need to be defined, namely enforcement mechanisms. In a scenario in which the borrower has used crypto as collateral and the collateralization ratio falls under a certain threshold, the smart contract will automatically initiate the liquidation process. Since the crypto collateral is usually locked in a smart contract, the same can be easily put for auction by the smart contract. When the same borrower has used their tokenized house as collateral, the liquidation process could prove cumbersome. Even if the smart contract locks the tokenized asset, the physical access, control and sale of the house would be complex. For this innovation to work in the future, off-chain and legally tied enforcement mechanisms will need to be leveraged.

Some of the old protocols are tailoring their crypto-native platforms to become compatible with tokenized assets as collateral, offering a combination of pools with different requirements.

AAVE

Aave was launched in 2017 by a team of coders led by Stani Kulechov. Initially launched as 'ETHLend', it was rebranded in September 2018 to its current name, which means 'Ghost' in Finnish. It originally launched as a peer-to-peer (P2P) lending protocol but later switched to a pooled protocol.

Lenders can supply liquidity to pools and earn interest while borrowers can withdraw loans from the same pools.

In 2020, Aave protocol initiated the move to a fully decentralized governance and is now fully governed as a DAO. Stani Kulechov stepped back, letting the community take the wheel through on-chain votes, and founded a software technology company called Avara (previously Aave Companies). In Aave, policies, changes and updates are determined by community votes. Both lenders and borrowers get governance tokens, AAVE tokens, when they supply liquidity and withdraw loans.

In 2021, Aave protocol partnered with Centrifuge, a centralized lending protocol, to provide the first RWA market (real-world, tokenized assets). Launching with seven pools, the market allows lenders to deposit USDC and borrowers to borrow tokens by depositing tokenized collateral. Aave users who until then were only able to lend against crypto-native assets could now earn yield against tokenized collateral.

Throughout the years, Avae went through a number of upgrades and pioneered innovative features like flash loans and collateral swap. Initially deployed on Ethereum, it has recently also launched on other blockchains, including Polygon and Avalanche. In 2023, Aave launched its stablecoin called GHO, after a community governance vote, which saw nearly 100 per cent of the 424 participating addresses vote in favour.[3]

The protocol has grown to become one of the most prominent crypto lending protocols, with a TVL of over $6 billion in 2023 across five networks and over 11 markets.

Centralized lending and borrowing

In recent years, a new form of protocol has emerged. These protocols implement centralized checks, due diligence procedures and credit checks, similar to the checks and concepts used by traditional financial institutions. Because they consider the creditworthiness of the applicants, they don't require over-collateralization, but instead loans are tailored according to applicants' credit. Often, they provide uncollateralized loans or under-collateralized loans, accepting tokenized assets as collateral.

Some protocols will have teams with years of experience in credit review that perform the checks while others will use external teams. Commonly, they will not directly originate the loans themselves, instead acting as a credit infrastructure between borrowers and lenders. Their main source of review is similar to decentralized protocols, which is a percentage of the interest revenue from outstanding loans.

Although such credit risk-assessment decisions may make certain aspects of these protocols more centralized than the ones discussed earlier, the reality is that these protocols still use many Web3 techniques and concepts, such as smart contracts automating the distribution of interest payments and using liquidity pools. From a traditional institution perspective, these types of protocols are more aligned with their needs and regulatory requirements while still using some new concepts that could provide efficiency.

Currently, they are mostly used by businesses in emerging markets and crypto-native institutions such as hedge funds and trading companies, which, given the industry in which they operate, tend to struggle to obtain loans from traditional institutions like banks. We will look at two examples, Goldfinch and Maple Finance, in the next few sections.

Lending and borrowing in action

Until now, lending and borrowing protocols have been mainly used by sophisticated investors and institutional investors, like hedge funds, for trading. Those investors have the levels of collateral required to be able to afford the over-collateralization requirements. They also have a greater risk appetite, which aligns with the high volatility in the crypto markets (especially in the early days).

Flash loans

Crypto arbitrage trading means that if you see a token trading at different rates on different exchanges, you can make money by buying it at one place and selling it at another. One use case that has become popular recently is flash loans, pioneered by Aave. Flash loans are a type of uncollateralized lending unique to the DeFi space. Users can borrow assets without collateral or credit checks as long as they pay back the loan in the same transaction. They are largely used to take advantage of arbitrage opportunities when two markets price an asset differently.

Let's look at an example. An investor spots that Ether (ETH, the Ethereum cryptocurrency) is priced at $2,000 on exchange A and $2,100 on exchange B. So, there is an arbitrage opportunity here. If the investor buys from the cheaper exchange (A) and sells it for more (in exchange B), she could make a profit.

She initiates a flash loan and borrows 10 ETH. With those 10 ETH she sells the same on exchange B, and closes the flash loan by paying it back. In this scenario, our investor makes a profit of $1,000 minus fees.

All these steps happen atomically within a single transaction. If any steps fail, the entire transaction is reversed, including the loan itself. Given that these types of transactions have low risk and low cost, some bad actors have used them to manipulate the market or exploit vulnerabilities. Such attacks can occur in mere seconds and still involve several protocols.

EULER FINANCE FLASH LOAN ATTACK

Founded in 2021, Euler Finance is a decentralized lending protocol built on the Ethereum network. Similar to other decentralized lending protocols, users can lend crypto or borrow crypto by using other cryptocurrency as collateral. In March 2023, Euler Finance suffered a flash loan attack, which resulted in over $195 million in losses. The attacker engaged in a number of attacks, draining various tokens from the protocol.

The first attack consisted of 20 transactions in the same block and drained around $8.9 million worth of DAI, the MakerDAO native stablecoin, from the DAI deposit pool. It was then repeated for other pools until the total amount was drained. The attacker borrowed a $30 million DAI loan from Aave and then exploited a vulnerable code in Euler Finance, tricking it into believing there were fewer collateral tokens than debt. Using a different entity, the attacker then liquidated the accounts and profited from the liquidation bonus.

After the attack, Euler Labs noted that it had worked with various security groups to perform audits of the protocol. While the vulnerable code was reviewed and approved during an outside audit, it was not discovered as part of the audit, remaining on-chain for eight months before it was exploited.

This attack caused a contagion to spread through multiple DeFi protocols, and at least 11 protocols in addition to Euler suffered losses due to the attack.

Over the following weeks, Euler sent on-chain messages to the Ethereum account holding the stolen assets, demanding the return of the funds. In a surprising outcome and to the great relief of many Euler users, the attacker returned the exploited funds.

Cross-border loans/investments

The new protocols that accept tokenized assets are particularly beneficial for borrowers who lack access to traditional financial markets or don't have a stable fiat currency in their country. The IFC (International Finance Corporation) estimates that 43 per cent of small and medium-sized enterprises (SMEs) in developing countries cannot access financing from traditional sources, with a gap of $4.1 trillion in unmet financing needs.[4] If we consider markets in which the native currency is frequently devalued, a loan based on a US-pegged stablecoin, for example, can provide much more stability and benefit than a fiat-based loan from a traditional bank.

GOLDFINCH

Goldfinch, a decentralized credit platform, was founded in 2020 to make crypto borrowing more accessible to individuals and businesses in developing countries. The founders, Mike Sall and Blake West, graduated from the University of Pennsylvania's Wharton School of Business and worked at Coinbase. After the publication of the Goldfinch Whitepaper 1.0, Goldfinch was officially launched in 2021. Gaining quick traction only one year later, Goldfinch had surpassed the $100 million mark in active loans,[5] distributed across 28 countries, including the US, Brazil, India, Indonesia, Mexico, Nigeria and others. It currently operates as an open marketplace for loans, fully collateralized by off-chain assets and income, and employs a decentralized loan underwriting process.

In essence, businesses in emerging markets can access funding from global lenders while providing non-crypto collateral. Businesses use their credit lines to draw down stablecoins, specifically USDC, and exchange them for fiat currency, deploying the funds on the ground to end-borrowers in their local markets. Investors can use Goldfinch to deposit crypto and receive yield. As the businesses make interest payments, the protocol immediately disburses them to all investors. This way, the protocol provides global access to capital, while leaving the end-borrower loan origination and servicing to the businesses best equipped to handle that in their own communities.[6] Currently, the protocol has supplied loans to a wide range of businesses. For example, Divibank, a data-driven financing platform offering Latin American businesses access to non-dilutive growth capital, borrowed a $5 million loan to fund the growth of its operations in Brazil.[7]

Incumbents and decentralized lending protocols

Most incumbents have not experimented with lending and borrowing protocols. The users' anonymity and lack of regulation, coupled with the attacks and hacks notoriously discussed in the news, have kept many traditional institutions at bay. Société Générale is one of the few traditional institutions that have performed experiments in this space, leveraging its digital asset-focused subsidiary, Forge.

SOCIÉTÉ GÉNÉRALE BACKS STABLECOIN LOANS WITH BONDS

In January 2023, Société Générale-Forge (SG-Forge) borrowed $7 million DAI from MakerDAO. MakerDAO is one of the largest and oldest decentralized lending and borrowing protocols. Borrowers deposit collateral into vaults and take out debt denominated in the protocol's native stablecoin called DAI. In simple terms, vaults are smart contracts which hold the borrower's collateral until all the borrowed DAI is returned. If the value of the collateral drops below a certain threshold, the vaults automatically liquidate the collateral through an auction process. MakerDAO is fully decentralized and organized as a DAO. Any new proposals require a community vote and the type of collateral that can be used by borrowers is determined by the DAO.

In 2020, MakerDAO voted to allow borrowers to post tokenized assets-based collateral to vaults, significantly increasing the protocols revenue. Two years later, MakerDAO made the first integration with traditional finance, by providing a loan worth up to $100 million to a community bank in Philadelphia called Huntingdon Valley Bank.

In 2022, after a community vote that passed with 76 per cent support, MakerDAO provided SG-Forge a credit limit of $30 million in DAI. The vault was backed by 40 million euro in bonds in the form of OFH tokens, making the loans over-collateralized. OFH tokens are tokenized securities issued on the Ethereum platform and backed primarily by home loans.[8]

Later, in 2023, SG-Forge repaid its debt to MakerDAO and labelled the experiment a success. A Forge representative said the experiment 'demonstrated that on-chain refinancing markets could be opened to real money asset owners, in full compliance with banking standards, with potentially significant improvements in financial terms, operational efficiency, settlement, and counterparty risks'.[9]

The permissionless nature of decentralized protocols on public blockchains is perhaps one of the main obstacles to incumbents' adoption. For regulated institutions, it remains impossible to meet KYC and AML requirements if they were to use decentralized protocols, putting them at risk of transacting in a protocol used for illegal activities. In order to bridge the gap between regulated incumbents and decentralized lending, some players in Web3 have created permissioned environments. Those environments allow regulated entities to engage with the innovation behind decentralized lending protocols, while ensuring that only onboarded and approved users can participate. Aave Arc is one of those notable experiments.

AAVE ARC

In 2022, Fireblocks, a centralized Web3 company and one of the governance token holders, submitted a proposal to Aave DAO. The proposal introduced the idea of creating Aave Arc, a permissioned version of Aave, aimed at facilitating the bridge between traditional regulated institutions and crypto markets. Permissioned would mean that the access was restricted to whitelisted institutions and users, i.e. institutions or users that went through due diligence procedures such as KYC and AML.

   The proposal was approved via community voting, and so the first permissioned DeFi protocol was available.

In a discussion with Stani Kulechov, founder and CEO of Avara (formerly Aave Companies), he told me how Aave Arc was received by the industry:

> Aave Arc has been well received by financial institutions, leading the way to JP Morgan and the Central Bank of Brazil to utilise Aave Arc contracts and being used to deploy other use cases such as real world assets.
>
>   Aave Arc was one of the first attempts at 'permissioned DeFi' and has attracted over 70 institutional users, driving Total Value Locked (TVL) to nearly $100 million. Notable among users are Coinshares, Canvas Digital, and GSR, all of whom were onboarded by Fireblocks – the initial whitelister. The success of these projects has opened the door to experimentation in DeFi among financial institutions and has led to conversations with large banks.

In terms of other opportunities with incumbents, Stani Kulechov sees a willingness to adopt stablecoins with a potential for liquidity pools that facilitate the supplying and borrowing of stablecoins:

> Businesses engaged in cross-border payments have shown an increased willingness to adopt stablecoins, indicating the potential for liquidity pools that facilitate the supply/borrow of stablecoins. This approach would also attract users beyond J.P. Morgan's clientele as well as those

who wish to avoid additional financial intermediaries. The partnership between traditional finance and Aave Companies was a milestone for the industry, and set a precedent for other banks to explore opportunities in the DeFi space, and on public blockchains.

Challenges and vulnerabilities

MAPLE FINANCE

Maple Finance, an uncollateralized lending and borrowing protocol, was founded in 2018 and launched in 2021. The founders, Sidney Powell and Joe Flanagan, with backgrounds in capital markets and traditional finance, saw the potential of building a decentralized alternative.

The team behind Maple Finance operates the credit platform but does not originate or underwrite the loans directly. Instead, Maple has pool delegates, who are third-party credit companies responsible for negotiating loan terms with borrowers, performing diligence, and liquidating collateral in the event of a default. Pool delegates also review a borrower's reputation, expertise and performance to evaluate the terms of the loan.

In 2022, Maple Finance hit the $1 billion mark, within less than 10 months of launch, and was looking to connect crypto mining borrowers with traditional asset managers. However, 2022 was riddled with a number of collapses in the crypto industry, changing the momentum for Maple and a number of other protocols across the industry. It all started in May 2022, when the project Terra-Luna, an algorithmic stablecoin, collapsed, taking with it hedge funds that had invested in the project. Three Arrows Capital (3AC), a Singapore-based hedge fund, was one of the first hit hard by the chaos. The hedge fund had invested in dozens of other crypto startups and borrowed from a number of lending protocols, and so, when it collapsed in 2022, loan defaults led to a mass contagion with many lending protocols, such as BlockFi, Voyager and Celsius, having to file for bankruptcy themselves.

While Maple did not have direct exposure to those companies, there were ongoing liquidity issues in the crypto market, affecting both lenders and borrowers. Later in the year, the collapse of FTX provided another blow to the industry, and Maple again found itself dealing with a potential liquidity crisis. Many of Maple's lenders and borrowers work or were connected with crypto and so were heavily impacted by the collapses and the value of cryptocurrencies going down and, as a result, were unable to pay for the loans. One notable example was Orthogonal Trading, a cryptocurrency hedge fund, which had loans with Maple and funds in FTX. With the FTX collapse, Orthogonal's funds were tied up and the hedge fund ultimately defaulted on its loans with Maple.

Based on the lessons learned from that event, the team at Maple is now looking to diversify its offerings. Besides uncollateralized lending, it is now venturing into tokenized assets-based collateral lending. For example, in 2023, Maple created a $100 million liquidity pool backed by tax receivables.

Additionally, it is also changing its risk management approach. Traditionally, Maple was not involved in the underwriting process, which was performed by third-party companies acting as pool delegates. But, in 2023, Maple established a new subsidiary to serve as the pool delegate for Maple Direct. Maple Direct, a new pool available on the platform, is a direct lending product designed to provide loans to Web3 infrastructure companies, asset management firms and liquidity providers. Maple Direct offers over-collateralized loans and all parties are subject to KYC and AML standards in order to participate.

Contagion events

Lending and borrowing protocols have attracted many investors looking for high yields. However, this space is still nascent and riddled with complexities and challenges. The events in 2022 underscored how lending protocols are mostly self-referencing in the crypto industry, creating contagion events. For example, much of the collateral used in decentralized lending is cryptocurrency, either the protocol native token or stablecoins, so, when the price of the cryptocurrency declines significantly, it puts pressure on lending protocols. Additionally, lending protocols are interconnected through cross-platform borrowing and lending. For example, many hedge funds borrow from lending protocols and invest in crypto companies and protocols (see Orthogonal Trading just mentioned). This intrinsic interconnectivity means contagion can propagate risks across multiple protocols quickly.

Vulnerabilities of uncollateralized loans

The same events have brought into focus uncollateralized lending vulnerabilities in such a volatile market. When an uncollateralized loan defaults, there aren't any assets that creditors can reclaim immediately, so creditors only receive partial compensation from the protocols and must resort to debt restructuring or go to court to recover their money. While some argue that uncollateralized lending is not viable in the young, volatile digital asset market, others believe there is still space for it. Maple, our use case, has realigned its strategy towards providing less risky alternatives (tokenized asset collateral instead of uncollateralized loans) and refining its risk management practices (doing this itself since it has a traditional background). Note that many centralized lending platforms do not perform credit underwriting themselves; instead, they act as credit infrastructure providers by connecting borrowers and lenders. While they may have some reputational risk in times of crisis, they do not bear the solvency risk themselves.

Inherent risks of automatic liquidation

Decentralized lending protocols do not face such issues since they are heavily collateralized. In situations in which the crypto assets pledged as collateral drop below a certain threshold, the collateral is automatically liquidated to repay the loan. Even during previous crypto market volatility, decentralized lending protocols operated as intended, with large amounts liquidated but minimal interruption. In mid-June 2022, during the sharpest downturns in the market, there were over $300 million in liquidation across the biggest decentralized lending protocols. Of course, automatic liquidation also has significant inherent risks. Since the smart contract will execute automatically and irreversibly, in situations of error, remediation is challenging. Additionally, there is also the risk of creating downward price spirals in crypto assets. If executed under stressed conditions, it can push collateral prices further down and spread contagion.

On-chain and off-chain transparency

Some critics in the industry argue that many issues seen in 2022 in the lending protocol space were due to a lack of transparency from centralized companies. Some centralized lending companies pledged off-chain assets as collateral, with some even using the same collateral multiple times. If an asset is pledged off-chain it is not transparent how much liability there is and how much risk undertaken. According to Robert Leshner, founder of Compound:

> The first reason why centralised lending businesses are imploding is because they are not in the advertised business of lending. All of these firms were operating, essentially, as proprietary hedge funds using customer money, and the reason this was able to occur was because these businesses were opaque. Nobody had any visibility.[10]

Regulation

Until recently, this space has been mostly left untouched by regulators. However, recent contagion events have intensified regulatory intervention. Many regulators are now starting to define frameworks that will undoubtedly impact this space. Initial frameworks are focused on centralized protocols and stablecoins, notoriously used as a collateral in this space given lower volatility versus other cryptocurrencies. However, as discussed earlier, this space is highly connected, so regulatory requirements for centralized protocols will most likely impact decentralized protocols as well. Because this ecosystem is so new, it is difficult to know the likelihood, timing and impact of some of these regulatory interventions.

Future outlook

In the early days, there were limited use cases to profit from crypto assets, but lending platforms unlocked new opportunities for investors. On-chain lending allowed investors to generate additional income from their crypto portfolios. However, the early features of protocols mostly facilitated speculation and trading with cryptocurrencies instead of real economy lending. Due to the anonymity of the players and high market volatility, many protocols adopted over-collateralization practices, which solved the solvency issues but restricted their ability to scale and be adopted by those that most needed access to loans.

Such problems inspired new players to approach decentralized finance from a different angle. Some leveraged traditional credit checks and underwriting mechanisms to provide uncollateralized loans or under-collateralized loans, using tokenized assets as collateral. Those protocols are undeniably already making progress in providing financial inclusion by expanding access to global investors. However, uncollateralized lending protocols are still a relatively new and untested concept, with critics arguing that the inherent risks are too high and they will eventually fail.

Looking ahead, the potential of lending protocols to serve the real economy is tied to leveraging tokenized assets as collateral and creating on-chain identity. Tokenization will be essential to expand lenders' and borrowers' profiles, outside crypto, overcoming its self-referential nature, but it requires both technological improvements and updated legal frameworks. Additionally, on-chain lending evolution relies on robust identity verification mechanisms that allow for credit scoring and reputation building. Such developments will likely push the industry towards more centralization, blurring the lines between DeFi and traditional finance.

As I was writing the concluding thoughts of this chapter, Goldfinch (the lending protocol for emerging markets discussed earlier) announced that it had written down a $5million loan provided initially to Tugende (a Kenyan taxi financier).[11] This story, alongside the events in 2022, showcased the inherent risks and complexity of lending. While some raised concerns about the need for more robust underwriting practices, others noted the issues of using tokenized assets as collateral, especially across the globe. The reality is that the same risk also takes place in traditional financial services, and loans often need to be written off. Being a new industry with new concepts and technology, risks and controls are still being defined. However, the innovation and opportunities are undeniable.

SUMMARY OF KEY POINTS

- In decentralized lending, lenders earn interest by providing money to a pool, and borrowers take instantaneous loans using the same pools.

- Early projects adopted over-collateralization, in which borrowers have to deposit more crypto collateral than the value of the loan they are taking. If the value of the collateral falls below a given threshold, the collateral is automatically liquidated.

- Centralized protocols implement centralized checks and provide uncollateralized or under-collateralized loans. Since the collateral value is lower than the loan, they are riskier than over-collateralized loans.

- Most incumbents have not experimented with lending and borrowing protocols due to lack of regulation, users' anonymity and numerous attacks and hacks in this space. In order to bridge this gap, some protocols have created permissioned environments in which only approved entities and individuals can operate.

- Downturn events have underscored how lending protocols are still riddled with complexities and challenges. However, the innovation and opportunities are undeniable. High yields will continue to attract investors, while innovative methods and operational efficiencies will benefit incumbents.

Endnotes

1   R Leshner. Introducing compound, the money market protocol, compound labs, Medium Blog, 31 January 2018, medium.com/compound-finance/introducing-compound-the-money-market-protocol-4b9546bac87 (archived at https://perma.cc/74AB-ECJV)

2 J Constine. Coinbase's first investment, Compound, earns you interest on crypto, TechCrunch, 16 May 2018, techcrunch.com/2018/05/16/cryptocurrency-compound-interest/ (archived at https://perma.cc/GG3W-J9B6)

3 B Liu. It's GHO time: Aave stablecoin passes community governance vote, Blockworks, 14 July 2023, blockworks.co/news/aave-stablecoin-gho-mainnet-launch (archived at https://perma.cc/UHG4-GH6B)

4 IFC. Banking on SMEs: Driving growth, creating jobs, *Global SME Financing Facility Progress Report*, 26 September 2022, www.ifc.org/en/insights-reports/2022/2022-global-sme-finance-facility-progress-report (archived at https://perma.cc/P8FT-22KA)

5 Dune analysis, dune.com/goldfinch/goldfinchdune.com/goldfinch/goldfinch)

6 A Simpson. Investing in Goldfinch, a16z crypto, 1 June 2022, a16zcrypto.com/posts/announcement/investing-in-goldfinch/ (archived at https://perma.cc/EX7M-U8S7)

7 Goldfinch. Goldfinch provides Divibank with a $5M debt facility to give LatAm businesses access to non-dilutive growth capital, Medium Blog, 12 November 2021, medium.com/goldfinch-fi/goldfinch-provides-divibank-with-a-5m-debt-facility-to-give-latam-businesses-access-to-ee5425a2d7e8 (archived at https://perma.cc/LS2Z-JNQ6)

8 C Wagner. Societe Generale withdraws $7M in DAI from MakerDAO vault, Blockworks, 12 January 2023, blockworks.co/news/societe-generale-withdraws-makerdao-vault (archived at https://perma.cc/KEP7-8447)

9 S Haig. MakerDAO to shutter SocGen's $30M credit line, *The Defiant*, 28 April 2023, thedefiant.io/makerdao-to-shut-socgen-vault (archived at https://perma.cc/7DT4-FYZF)

10 B Dale. Compound's founder is unworried about DeFi defaults, Axios Crypto, 1 July 2022, www.axios.com/2022/07/01/compound-defi-defaults-decentralized-leshner (archived at https://perma.cc/QP6X-WGHY)

11 S Haig. Goldfinch writes down failed $5M loan to Kenyan taxi financier, *The Defiant*, 9 August 2023, thedefiant.io/goldfinch-writes-down-failed-usd5m-loan-to-kenyan-taxi-financier (archived at https://perma.cc/CCD7-YLWL)

07

Digital identity

'*Who are you?*'

On the surface, the answer seems simple. Instinctively, you may answer that question by saying your name, age and nationality. The reality is that you are more complex than what your ID says. Identity encompasses your professional skills, knowledge, relationships, hobbies and interests. It includes how you express yourself creatively and the communities you belong to. Your identity is shaped by your inherent traits and lived experiences. In the digital world, identity becomes fragmented across countless profiles based on usernames, passwords and biometric data. Parts of your identity are scattered across social platforms, apps and devices owned by centralized entities. In finance, identity often comes down to a credit score, income level and transaction history. Parts of your identity exist in silos across banks, lenders, credit bureaus and regulators.

QUEST FOR FINANCIAL IDENTITY

Meet Jane, a finance professional who emigrated from Colombia to the US.

Jane studied economics and became a market analyst at a renowned investment bank. Through work, she moved to the US a couple of years ago and is now looking to buy her first house, but realizes her experience in Colombia is not reflected in her US credit history. She lacks the financial identity to get approval for a mortgage. Not being one to wait, she decides to take the problem into her own hands. She registers for a decentralized identity wallet and applies for verifiable credentials to validate her Colombian academic degree, early career and expertise. With those credentials anchored to her wallet, she can selectively share a fuller picture of creditworthiness and economic insight with lenders and banks.

This story, while imaginary, showcases what is on the horizon for identity and financial services. Decentralized identity models can make identity more holistic, inclusive and purposeful. As the financial sector explores Web3, identity ownership becomes pivotal, not just for compliance, but for the very foundation on which decentralized finance rests.

Legal identity

Proving your identity is, for many in centralized countries, a given. Legal identity plays a pivotal role in society, and being able to verify your identity is a gateway to access services, benefits and opportunities. The United Nations defines legal identity as 'the basic characteristics of an individual's identity, e.g. name, birthday, sex and place of birth conferred through registration and the issuance of a certificate by an authorized civil registration authority'.[1]

However, according to the World Bank, roughly 850 million people worldwide do not have legal identification. This restricts them from fully engaging in society, making it harder to get a SIM card, vote in elections, receive healthcare or even open a bank account.[2] In 2020, of the 1.7 billion underbanked adults worldwide, 26 per cent cited lack of documentation as the primary barrier.[3]

At the same time, those with IDs lack privacy and control over how their data is shared. The identification method is often inefficient, centrally stored and vulnerable to misuse or theft. How often has a hotel receptionist scanned your passport and kept the copy in an unlocked/unprotected drawer? Or, how often have you been asked to share a copy of your passport via unsecured channels like email?

Digital identity

As our lives have moved increasingly online, creating a digital ID or proving your identity digitally has become necessary. Digital identity represents the attributes that define our legal identity, like a name and date of birth, and how a person or organization expresses themselves online. One of the first primitive digital identities still widely used today is the email address. As the internet grew, we saw the emergence of various authentication and login solutions issued by different platforms such as Google, Apple and Facebook. Those prominent players become the gatekeepers and controllers of digital identities. In this model, the user is entirely dependent on the platform, and the platform's ability to secure the data and defend against hacks and cyber-attacks, their decisions around sharing and selling data and control over accessibility and censorship.

Over the years, stories demonstrating the limitations of this centralized model have come to the surface. From Facebook exploiting users' data for targeted advertisement, to data breaches of password management providers like Last Pass (whose primary goal is to protect user's data securely)[4] and users getting locked out of platforms. Just as I was writing this book, I saw two colleagues locked out of LinkedIn. LinkedIn blocked their accesses because of 'suspicious activity'. They both had to contact, email and call different teams on LinkedIn to get access back.

Now, you would assume that if you lose your data on LinkedIn, it is not so bad. And while personal information, like your education and professional data, can be easily re-added by the user, the followers, previous content and engagement could be lost for ever. And the reality is that this is not a unique story; countless similar stories take place on many other platforms that have a centralized model.

Identity in financial services

Identification in financial services is critical, but processes are still complex and costly and vary by country and organization.

Authentication procedures are still a mix of old and new technologies. For example, in some countries, the bank still requires a copy of your passport to open a bank account. In others, fintechs and neobanks use video-call-based onboarding or biometrics, and the account is open in days.

Organizations must ensure compliance with Know Your Customer (KYC), anti-money laundering (AML) and other due diligence processes – processes that are highly complex, time-consuming and costly. In 2022, the total cost of compliance against financial crime across financial institutions worldwide was \$274.1 billion.[5] Additionally, financial institutions also bear the risk of holding sensitive data and facing cyber-attacks. Such attacks are not only costly but also damage the reputation of an industry in which 'trust' is critical.

Cross-border authentication

Global institutions face the challenge of completing the same due diligence process multiple times, resulting in increased costs and poor customer experience. However, cross-border authentication is a very complex problem due to different regulations and processes.

Let's look at an example. Imagine a customer who has a UK bank account wants to open an account in the US with the same bank. When contacting their bank, the customer is perplexed to have to provide ID and other documentation again since they are already a client in the UK. This leads to frustration and a poor user experience for clients interested in cross-border banking. To simplify the user experience, the global institution would have to redesign the existing process and create a global onboarding process in the future. With the new global process in place, the client would provide the ID once, and processes in the UK and US would be done from that documentation. This could be done by the bank holding the ID and then sharing the information internally, across countries, or by using a third party that holds the ID, with each team, UK and US, accessing the information via the third party.

Now, different countries (UK and US) have different compliance requirements, so the same bank will need to look at different data sets to fulfil different requirements. Should the bank collect all data at once? This would mean collecting more data than initially needed. Should banks share the data internally? There are currently restrictions on what data can be shared across countries. There is also a need to do it safely so no data breaches take place.

This example showcases the complexity and considerations for the creation of an authentication process at a global level vs a local one; a gap that the European Commission aims to close in Europe with the launch of the European Digital Identity.

EUROPEAN DIGITAL IDENTITY

The European Commission aims to make cross-border e-ID a reality by 2024. The European Digital Identity will be available to EU citizens, residents and businesses who want to identify themselves or provide confirmation of certain personal information. It will be available for online and offline, public and private services across the EU.

With the EU Digital Identity wallet, users will be able to prove, across the EU, their identity where necessary to access services online, share digital documents or simply prove a specific personal attribute, such as age. Well-known examples include requesting birth certificates, filing tax returns, applying for a university in another member state, and storing a medical prescription that can be used anywhere in Europe. The opportunities will be endless, including significant opportunities for financial institutions, such as using the same e-ID for opening bank accounts or requesting loans.

The rollout of the e-ID aims to provide benefits to both individuals and businesses. Processes will be streamlined and sped up, reducing operational costs and increasing efficiency, while providing a better customer experience and increasing trust in the services provided. Ultimately, it will enable innovation across the EU, for example a Portuguese citizen will be able to buy a phone sim plan from a French company if the rates are more advantageous.

In her State of the Union address on 16 September 2020, Ursula von der Leyen, President of the European Commission, stated:

Every time an App or website asks us to create a new digital identity or to easily log on via a big platform, we have no idea what happens to our data in

> *reality. That is why the Commission will propose a secure European e-identity. One that we trust and that any citizen can use anywhere in Europe to do anything from paying your taxes to renting a bicycle. A technology where we can control ourselves what data is used and how.*[6]

Innovative solutions

Many financial services organizations have multiple ongoing projects that aim to improve identity verification processes, assess new technologies and streamline existing processes. However, those projects are very complex to implement and can take years to be completed. Another common approach is for banks to participate in consortiums, composed of other banks, regulators and fintechs, to create an industry framework. Such consortium initiatives are common when the problem goes across multiple players, and an industry solution would benefit everyone. The problem with consortiums, however, is that having many players and decision-makers in one room may lead to long decision times.

Many fintech companies have been at the forefront of driving innovation in identity to streamline processes and enhance privacy. Companies like Trulioo and Onfido are well-known for streamlining identity verification processes by offering real-time, multi-source verification services, thereby reducing the time and complexity traditionally involved in such tasks. Companies like Nuggets and Civic have recently emerged and are focused on leveraging self-sovereign identity to provide individuals greater control and ownership of the data. Even tech giants are getting in on the action. For example, Microsoft launched the decentralized identity toolkit ION, while Amazon Web Services offers managed blockchain for identity.

Decentralized identity

Decentralized identity will be essential for the adoption of Web3 solutions, especially by regulated entities, but could also be used for

Web2 solutions since it addresses the limitations of centralized solutions. Decentralized identity flips the model from big platforms to self-sovereignty. Individuals will be able to own and control their data, both in terms of whom they share it with and how much of that data they share, moving to a 'need to know' basis.

The World Economic Forum defines decentralized identity as a 'form of digital ID that allows individuals to control to whom and how they share their data while allowing entities to issue credentials'.[7] From a financial institution's perspective, decentralized identity will address the vulnerabilities of centralized identity systems, such as data breaches and fraud, and streamline regulatory compliance and operational processes, resulting in significant time and cost savings. Critically, decentralized identities could also promote financial inclusion and access. Underserved groups like refugees and small businesses in emerging countries would only need access to the internet and a smart device to create proof of existence.

How does it work in practice?

In this emerging concept, users would be able to access and store their social credentials, digital assets, personal accounts and biometrics data in a Web3 Wallet. They would be able to receive credentials issued by credential providers, like governments and universities, and accept or reject requests to share information with third parties.

Let's imagine how this might work. A recent graduate is looking to start a new job and is currently undergoing background checks. As a final check, the HR department asks her to share her university credentials. She opens her decentralized identity wallet app on her phone, where she has the university degree credential, her government ID credential, her credit score, her NFT (non-fungible token), and the proof of attendance from a recent fintech event. She selects the university credential in the app and shares it with the HR department. The company automatically sees that the credential is authentic, and the background check is completed quickly.

The end-to-end process took a few minutes instead of weeks. The graduate is in full control and able to share only the information needed instead of sharing all her private information. From the company side, it was able to verify the information in seconds without having to contact the university. Imagine how much time and resources you can save if you are able to complete onboarding and background checks this quickly. Additionally, since companies no longer need to store user data, the risk of cyber-attacks is reduced significantly.

The same concept can be applied to the verification of new applicants for mortgages and other loans, for new accounts, and for transferring money. Faster verification and authentications could save time and cost and increase liquidity. As you can see in our example, there is still a need for centralized parties in identity, namely the issuance and verification of credentials, but the role they play and the way activities are performed have changed. This is a trend seen across the use cases in this book. Web3 tools will enable faster and cheaper processes, and while the role of existing players may change, there is still an opportunity for players to operate even if in a different format.

Digital identity elements

As we saw in our example, our graduate had a combination of identity elements in her wallet, which reflects the complexity of one's identity. Let's think about it. Besides your name, age and email address, what else is part of your identity? The degree you earn, your job, memberships, the people you know, and your reputation are all part of your identity. In decentralized identity, there are currently a number of different options to reflect each of those components of your identity.

Let's look at a few examples.

IDENTIFIERS

Identifiers represent a way to identify an individual. Your mobile phone, for example, is a form of centralized identifier assigned to you by the phone company, so it keeps track of who owns what.

- Ethereum Name Service (ENS) is a well-known identifier in Web3, a domain naming system built on the Ethereum blockchain that converts public addresses into more easily recognizable words, like the name of a person or brand. For example, users are able to send payments to friends using their ENS (yourname.ens) instead of using the Ethereum address (a long alphanumeric string of letters and numbers). This is a similar concept to Web2, in which users can send payments to friends using their telephone number or name instead of bank account details.

- Similarly, decentralized identifiers (DIDs) are cryptographically verifiable identifiers created and owned by the user. They are unique. For example, let's consider the name Annabella Smith. There are thousands of Annabella Smiths worldwide, so using a unique identifier like DID would ensure no cases of mistaken identity. DIDs are a recognized standard within the World Wide Web Consortium (W3C), an international community working together to develop web standards.

IDENTITY CLAIMS

Identity claims represent data points or records about an individual or entity, for example what school you went to, what company you have worked at, what assets you own and so on.

- Verifiable credentials (VCs) are a digital, cryptographically secured version of physical and digital credentials. Examples include passports, driver's licences, professional experience and employee status. A third party will cryptographically sign a claim about an individual. For example, Oxford University could issue a VC claiming that someone attended their fintech course.

- Soulbound tokens (SBT) were proposed by Ethereum founder Vitalik Buterin. They represent a fact or claim about an individual, similar to a VC, but the claim is public, permanent and non-transferable. Once a SBT is issued to the wallet, the SBT is bound to that wallet forever. The fact that they are permanent, lack privacy and aren't recoverable (*What would happen if an individual loses access to their wallet?*) has raised concerns and limited adoption.

- Non-fungible tokens (NFTs) are similar to SBTs but can be transferred. Initial use cases were formed around education certifications, ownership of specific art items, digital collectables or proof of attendance (e.g. a token that states an individual has attended a conference).

Each of these components has its own advantages and disadvantages. Institutions thinking about exploring digital identity should consider privacy, control and scalability needed for their use cases.

Decentralized identity in action

Over the last few years, we have seen tremendous growth in the decentralized identity space, fuelled by concerns about identity theft, data breaches, new government regulations and investment into new technologies. The global decentralized identity market is expected to reach $102 billion in 2030, according to recent research.[8] From bigtech, banks, fintechs and Web3 native companies, all stakeholders are looking to leverage decentralized solutions.

Let's look at a few examples.

Financial services experiments

Identity and privacy are crucial for financial services experiments. Regulated traditional institutions are required to perform onboarding, KYC and AML processes while ensuring the privacy of client data and information. The fact that public blockchains lack privacy and are often used by anonymous users is a barrier for adoption by many traditional institutions. That is one of the reasons why they will often experiment and create solutions in private blockchains or closed environments (in which only pre-approved and reviewed players can participate, similar to Aave Arc, which we discussed in Chapter 6).

One great example of an experiment that dealt face on with this issue is Project Guardian. It is often used as a reference for innovative projects that touch many aspects discussed in this book (tokenization, public blockchains and identity).

PROJECT GUARDIAN

Project Guardian, initially designed by the Monetary Authority of Singapore (MAS), is a collaborative initiative with policymakers and financial industry that seeks to test the feasibility of applications in asset tokenization and decentralized finance (DeFi). The first pilot, completed in 2022, aimed to determine if tokenized real-world assets and deposits could be transacted on a public blockchain leveraging DeFi protocols, in a compliant manner.[9]

In that pilot, J.P. Morgan and SBI Digital Asset Holdings successfully completed a cross-currency trade. Tokenized Singapore dollar deposits were exchanged for tokenized Japanese yen on the public blockchain Polygon, utilizing a modified version of the Aave protocol[10] (Aave's Arc, a permissioned version of Aave – see Chapter 6). Onyx by J.P. Morgan explored how digital identity can be used to enable financial institutions to safely gain access to DeFi protocols on public blockchain networks. Onyx created a VC-based digital identity solution and institutional wallet offering that enabled traders from J.P. Morgan and SBI to execute trades in a way that allowed them to prove aspects of their identities while still preserving privacy.

In a discussion with George Kassis, Digital Identity Lead at Onyx by J.P. Morgan, he told me about the experience with Project Guardian and how the team considered identity and privacy using a public blockchain:

Permissioned blockchains such as Onyx Digital Assets are necessary for many financial services use cases, however we also recognize the need for individuals and entities to potentially operate on open, public blockchains in a regulated and compliant way. This is where we look to the idea of a system that combines the power and efficiency of DeFi protocols with a level of safeguards to meet regulatory compliance and customer-safety requirements. Currently, many DeFi protocols lack identity solutions to meet anti-money laundering (AML), know your customer (KYC), and combatting the finance of terrorism (CFT) requirements. Cybersecurity is another major risk, as recent high-profile hacks demonstrated.

When working on the Project Guardian we researched several potential identity solutions, from Verifiable Credentials (VCs), soulbound tokens (SBTs) and others to understand what was available and which one could best solve the problem at hand. We chose VC for various reasons with the key ones being that it is based on W3C standards, enables the use of strong governance models, allows for privacy, and has been extensively tested in prior work.

In terms of architecture, George explained that before the trade, VCs were issued by the financial institutions acting as Trust Anchors. Trust Anchors, in project Guardian, were regulated financial institutions (i.e. J.P. Morgan and SBI) that issued and verified VCs to participating traders, enabling them to transact on the public blockchain while ensuring that all trades were conducted within a controlled and compliant environment.[11]

In simple terms, J.P. Morgan issued a VC to a J.P. Morgan trader, stating that he was an employee of the company and a verified trader with specific risk limits. Once issued, the J.P. Morgan trader claimed that VC and held it in his custom-built digital wallet. The same process took place for SBI.

The custom-built institutional wallets enabled VCs to be shared along with trade instructions. The verification of VCs was done on-chain by smart contracts before the system forwarded the trade instruction to the smart contracts that held the on-chain tokenized deposits. Traders never had direct access to firms' funds and their personal information was never stored on-chain. George Kassis explained:

> *We defined the architecture this way to ensure there was segregation between the wallets used by the traders, the on-chain identity smart contracts, the tokenized smart contracts and the DeFi pool. This method of modular design enables a higher level of controls and helps with ease of scalability.*

Once the trade was instructed, on-chain identity smart contracts would ensure that the VCs were not revoked and were issued by the appropriate Trust Anchor. If the rules just discussed held true then the identity verification would succeed and the trade instruction sent by the trader would proceed. This would then enable the movement of tokenized deposits to and from the DeFi pool.

In terms of lessons learned, George Kassis shared:

> *The pilot was a success: we were able to prove that traders can instruct real transactions on public blockchains using a framework that enables their identity to be verified at the time of trading, without revealing personal information. We confirmed our strong belief that identity has a significant role to play in Web3.*

Central banks' experiments

CBDCs are another area where the balance between authentication and privacy is critical. Many worry about the inherent privacy and security challenges, arguing that the government could easily turn them into surveillance and monitoring tools.

DIGITAL POUND

The Bank of England (BoE) launched a consultation on a CBDC (the digital pound) in February 2023, with the final decision taking place no earlier than 2025. As part of the evaluation process, BoE announced a partnership with Nuggets, a fintech that leverages self-sovereign identity. The BoE is working with Nuggets to investigate and design the privacy and identity layer for the potential digital pound, a key component in the final decision.

Nuggets is looking to implement zero-knowledge proofs (ZKPs) on the privacy layer, a technology that allows third parties to test encrypted data for limited facts without exposing the underlying data. For example, nowadays, to buy an alcoholic drink at the supermarket, you may be asked to show an identification. But in doing so, you are showing more information than needed. You would be showing a considerable amount of your private information, like your name, date of birth and driving licence number.

With ZKPs, the supermarket would simply ask, 'Is this person above 18 years old?' and would merely receive the answer, 'Yes, this person is above 18.' No personal information, not even your date of birth, would be shown. This is very much a simplification of how the technology would work, but shows the opportunities ZKPs could have for users. ZKPs are being explored by many protocols in Web3 to provide a privacy layer in public blockchains.

Industry frameworks and solutions

Recognizing the need for authentication and privacy, many players in Web3 are already working together to find solutions and frameworks that can be used at the industry level.

INDUSTRY FRAMEWORKS: TRUST AND VERITE

In 2021, the largest US cryptocurrency exchanges and custodians, BitGo, Coinbase, Gemini, Kraken and Fidelity, came together to propose a solution for the new regulatory requirement known as the Travel Rule. The Travel Rule is a set of guidelines to prevent money laundering and terrorist financing and requires financial institutions to share certain basic information about customers when sending funds to another financial institution. Although transferring personal data between financial institutions has been long established, the Travel Rule is a relatively new requirement for the crypto industry. Web3 companies, like custodians, brokerages and exchanges, will have to satisfy this rule, which applies to many countries, including the US, UK and the European Union member states.

The initial group of five has now increased to more than 30 industry-leading global companies. This unprecedented broad effort led to a jointly designed solution called TRUST (Travel Rule Universal Solution Technology). TRUST aims to provide a 'comprehensive compliance solution to be used across the industry', with its current focus on continuing to expand to other jurisdictions.[12]

Similarly in 2022, Circle, Coinbase, Block and others collaborated on the launch of Verite, a set of decentralized identity standards that enables organizations to issue and verify digital identity credentials for users and institutions participating in the Web3 economy. The potential benefits are wide-ranging, including allowing those who lack traditional forms of identification to participate in the global financial system and making it safer for people to participate in DeFi.[13]

Holistic identity for Web3

Currently, users do not have a single identity. Every time they interact with a new platform, they must create a new wallet, which means users end up with a multitude of wallets and addresses across each chain, limiting the scalability of Web3. NFT3, a decentralized identity company, aims to solve this issue and create a holistic identity.

NFT3

NFT3 is creating a secure, decentralized and verifiable identity layer in Web3, acting as a unified virtual identity framework across all application layers.

NFT3 is creating a user-centric identity management system where users have complete control over their own digital identity (including their social profile and information currently scattered across various chains). Additionally, NFT3 established the first credit system for Web3, by introducing NCredit, a sophisticated on-chain credit scoring system based on a user's social account information and on-chain data (like historical transaction information and balance on multichain addresses).

This Web3 on-chain identity and credit system can be used for financial services onboarding and due diligence, while preserving user's privacy. What's more interesting is the fact that a user's identity is now composed of online and offline interactions and assets, providing a fuller view of the user and allowing companies to provide more tailored services.

Financial inclusion enabler

Identity is a crucial enabler for the adoption of Web3 and financial inclusion.

Decentralized identity has the potential to include underserved communities in our society and financial services, by leveraging not only traditional forms of identity like your ID and driving licence but also new forms of identity like interactions and investments on-chain.

As we have seen throughout this chapter, identity is already a priority in the industry. Many Web3 players are exploring new technologies like ZKPs, partnering with identity providers, and joining consortiums to create industry-wide frameworks. Circle is an excellent example of a Web3 company focused on identity, even though at first glance its core service is not aligned to identity but to the issuance and governance of stablecoins and Web3 services. Besides joining the TRUST consortium, Circle has also announced it was the principal architect of Verite: a set of decentralized identity standards developed with support from Coinbase, Block and others.

Dante Disparte, Chief of Strategy Officer and Head of Global Policy of Circle, explained to me why identity is a crucial focus for the company:

> You know the expression: if the product is free, you are the product? In financial services, in most countries around the world, individuals have to satisfy a KYC requirement to get access to the formal economy. In the United States and many advanced economies, global credit bureaus collect individual's personally identifiable information, like Social Security numbers or IDs, in exchange for providing a credit score. Such scores determine whether or not loans will be approved, and if so, at what interest rate for the rest of our natural life.

> In 2017, Equifax (a US credit bureau) had a data breach that exposed the personal information of 150 million people, larger than the US workforce. Those people now have an identity theft risk for the rest of their lives since their data is correlated to their financial choices, and their Social Security number will never change.

> And so, if ever there was an argument for cryptography, self-sovereign identity, privacy-preserving information stored in little tiny packets, where if the loss of a single packet of information wouldn't be catastrophic to the entire system, this is it. Blockchain is part of the answer.

> There is a need for a national digital identity strategy in the United States that architects away from this honey pot. From a single source of failure database model to a model in which the failure of any one part of the system wouldn't be catastrophic to the entire system. In fact, my early foray into the blockchain world was from the lens of national security and cyber resilience, and it remains, I think, a piece of unfinished business.

> Additionally, there are billions of people who are born in the shadows, who do not have national IDs, and internally displaced

peoples and refugees who will never, ever meet the criteria to enter the formal economy. And so, there is a need to develop scaled ways of ensuring financial access and trust.

As a real example, almost as soon as hostilities began in Ukraine, a digital wallet was established accepting a range of crypto assets directly supporting the Ukrainian government. Since its inception, this wallet has raised over $60 million worth of crypto assets.

Decentralised identity is an architecture that gives policymakers no more excuses for why people in Argentina, sub-Saharan Africa, Iraq and Afghanistan, very complex places, have to remain persistently on the margins. There is no technological excuse for why they have to remain persistently unbanked. However, the tech is the easy part, the governance, coalitions and the value chain – that is the hard part.

Future outlook

Identity plays a significant role in all financial services interactions, and, while many players are looking to simplify verification and onboarding issues, processes are still complex and costly.

Traditional financial services are well-positioned to tackle this problem. In a discussion with George Kassis, Digital Identity Lead at Onyx by J.P. Morgan, we focused on why identity is a crucial area for the team:

If you look at JP Morgan from a technology innovation standpoint, we invest across the board. Whether through Onyx and blockchain or other types of new technology, we are always looking ahead to identify what emerging technologies we should research and explore. The reality is that no one can be sure which technologies will stand the test of time, for example, we don't know what identity standards will prevail in the future. And so, we focus on continuously trying and testing to develop solutions to benefit our clients and the firm. Innovation is embedded in our culture.

Now, why is Identity important to us? Identity touches upon everything, every line of business and function. From merchant services, fraud, onboarding, supply chain, healthcare, markets, pre-trade and post-trade, Identity is often a pain point in all of these categories. We believe we are well-positioned to be able to solve it, or at least contribute to how to solve it.

Identity for regulated institutions is not just an opportunity but a necessity. Traditional financial institutions will only engage further in Web3 if they are able to perform traditional controls required by regulation, such as KYC, AML and others. Similarly, as more regulation is defined, any Web3 companies providing financial services will have to perform similar controls and checks. But the good news is that identity solutions are being created and tested, and new innovations like ZKPs are showing value. By adopting those solutions, traditional and new players will be able to streamline and speed up compliance and control processes while reducing the risk of holding private data.

New identity solutions also present an opportunity to reimagine digital identity from the ground up. An individual's identity is complex, contextual and nuanced. Yet, in finance, individuals are often reduced to credit scores, transaction logs and centralized data silos. By expanding identity to include on-chain information, unbanked and underrepresented communities will be able to start creating a digital footprint that can be used to access financial services and other societal benefits.

Though decentralized ID offers an opportunity for inclusion, effectiveness, control and privacy, there is still work to be done and a lot at stake. Some countries have developed their own systems of digital identity, but these are disparate, national schemes. Finding something that works for every country and across borders is a significant challenge. Users will need to feel comfortable that they can express their identity without accidentally making sensitive information public on the blockchain. Lending protocols reviewing individuals' identities for loan applications need to be satisfied that the applicant is not hiding adverse reputation claims. Additionally, for any form of identity to be broadly adopted, it is essential that it is recognized both in a centralized and decentralized world, enabling users to access services in the digital and physical borders seamlessly.

The future of identity is promising, but many challenges still need to be solved. George Kassis shared with me how he sees the future of identity:

We talk about Web2 as the movement of information and Web3 as the movement of things of value (in that I include our personal data). In the future, I potentially see a world where citizens hold Identity wallets that include their scuba diving licence, university degree, books they read, awards received, loyalty points and more. Everything about their Identity could be included in the wallet, and they own and control their own data. Both online and in-person interactions should be frictionless and straightforward.

SUMMARY OF KEY POINTS

- Legal identity plays a pivotal role in society, being a gateway to access services, benefits and opportunities. However, there are 1.7 billion underbanked adults worldwide, without a legal identification.

- Those with IDs lack privacy and control over how their data is shared. The identification method is often inefficient, centrally stored and vulnerable to misuse or theft.

- Decentralized identity flips the model from big platforms to self-sovereignty. Individuals will be able to own and control their data, both in terms of whom they share it with and how much of that data they share, moving to a 'need to know' basis.

- Identity and privacy are crucial for financial services' adoption of Web3. Project Guardian is a good example of how financial institutions could use Web3 while ensuring privacy and security.

- Decentralized identity has the potential to include underserved communities in our society and financial services, by leveraging not only traditional forms of identity (such as an ID or driving licence) but also new forms of identity like interactions and investments on-chain.

Endnotes

1 United Nations. Legal identity agenda, unstats.un.org/legal-identity-agenda/ (archived at https://perma.cc/WU6L-YVN7)

2 World Bank. ID4D global dataset, 2021, id4d.worldbank.org/global-dataset (archived at https://perma.cc/37WC-5V8B)

3 Financial Action Task Force. FATF guidance on digital identity, March 2020, www.fatf-gafi.org/content/dam/fatf-gafi/brochures/Digital-ID-in-brief.pdf. coredownload.pdf (archived at https://perma.cc/SFQ8-97KV)

4 LastPass. Notice of recent security incident, 22 December 2022, blog.lastpass. com/2022/12/notice-of-recent-security-incident/ (archived at https://perma.cc/ B5YD-KFGE)

5 LexisNexis. LexisNexis® Risk Solutions 2022 true cost of financial crime compliance study – global summary, 2022, risk.lexisnexis.com/global/en/ insights-resources/research/true-cost-of-financial-crime-compliance-study- global-report (archived at https://perma.cc/PQ9J-AHDB)

6 European Commission Digital identity for all Europeans, commission.europa. eu/strategy-and-policy/priorities-2019-2024/europe-fit-digital-age/european- digital-identity_en#benefits-of-the-european-digital-identity (archived at https://perma.cc/6ETR-EY68)

7 World Economic Forum. Reimagining digital ID, 7 June 2023, www3. weforum.org/docs/WEF_Reimagining_Digital_ID_2023.pdf (archived at https://perma.cc/5YAQ-X26V)

8 Globe Newswire. Global decentralized identity market size & trends analysis report 2023: Market to surpass $100 billion by 2030, growing at a staggering CAGR of 90.3% – BFSI Leads in Implementing Solutions, 25 October 2023, globenewswire.com/en/news-release/2023/10/25/2766325/28124/en/Global- Decentralized-Identity-Market-Size-Trends-Analysis-Report-2023-Market-to- Surpass-100-Billion-by-2030-Growing-at-a-Staggering-CAGR-of-90-3-BFSI- Leads-in-Implementing-Solution.html (archived at https://perma. cc/3MPB-G7EN)

9 J.P. Morgan. Institutional DeFi: The next generation of finance?, 24 November 2022, jpmorgan.com/insights/payments/wallets/institutional-defi (archived at https://perma.cc/95FB-XP5M)

10 J.P. Morgan. Institutional Defi Report, 2022, jpmorgan.com/onyx/documents/ Institutional-DeFi-The-Next-Generation-of-Finance.pdf (archived at https:// perma.cc/N7SD-4B86)

11 J.P. Morgan. *Institutional Defi Report*, 2022, jpmorgan.com/onyx/documents/ Institutional-DeFi-The-Next-Generation-of-Finance.pdf (archived at https:// perma.cc/N7SD-4B86)

12 Coinbase. The standard for Travel Rule compliance, coinbase.com/travelrule (archived at https://perma.cc/V7K4-G4QM)

13 Businesswire. Centre announces Verite – a decentralized identity solution for crypto finance, 17 February 2022, businesswire.com/news/home/2022021700 5290/en/Centre-Announces-Verite---A-Decentralized-Identity-Solution-for-Crypto-Finance (archived at https://perma.cc/6YNX-S8FM)

PART THREE

The major players in Web3

Opportunities, challenges and implications

08

Traditional institutions and the adoption of Web3

J.P. MORGAN'S JOURNEY INTO BLOCKCHAIN

In 2014, J.P. Morgan, one of the largest banks in the United States, embarked on a transformative exploration of blockchain technology. Initially, the efforts were led by a handful of individuals who believed blockchain platforms could have a meaningful impact on how financial businesses could evolve. This marked the beginning of a remarkable journey that has since evolved into the creation of a dedicated business unit within J.P. Morgan called Onyx. Onyx currently includes four verticals: Onyx Digital Assets, JPM Coin Systems, Liink and Blockchain R&D.

In the early days, J.P. Morgan joined a number of blockchain consortiums alongside several other banks and financial institutions. For example, in 2015, J.P. Morgan made the news by joining a consortium led by the R3 blockchain company alongside Santander, HSBC, BBA, Barclays and many others. The consortium aimed to help the financial sector develop shared blockchain technology to streamline and improve complex and cumbersome processes. However, J.P. Morgan eventually left R3 two years later to pursue its own strategy.

In 2016, the bank launched its own blockchain protocol called Quorum, an enterprise-focused version of the Ethereum blockchain, designed to facilitate private and secure transactions between institutions. Quorum's evolution continued, ultimately leading to its acquisition by Consensys in 2020.

Continuing its blockchain journey, in 2017, J.P. Morgan piloted the Interbank Information Network (IIN), which was initially designed to reduce the friction between cross-border payments using private blockchain technology. Later, in 2020, INN was rebranded and launched into the market as Liink. The rebrand included an increase in scope to enable peer-to-peer information exchange. In 2023, Liink had over 100 participants using the network to exchange payment-related information.

Two years later, in 2019, J.P. Morgan launched JPM Coin, a blockchain-based bank account. When clients open a JPM Coin account, they are, in simple terms, opening an account at J.P. Morgan that enables payments over blockchain, taking advantage of this 24/365 infrastructure that can move money internationally more quickly and cheaply. In 2023, JPM Coin was handling $1 billion of transactions daily.

Finally, in 2020, J.P. Morgan launched Onyx Digital Assets, an asset tokenization platform, which has processed over $900 billion of intraday repo transactions. In 2022, the team expanded the platform further by broadening tokenized assets beyond US Treasuries and signing global clients such as Goldman Sachs, DBS and BNP. In 2023, it added a new collateral mobility product with BlackRock as the first client, and announced it would explore how tokenization could be used for private assets, under the next phase of MAS Project Guardian, in collaboration with Apollo.

Throughout the years, alongside experiments and solutions development, J.P. Morgan has made notable investments in this space, including joining Elliptic Series C funding in October 2021 and TRM Labs Series B funding in 2022.[1]

In a discussion with Tyrone Lobban, Managing Director at J.P. Morgan and head of Blockchain & Onyx Digital Assets, he described the early days as pure experimentation. The team was trying to understand blockchain and the real value it could bring:

> In 2015 and 2016, we took a very broad view because we wanted to understand the true opportunities and value propositions across the breadth of our businesses. It was an extremely constructive phase that helped us define where we see blockchain being applicable.
>
> In those early days, there was a lot of large-scale collaboration. The thinking at the time was that this is a network technology that requires multiple participants, and so the natural approach was to get everyone

around the table. Banks, broker-dealers and custodians all came together to define how we would implement this shared ledger.

While Tyrone Lobban believes that was probably the right approach at the time, the team has since changed the model to focus on smaller and specific use cases with key partners. This change of direction reflects a lesson learned early on, that designing and working with a large group of stakeholders can be a complex and lengthy process. Tyrone explained:

We learned that you can't really design by committee, and it's difficult to bring together a set of participants where incentives may not be aligned. For example, some may be there just to learn or can't contribute as quickly due to the smaller size of the team.

So, nowadays, we are much more streamlined in our focus. We identify a clear problem that we want to tackle, and work out the smallest set of steps that we can take to quickly test and get learnings from. Then we identify 1 to 2 motivated, progressive, forward-thinking partners to execute with.

With this approach, J.P. Morgan is seeing a model for success because it can test and learn quickly in collaboration with key partners. Results are then showcased to the industry, and discussions on scaling out are progressed. Tyrone Lobban reflected:

The key thing now is that there are more live products. There are more examples of how this technology is being used in production and making a difference. By default, that was not the position when we started because we were still in learning mode.

Banks and traditional financial institutions have quietly been testing and exploring Web3 concepts and technologies for years. And while only a handful of banks and use cases are regularly discussed in the news, the work happening behind closed doors is further along than many may expect.

But how far will the Web3 disruption go?

- Will incumbents be replaced by new, innovative players?
- Will value chains be reconfigured in a way that no intermediaries are required at all?

While it is impossible to predict the future, the companies that will succeed are the ones that are ready to leverage this new technology, have a strategy in place and know what role they want to play in this sector in the future. Bain & Company views the adoption of Web3 as similar to the emergence of electronic trading. According to the consulting company, electronic trading disruption 'created efficiencies for participants, spurred higher transaction volumes and unlocked a variety of new products'. Companies that invested and learned earlier succeeded, while others had to catch up and even lost market share.[2]

As seen throughout the use cases chapters in Part Two, Web3 can undoubtedly bring efficiencies and benefits to incumbents. From eliminating reconciliation processes, reducing operational risk and transaction costs, to providing new revenue streams fuelled by innovative offerings.

However, the risks are also substantial. From potential disintermediation driven by DeFi players to impact on commercial banks' business models if retail CBDCs are designed to compete with bank deposits and other forms of money, there are many potential risks. (Note that the collapse of the business model of commercial banks due to retail CBCDs is a worst-case scenario and one that we do not envision occurring.)

However, traditional institutions are well placed to capture the opportunities and navigate the risks. They have a history of working with regulators, embracing innovations and navigating disruption faced by fintechs and bigtechs. As new regulation is defined and new players continue to implement components of Web3, the central question for each bank and traditional institution is no longer whether to explore Web3 but how to do so and capitalize on the opportunities presented to them.

Incumbents leading the way

Institutional interest and experiments in Web3 started around 2013 and 2014. Back then, only a small number of institutions were exploring blockchain technology. Teams were still small, composed of a handful of individuals, and experiments were mostly done behind closed doors, not publicly discussed or communicated.

From 2017 to 2020, experiments started to flourish and increase in scope. Team size increased significantly, with some teams spinning off as separate entities or business units. This increased interest can be seen in the number of crypto assets and other blockchain-related patents submitted during that period: 4,500 patents were filed in 2017 and almost 6,000 in 2019, from almost nothing in 2014. Major payment processors (including Mastercard, Visa and Alipay), banks (Bank of America and Capital One) and various retailers and technology conglomerates were among the top applicants for patent filings in this space.[3]

The year 2022 was marked by tight monetary and fiscal policies around the world, which led to sell-offs, volatility and collapses in the crypto industry from the implosion of the project Terra and, as a consequence, the bankruptcy of Celsius Network and Voyager Digital and the notorious fallout of FTX. That gloomy environment, aligned with slower economies and recession potential, resulted in incumbents and big enterprises retreating their experiments once more behind primarily closed doors.

However, the summer of 2023 brought new winds, with incumbents and new players doubling down on their experiments with numerous announcements in the news. Payment players, for example, significantly expanded their acceptance of stablecoins, with a major announcement from PayPal of the launch of its own stablecoin, backed by the US dollar, to facilitate payments.[4] A number of incumbents also announced new tokenization initiatives, among them Citi and the London Stock Exchange. Citi launched Citi Token Services for cash management and trade finance,[5] and the London Stock Exchange revealed plans to launch a blockchain-based digital asset exchange targeting private markets.[6] New consortiums were launched to foster further collaboration and innovation. One such consortium was Canton, aiming to be a privacy-enabled interoperable blockchain network designed for institutional organizations. It included the partnership of financial giants like BNP Paribas and

Goldman Sachs, along with leading technology companies and Web3 companies.[7]

In June 2023, Bloomberg estimated that up to 30 Bitcoin exchange-traded funds (ETFs) were filed by incumbents and new players, including big names like BlackRock (whose CEO had previously voiced his concerns against the industry).[8]

ETFS SAGA

In 2013, the Winklevoss twins – you may know them for suing Mark Zuckerberg for stealing their idea for Facebook – submitted the first exchange-traded fund (ETF). They aimed to provide mainstream investors with a regulated avenue to invest in this new asset class without holding Bitcoin. In the following years, many other high-profile companies submitted ETFs.[9] However, the SEC (US Securities and Exchange Commission) rejected every single Bitcoin ETF application, citing concerns about market manipulation, liquidity and investor protection.

Fast forward a decade, to 15 June 2023, and BlackRock submitted a spot Bitcoin ETF to the SEC. As the world's largest asset manager, BlackRock's submission signalled a remarkable turning point in institutional investors' interest in digital assets. Other notable submissions followed, including a resubmission to the SEC from Fidelity. The market saw this new wave of submissions as a potential catalyst to legitimatize the entire industry and increase liquidity due to broader acceptance and adoption from large institutions. Some estimated billions of dollars could flow into a spot market Bitcoin ETF.

In October 2023, a mere rumour that BlackRock's Bitcoin ETF was going to be approved made the crypto markets climb $2,000, and then drop when the news was revealed as fake.[10] On 9 January 2024, a post on the SEC official X account, announced the approval of the spot Bitcoin ETFs. The price of Bitcoin jumped briefly until an SEC spokesperson announced later that the message was unauthorized, and the SEC account had been hacked.

After months of speculation, the SEC approved all 11 spot Bitcoin ETFs under review on 10 January 2024.

Similar exchange-traded products already existed in Canada and Europe; however, the approval of ETFs in the US was a turning point leading to more transparent and favourable regulations surrounding digital assets in the country.

'So, what led to that sudden interest from traditional institutions?' you may be thinking.

The truth is that the interest is not sudden. On the contrary, it reflects years and years of internal experiments and explorations by banks and traditional institutions.

When speaking with others in the industry while I was working at HSBC, many were surprised that we were doing experiments or projects in this and other innovative areas. 'When did you announce this?' they would ask in surprise. The reality is that often, we didn't announce it to the market. Traditional financial institutions are cautious about their communications related to innovation and experiments. Most institutions still have a conservative approach to comms since both positive and negative news tend to be exaggerated by media outlets and can lead to reputational damage. And so, teams are careful about what they announce publicly, especially in the early stages of pilots and testing.

After a few years of experimentation, many teams in 2023 were more comfortable with the new technology, the benefits that they could take from it and how to mitigate the risks. They were faster at making decisions and progressing into the next phase. The pace of innovation and investment was also fuelled by the introduction of new regulations, such as the European Union's Markets in Crypto Assets (MiCA) Regulation, which was introduced in 2023 and aims to support market integrity and financial stability. Regulation clarity was always going to be an essential requirement for incumbents to join and engage with Web3.

One example of incumbents leading the way is J.P. Morgan, which we reviewed at the start of this chapter. Additionally, Santander also started its exploration in 2015 and continuously drives change by adopting blockchain technology.

SANTANDER'S JOURNEY INTO BLOCKCHAIN

Banco Santander, the 160-year-old Spanish bank, began exploring blockchain around 2015. In an interview with *Business Insider*, Mariano Belinky, head of Santander InnoVentures, said at the time that it had 'internally identified 20 to 25 use cases where this technology can be applied'.[11]

One year later, the bank decided to double down and hired John Whelan, a Silicon Valley entrepreneur, to lead its blockchain lab. The same year, it announced the launch of One Pay FX, an innovative app that would make instant payments up to £10,000. The app was built using Ripple's technology, a blockchain company that the bank had invested in.[12]

In 2018, Santander expanded its efforts and set up a Digital Investment Unit. This unit, led by John Whelan, aimed to ensure the bank was using the latest technology to improve efficiencies while exploring the use of tokenized securities in the capital markets, derivatives and other financial products. At the time, the bank was already a founding member of several consortiums, including Enterprise Ethereum Alliance, Alastria, we.trade and Utility Settlement Coin.[13]

Over the years, Santander's perspective on blockchain evolved from focusing on the technology to exploring practical use cases. In September 2019, it led explorations in the tokenization space by issuing the first end-to-end tokenized bond worth $20 million. In 2020, the bank joined other leading Spanish firms to develop a self-managed digital identity model with blockchain technology, under Project Dalion. Two years later, the project successfully completed its Sandbox pilot.[14]

In 2023, in a bold move for an incumbent, Santander introduced Bitcoin and Ethereum trading for clients in Switzerland. The same year it launched a Digital Assets 101 educational series to demystify the fundamentals, benefits and implications of this transformative technology.[15]

Most incumbents leading the way have been learning and investing in this space for almost 10 years or more. Initially driven by requests from their clients, institutional investors looking to invest in crypto, or interest in the technology itself.

One key thing they all have in common, however, is their innovative mindset and vision. They are not afraid to explore new ideas, even if those have the potential to disrupt existing business models. They have continuously invested in innovation and research by making small bets across a number of new technologies. They look for new solutions that can bring commercial value to them and their investors.

J.P. Morgan, for example, invests $12 million per year in a broad number of new technologies. Larry Feinsmith, Managing Director and head of Global Tech Strategy, Innovation & Partnerships at J.P. Morgan Chase, notes, 'Because technology changes so quickly, we are not only developing technology for today, but we are also anticipating the technology needs of our consumers 5–10 years down the road.'[16]

Public vs private blockchains: which will prevail?

When discussing institutional adoption, the question of public vs private blockchains always arises. *Why do banks use private blockchains? Is that even Web3?*

The vision of Web3 was based on public blockchains. Bitcoin and Ethereum, both public blockchains, were developed around decentralization, openness and transparency. However, most traditional institutions have instead adopted private and permissionless blockchains.

Before we dive deeper, let's understand the concepts.

DEFINITIONS TYPES OF BLOCKCHAINS

Public blockchains are permissionless in nature and allow anyone to join, read, write and validate data. Popular public blockchains include Bitcoin, Ethereum and Solana.

Private blockchains are permissioned in nature, i.e. participants require an invitation and approval to join the network. The central entity authenticates and verifies participants using their identity or other approved information. In this essence, private blockchains provide more privacy, as only approved participants can see, edit and validate the data. Known blockchains used in financial services include Ripple and Hyperledger.

Consortium blockchains are formed when a group of organizations with a common goal seek to work together. Consortium blockchains tend to be

> permissioned, allowing only pre-authorized users to access the
> network. In contrast to private blockchains, each consortium member is
> granted equal control. Popular examples in financial services include R3
> and Canton Network.
>
> All types of blockchains have advantages and disadvantages, and leaders
> should select the type of blockchain based on their use case and
> requirements. In financial services, leaders tend to focus on performance,
> privacy, security and cost.

Financial services requirements

Financial services companies handle vast amounts of sensitive customer data and trade secrets. The transparency provided by public blockchains could expose confidential and important information, putting vulnerable customers at risk. Additionally, companies may want to keep certain information private from competitors, for example supply chain information and negotiated prices. By starting in a private or permissionless network, institutions can ensure that only trusted participants, such as other banks or regulatory authorities, can access the data, protecting sensitive information from public exposure or potential breaches.

Regulated financial institutions also need to comply with legal and regulatory requirements, such as KYC and AML. In private environments, they have higher control and are able to perform those actions more easily. Institutions can define governance models, access controls and data-sharing protocols for their specific needs. At the time of this writing, some regulators are also voicing their preference, in some cases mandating, for the usage of private blockchains over public ones.

It is important to note, however, that several solutions are emerging that aim to enable privacy and regulatory requirements in public blockchains.

The hybrid model

Over the years, hybrid models have been created to try to leverage the benefits of both private and public blockchains.

Aave Arc, discussed in Chapter 6, is an excellent example of a hybrid model. As you may recall, the Aave protocol is a set of smart contracts running autonomously on Ethereum, Avalanche and Polygon – all public blockchains. As the demand for DeFi grew, so did institutional market interest and, in 2021, Aave Arc was introduced to meet that interest and demand. Aave Arc is an isolated market, within Aave, in which only 'whitelisted' users can participate. Whitelisted users are those that go through Know Your Customer (KYC) or Know Your Business (KYB) onboarding procedures.[17]

This new set of onboarding processes allows institutional regulated companies to meet regulatory requirements while using a DeFi protocol on a public blockchain.

Another interesting example is the introduction of 'subnets' in Avalanche. Subnets are a distinctive feature of the Avalanche network that allow the creation of custom blockchains tailored for specific use cases. In 2023, Ava Labs launched Avalanche Evergreen Subnets, a suite of institutional blockchain deployments, tooling and customizations designed to address company-specific requirements for financial services.[18]

In contrast to default subnets, Evergreen Subnets have certain built-in features, providing a ready-made product for institutional blockchain deployments, such as user and validator permissioning, jurisdictional-based geofencing, custom gas token selection and Ethereum Virtual Machine compatibility.[19] In essence, Evergreen Subnets provide a controlled environment while providing the benefits of public blockchain development.

Which blockchain will prevail?

The discussion between private and public blockchains is an interesting one.

Private blockchains can enable process simplification and reduction of operational costs, something that many institutions have tried to achieve for years with transformation programmes such as cloud projects and implementation of automation and workflow tools. But private blockchains lack the benefit of network effects and industry-wide transparency provided by public blockchains.

Private blockchains can also be expensive to set up and maintain, so we must consider if the benefits of using a private blockchain outweigh databases or even transformation projects.

Mauricio Magaldi, Head of Product for Midnight, has worked for a number of years with a multitude of financial services institutions, both at IBM and at 11FS, to implement transformation and blockchain projects. Given his experience, Mauricio advocates for the benefits to be considered on a wider spectrum:

> There might be benefits from using private/permissioned blockchains, especially in niche use cases, in sections of an extended supply chain. If that's the case for a particular industry or segment, it might be the fastest way to tap into the efficiencies blockchains can provide, even if it's not at a global scale, with access to global liquidity.

Morgan McKenney, former CEO of Provenance Blockchain Foundation, believes that banks are working with private permissioned blockchains given regulatory requirements, but does not believe that should be the target end state in the longer term. Morgan speaks from direct experience, having successfully implemented two private blockchain projects with Nasdaq, Alibaba and Ant Financial and, more recently, as CEO of Provenance Blockchain Foundation working to establish private permissioned zones of Provenance for specific financial use cases.

> Blockchain is still intensive to implement, and creating private permissioned blockchains replicates the highly permissioned ecosystem we already have today without the benefits that public blockchains offer, including reduced costs of intermediation, open innovation, and broader participation.
>
> However, for regulated industries like banking, private permissioned blockchains are currently necessary to ensure regulatory feasibility. And so, solutions are being built that support regulatory requirements while retaining the possibility for future openness.
>
> Provenance Blockchain, for example, was built using Cosmos SDK. The Cosmos ecosystem enables builders to stand up blockchains for specific use cases that are interoperable with each other. So Provenance

Blockchain was built specifically to support regulated financial services. Therefore, banks are able to create private permissioned zones of Provenance that can later be transitioned to being more open.

This question seems to divide the industry. In a discussion with Tyrone Lobban, Managing Director at J.P. Morgan and head of Blockchain & Onyx Digital Assets, we covered private vs public blockchains. While J.P. Morgan has its own private blockchain (Quorum), it has actively tested with public blockchains, namely during the first phase of Project Guardian (see Chapter 7 for more details).

My view is that public blockchains are and will probably remain an important aspect of the next generation of financial rails. This idea of borderless, virtually frictionless, continuously available infrastructure is quite a powerful concept. With Project Guardian, we wanted to really understand the boundaries and how we, as a regulated entity, could utilise that infrastructure.

Now, the requirement for a bank to know their customers, prevent money laundering, and prevent dealing with sanctioned entities will never change. That's how regulated entities operate and will operate in the future. And so, we need to consider how we can operate with those constraints and which technology can support those requirements.

Today, those constraints can only be met in private, permissioned blockchains, which is something we do through the Onyx Digital Assets platform. We can perform KYC, AML, sanctions checks, and so on through the Onyx Digital Assets platform since it is fully integrated into our banking systems.

However, Tyrone Lobban sees a future in which public blockchains can be potentially used by regulated institutions if those blockchains are upgraded to support regulatory requirements:

Will we get to use public blockchains? Possibly, if those requirements can be met, and we can operate in a compliant and safe way.

I believe public blockchains are going to continue to evolve. In fact, if we look back to the early days, those blockchains have changed even since 2015. Back then, it was primarily Bitcoin and Ethereum

(Ethereum had recently been launched). Ethereum was a Proof-of-Work (PoW) chain and has now evolved into a Proof-of-Stake (PoS) chain. Nowadays, there are several alternative layer 1 blockchains and some of those offer permissioned zones or subnets where you can have privacy but still operate on a public blockchain.

So, I believe this evolution will continue, and operating on a public blockchain will mean something slightly different from what it means today.

How to respond and extract value

Only 13 per cent of executives rate their companies as very effective at deploying emerging technologies, according to an MIT CISR survey.[20] Yet, mastering cutting-edge innovations and technologies can be a competitive advantage, significantly correlated with growth and profitability.

Most leaders face the challenge of balancing BAU (business-as-usual) activities with exploring emerging technologies and ideas. Although in the long run some emerging technologies may become profitable, the reality is that many bets and pilots will lead to failures and written-off investments. While early adopters and leading companies may be willing and have the capacity to face risks, not all companies will want to do so. Different executives will want to pursue different approaches, weighing opportunities and risks for their own market and business model.

Some executives may even want to adopt a 'wait and see' approach, leaving early experimentation for other companies and only joining in when there is more precise regulation and technology has been developed further with risks mitigated. While caution may seem prudent to some, this approach also comes with a set of risks. It can result in the loss of key talent and a lack of organizational experience and foundation capabilities. So, for leaders who do not want to join experiments at this stage, I still advise them to focus on internal education for key staff. Education can be done by providing 'lunch and learn' sessions, bringing on-demand courses from universities or providing external speakers sessions. Ignoring Web3 risks falling behind and not being ready to leverage opportunities when they arise.

Executives ready to start exploring Web3 will be faced with the question of how to build the capabilities while managing associated risks. While there is no one-size-fits-all in terms of driving innovation, there are strategic frameworks and considerations that can be leveraged.

Vision and strategy

While there are many different perspectives on the potential of Web3 disruption, the reality is that still no one knows how disruptive it will be and what business models will be impacted the most. Each institution should tailor its strategy based on specific markets, businesses and clients.

Leaders must use a scenario-based exercise to evaluate all options, impact on existing business, risks and opportunities. This exercise on what the future could look like will help them identify how their business could be impacted and what role they would like to play. It will enable them to create a roadmap for where they want to invest and explore further.

For example, the DBS CEO does not believe in the 'utopian' scenario in which DeFi replaces banks. Instead, he believes blockchain technology 'will power the back-office in 5-10 years'. This vision drives how DBS invests and experiments in Web3.[21]

Given the rapid evolution of this space, this exercise will need to be continuously revised.

Operating model

The level of organizational support and engagement is crucial for the success of such disruptive initiatives. While some institutions choose to centralize Web3 experiments in one team, others spread capabilities by use case across existing teams.

For example, Fidelity launched a separate entity called Fidelity Digital Assets that focuses solely on Web3 initiatives, while DBS leverages an ecosystem approach to engage in Web3 initiatives across the organization. They have ensured that teams combine different skills, such as risk, compliance, IT and product, instead of experiments being done in siloed environments.

This operating model can also evolve over time as hypotheses are tested and the teams learn more. For example, Fidelity and J.P. Morgan started with a handful of people initially and only years later launched separate entities once they had a better view of the potential of the technology.

Delivery model

Similar to other innovation initiatives, institutions will adopt different delivery models leveraging a combination of build, buy, partner and invest.

HSBC and Standard Chartered, for example, have a separate team that invests in innovative startups. J.P. Morgan has built a number of internal solutions via the Onyx team while partnering and investing with startups. HSBC, Citi, Standard Chartered and a number of others continuously participate in numerous consortiums led by regulators and other institutions to explore and test new solutions.

Legacy interoperability and governance

The uniqueness of Web3 disruption requires leaders to ensure proper governance set-up as they go on this journey. One of the key considerations is how the new solutions and changes will work alongside existing legacy systems, legacy risk and compliance frameworks and processes. This consideration should be done for the short and long term. Some leaders believe they may have to run two distinct 'businesses' in parallel for a long time until they have a unified solution. What would this mean for processes, governance and teams?

Future outlook: end state

So, what is the end state?

While currently, traditional institutions' experiments and solutions are focused on individual pieces of the technology and use cases, leaders and executives must take a step back and consider the end state.

If the Web3 vision materializes, how will it impact incumbents' roles, business models and services?

I recently had a discussion with Marcus Grubb, former Global Head of Product at State Street, whose insights serve as a formidable guide for what is to come. Marcus believes that the end state will lead to a radical reimagining of financial markets:

> We are really talking about automating and re-platforming banks, asset managers and even insurance companies. The implication is that you probably don't need many thousands of people anymore.
>
> Nowadays, banks have a high failure rate of transactions, and the only way to fix them is through manual reconciliation. And so, they have thousands of people manually reconciling and fixing transactions.
>
> A single golden source (like blockchain) will reduce failures and issues substantially. Failures that take place will be visible in a matter of minutes instead of days, eliminating interest rate costs.

Marcus believes the benefits will be felt by individual institutions and across the whole value chain, including more transparency to regulators and auditors:

> If you look at the whole value chain and the way financial markets work today, all the different pieces are segmented in all parts of the financial system, whether it's funds or collateral or cash and payments and foreign exchange or bonds or equities or private markets. All the value chains are sliced up with different providers and a multiplicity of different systems.
>
> Now, imagine being able to do price discovery, price dissemination, trading, matching, settling and clearing all on a single platform in minutes. In this end state, if there is any problem at all, everyone will

> know within minutes after the transaction. Everyone can view the
> Ledger provided they're on the network, i.e. have access to the right
> nodes. Even the regulator could be on the network as they want it to be.

In terms of infrastructure, Marcus believes each bank will have its own set of solutions, potentially even its own licensed and regulated stablecoin, which will be used internally.

Across the industry, there will be a blockchain layer that will allow the transfer of assets and payments across institutions, i.e. a common translation, legal and business domain and interoperability. That blockchain layer will allow for interoperability across institutions and clients, linking back into each banking rails easily. Value (digital cash) will be exchanged on a stablecoin exchange or network.

However, for this industry-wide end state, Marcus believes that the mindset in the industry needs to move from a competition to a collaboration approach.

Impact on business models and roles

Marcus's vision of the end state highlights well how financial markets will be much more streamlined, automated and efficient, run on decentralized technologies. This new paradigm will change existing roles and business models.

'What will be the new role of banks and traditional institutions?' you may ask. And that's a difficult question to answer because it depends. For example, an investment bank operating in private markets and primary issuance will have a different answer from that of an asset servicing and custody bank. This new role will also vary depending on how widely Web3 is adopted across other industries.

Let's consider digital identity as an example. Imagine we are many years in the future; technology has evolved, and digital identity has been adopted. Individuals' digital identities include their names, addresses, movie tickets, career histories, memberships, pensions and financial assets. And so the digital identity wallet would be used for participation in society and not just financial services.

In this scenario, would it make sense for the bank to provide custody of your private keys? Probably not. Instead, individuals would probably use digital identity management services. In this scenario, the role of a custodian bank will change drastically.

Swen Werner, former Global Head of Digital Custody and Payments at State Street, explains it simply:

> Custody is more than just keeping the assets safe, in fact, a custodian bank's effort and cost base is related to asset servicing (lifecycle events from income to tax processing, etc.)
>
> Banks will still be doing those services, but they don't necessarily have to do it directly. For instance, the bank could provide the tax status of a certain client to a smart contract that is then calculating it.
>
> This would mean a big shift in the business models. While nowadays everything happens within the four walls, in the future, they will be orchestrating services. And so, in that sense, business models will be about data and data standards.

This shift in the business model is one that I heard from a few experts. Banks would move from managing 'money' to managing 'data'.

But this is a paradigm shift from what they do today. We can say that banks would become more like 'IT companies', and so skills and teams would have to be updated to reflect this new model.

Such a change of skills and team composition is not something new in the finance world. In 1999, an age in which trading was still done human-to-human, either on trading floors or trading pits, traders were tall and loud. In a packed room, their voices had to be heard and their bodies seen above the crowd.

Later, automated trading systems arrived. Humans no longer traded directly with other humans; instead, programmed computers would trade with other computers. By removing humans, trades were made faster and more frequently than ever before. And so, the skills needed to change. Instead, individuals who could code and give instructions that could be codified were hired.

Similarly, recently, with the advent of artificial intelligence (AI) and ChatGPT in the banking sector, job roles and skills requirements are poised to change. This ongoing evolution underscores the importance of continuous learning and adaptability within the banking work-force.

Right now, you may believe that this end state is impossible. 'The technology is not ready, and, without regulation, this industry will not prosper,' you may ponder. The reality is that regulatory clarity will come, and technology will be improved. Remember, this is an open-source technology that teams and individuals across the globe are working on.

So, leaders need to be prepared and ready to leverage the disruptive potential of Web3 and what it represents.

SUMMARY OF KEY POINTS

- Traditional financial companies have been learning and performing experiments quietly since 2013. A decade later, many are now actively engaged and building solutions that take advantage of Web3.

- Leading companies have in common an innovation mindset. Leaders are continuously exploring new technologies and ideas, disrupting their own business models.

- Different types of blockchains (public, private and hybrid) have their own advantages and disadvantages. Leaders should select the type of blockchain based on their use case and requirements.

- Executives should take a step back from existing experiments and consider what the end state could mean for the current business model, products and services, skills and team composition.

- The central question for each traditional institution is no longer whether to explore Web3 but how. Companies that do not take advantage of this new technology could be left behind and disrupted by new players.

Endnotes

1 Blockdata. What JP Morgan is doing in blockchain and crypto, 8 September 2022, blockdata.tech/blog/general/what-jp-morgan-is-doing-in-blockchain-and-crypto (archived at https://perma.cc/5RRJ-GYPR)

2 Bain & Company. Web3 experiments start to take hold in banking, 14 December 2022, bain.com/insights/web3-experiments-start-to-take-hold-in-banking/ (archived at https://perma.cc/TU5B-69MK)

3 R Paul, G Discher and M Nonaka. Patenting for Blockchain and crypto tech, Convington, 18 August 2023, insideglobaltech.com/2023/08/18/patenting-for-blockchain-and-crypto-tech/ (archived at https://perma.cc/XD8R-METE)

4 PayPal. PayPal launches U.S. dollar stablecoin, 7 August 2023, newsroom.paypal-corp.com/2023-08-07-PayPal-Launches-U-S-Dollar-Stablecoin (archived at https://perma.cc/9Y3N-3S87)

5 Citigroup. Citi develops new digital asset capabilities for institutional clients, 18 September 2023, citigroup.com/global/news/press-release/2023/citi-develops-new-digital-asset-capabilities-for-institutional-clients (archived at https://perma.cc/KCJ9-9RTP)

6 M Meichler. London Stock Exchange Group plans blockchain-powered digital markets business, Decrypt, 4 September 2023, decrypt.co/154852/london-stock-exchange-group-plans-blockchain-powered-digital-markets-business (archived at https://perma.cc/6A3A-89H6)

7 Canton Network. Press release: Introducing the Canton Network: a blockchain financial institutions can say 'yes' to, 9 May 2023, www.canton.network/press-release (archived at https://perma.cc/FCH3-QS5G)

8 V Hajric and K Greifeld. Fidelity joins Spot-Bitcoin ETF race with fresh SEC filing, 29 June 2023, Bloomberg, bloomberg.com/news/articles/2023-06-29/fidelity-jumps-into-spot-bitcoin-etf-race-with-fresh-sec-filing (archived at https://perma.cc/2PC8-GYW5)

9 M Doyich. The ripple effects of a spot market Bitcoin ETF, Coindesk, 16 October 2023, coindesk.com/consensus-magazine/2023/10/16/the-ripple-effects-of-a-spot-market-bitcoin-etf/ (archived at https://perma.cc/7WXN-24TP)

10 D Kihn. What's all the fuss about Bitcoin ETFs?, Coindesk, 16 October 2023, coindesk.com/consensus-magazine/2023/10/16/whats-all-the-fuss-about-bitcoin-etfs/ (archived at https://perma.cc/7W5M-MJZH)

11 O Williams-Grut. Santander is experimenting with bitcoin and close to investing in a blockchain startup, *Business Insider*, 17 June 2015, www.businessinsider.com/santander-has-20-25-use-cases-for-bitcoins-blockchain-technology-everyday-banking-2015-6?r=US&IR=T (archived at https://perma.cc/KQ9P-AQMZ)

12 Santander. Santander becomes first UK Bank to introduce blockchain technology for international payments with the launch of a new app, 27 May 2016, santander.co.uk/about-santander/media-centre/press-releases/santander-becomes-first-uk-bank-to-introduce-blockchain (archived at https://perma.cc/4893-EVN7)

13 H Vilar. Santander sets up digital investment unit for blockchain, FinTech Futures, 16 July 2018, fintechfutures.com/2018/07/santander-sets-up-digital-investment-unit-for-blockchain/ (archived at https://perma.cc/2ACT-SVZB)

14 Santander. Ten Spanish companies join forces to promote digital identity using blockchain technology, Santander Press Release, 5 November 2020, santander.com/en/press-room/press-releases/2020/11/ten-spanish-companies-join-forces-to-promote-digital-identity-using-blockchain-technology (archived at https://perma.cc/2D8F-TY3G)

15 M Koss. Spain's largest bank begins educational series on Bitcoin, Digital Assets, *Forbes*, 26 June 2023, forbes.com/sites/digital-assets/2023/06/26/spains-largest-bank-joins-list-of-financial-institutions-exploring-bitcoin/ (archived at https://perma.cc/ML4S-U7ZG)

16 J.P. Morgan. This $12 billion tech investment could disrupt banking, jpmorganchase.com/news-stories/tech-investment-could-disrupt-banking (archived at https://perma.cc/5CER-5W5Y)

17 Aave. An introduction to Aave Arc whitepaper, 2021, github.com/aave/protocol-v2/blob/feat/permissioned-market/aave-arc-whitepaper.pdf (archived at https://perma.cc/L4NC-RKZN)

18 Avalanche. Avalanche launches 'Evergreen' Subnets for institutional blockchain deployments, 6 April 2023, medium.com/avalancheavax/avalanche-launches-evergreen-subnets-for-institutional-blockchain-deployments-8cb75cfcc151 (archived at https://perma.cc/8LQJ-F3MP)

19 H Partz. Avalanche introduces 'Evergreen' Subnets to connect institutions on blockchain, 6 April 2023, *Cointelegraph*, cointelegraph.com/news/avalanche-introduces-evergreen-subnets-to-connect-institutions-on-blockchain (archived at https://perma.cc/N2J6-K97T)

20 G Benedict, I Sebastian and S Woerner. Creating value from WEB3: Four approaches to adopting blockchain, MIT CISR, 16 March 2023, cisr.mit.edu/publication/2023_0301_AdoptingBlockchain_BenedictSebastianWoerner#fn_2 (archived at https://perma.cc/4WHT-GRCE)

21 I Tham. Blockchain will power world's back office in 5-10 years, *The Straits Times*, 19 June 2022, www.straitstimes.com/opinion/blockchain-will-power-the-back-office-of-the-world-in-5-to-10-years (archived at https://perma.cc/Q57U-WKAH)

09

How DeFi is reimagining finance

MEET UNISWAP

In July 2017, Hayden Adams, a young mechanical engineer, was laid off from Siemens, his first job out of college. Unsure about his next steps, he reached out to his friend Karl Floersch, who at the time was working at the Ethereum Foundation. Karl encouraged him to dive into the Ethereum blockchain, in his view an untapped and future market. 'Ethereum is the future and you're still early. Your new destiny is to write smart contracts!' said Karl.

Despite lacking the necessary coding skills, Hayden spent the next couple of months learning the basis of Ethereum, the Ethereum programming language called Solidity and Javascript, a common programming language. At this point, Hayden was looking to put his learnings into practice, and Karl suggested that Hayden work on creating an automated market maker (AMM), a concept described by Vitalik Buterin, Ethereum's founder, in a 2017 blog post. In November 2018, after receiving a grant from the Ethereum Foundation and working on the project for over a year with a small team and a few advisors, Hayden launched Uniswap v1, a decentralized exchange (DEX) that enables users to buy and sell tokens. Unlike traditional exchanges that rely on order books, Uniswap uses AMMs, an innovative approach to asset exchange.

In simple terms, in traditional and centralized exchanges, trades occur through an order-book system, in which buyers and sellers place orders, specifying the price and quantity they wish to buy or sell; these orders are then matched. The AMM model uses liquidity pools created by users, called liquidity providers, who deposit a pair of tokens. For example, liquidity providers deposit ETH and USDC. Traders can then trade ETH for USDC, or vice versa, directly through the liquidity pool. The AMM algorithm adjusts the prices based on the supply and demand dynamics within the pool.

Around 2018, a for-profit company called Uniswap Labs was incorporated, composed of the team that created Uniswap v1 (and later v2, v3 and v4). In April 2019, the company received a $1 million seed investment from Paradigm, a venture capital (VC) company, which was used to develop and launch Uniswap v2 in May 2020. Version 2 of the DEX removed the need for token pairs to trade via ETH and introduced further upgrades and enhancements. Only a few months later, in June 2020, the company raised $11 million in a series A funding round led by a16z, Paradigm and other VCs.[1]

In September 2020, Uniswap announced the launch of its new governance token called UNI. A total of 1 billion UNI tokens was allocated: 60 per cent to the community, 21.5 per cent to the team and future employees, 17.8 per cent to investors and 0.69 per cent to advisors. Any users who had previously used the exchange also received UNI tokens, compensating early adopters.

From the start, Uniswap wanted to provide an open and transparent financial system. Uniswap does not hold or control users' assets. Instead, participants manage their private keys and assets directly via non-custodial wallets. Additionally, Uniswap is open and transparent by default, allowing anyone to inspect the project and confirm that things are working as planned. However, it also allows for anyone to copy existing projects, referred to as 'forking'. Many other projects have been created using Uniswap code, including food-named competitors like PancakeSwap and SushiSwap.

Throughout the years, Uniswap launched new versions improving on previous features and adding flexibility. Uniswap is currently one of the largest players in the DeFi industry.

Reimagining finance

The origins of financial institutions go back centuries, starting when the first currencies were minted and a need to store and exchange money emerged. Over the years, the financial system has matured and diversified, and several financial crises have led to increased regulation.

Fast forward to the modern era, where the financial ecosystem has morphed into a complex network of institutions working together to transfer capital from one place to another or from one function to another. Central banks steer the monetary policy, while traditional financial institutions facilitate the borrowing and lending of money. In recent years, a digital wave has emerged driven by fintechs, bigtechs and neobanks and the advent of new cutting-edge technology disrupting the financial ecosystem. Yet, despite the evolution and disruption over centuries, one common thread has remained unchanged: the centralization of services and products. Banks, fintechs, insurance companies, asset managers or central banks, and central institutions have always been at the core of financial services.

However, the Web3 vision has shaken the paradigm and challenged the notion that centralized entities are required for services and products. The invention of smart contracts has enabled the provision of financial services without such entities. And so, decentralized finance (DeFi) has emerged. CEOs, brokers, custodians and clearing firms can be replaced by smart contracts, enabling any users to participate.

DeFi represents an emerging ecosystem of financial applications that operates on decentralized networks (decentralized applications, or DApps). Transactions are transparently recorded and often executed through self-executing smart contracts. In essence, DeFi not only leverages emerging technology and new concepts to provide new and existing products, but goes one step further and disrupts market structures, disintermediating traditional finance.

And while the benefits abound, DeFi is still highly complex and requires a lot of risk-taking from users. In traditional finance, if you have an issue, you call a help desk or message the same via your bank app. If a financial crisis occurs, the country's regulators protect individuals up to a certain amount. However, in DeFi, individuals have no one to call or ask for support; remember that technology provides the service. Currently, DeFi is mostly unregulated, lacking the traditional consumer safeguards that exist in traditional finance. In DeFi, users trust the computer code enforced by a decentralized network, instead of individuals and institutions: a drastic change to existing financial paradigms.

Evolution of the DeFi ecosystem

The term DeFi was born in August 2018 in a Telegram chat. In the chat, Ethereum developers and Web3 entrepreneurs were discussing what to call the movement of open financial applications being built on Ethereum. Some options considered included Open Horizon, Lattice Network and Open Financial Protocols. After deliberation, the group decided to go with DeFi. Blake Henderson of 0x said at the time that he liked DeFi, as it sounded like 'DEFY'.[2]

Web3's starting point can be traced back to the launch of Bitcoin in 2009. However, the foundation for DeFi protocols should be traced back to the introduction of Ethereum in 2015. Created by Vitalik Buterin, Ethereum introduced the groundbreaking concept of programmable money, the automatic transfer or movement of money when pre-determined conditions are met, via smart contracts. As discussed in Chapter 2, smart contracts are self-executing contracts with the terms of the agreement written in the code, an innovation that enabled more complex financial transactions to be conducted in a decentralized manner, i.e. without the need for human input.

In 2016 and 2017, early projects started gaining prominence in the Ethereum network. One of the flagship projects that came into existence was MakerDAO in 2017, a decentralized lending protocol with its own stablecoin (DAI). DAI was one of the first decentralized stablecoins pegged to the US dollar, an innovative concept for its time. A dozen other DeFi applications followed, from decentralized exchanges like Uniswap to other lending platforms like Compound (lending platforms were discussed in Chapter 6). DeFi platforms offer various financial services, all accessed via permissionless platforms.

ICO boom

In 2017 and 2018, initial coin offerings (ICOs) surged in popularity. This form of crowdfunding, i.e. selling tokens to fund the development or launch of a project or application, would typically include the publication of a whitepaper that described the token sale, underlying blockchain and the vision and business model for the project. Available ICO standards, such as the ERC-20 token based on Ethereum, enabled even non-technical founders to issue tokens and collect funds with minimal effort and resources. In their article 'Why do startups pursue initial coin offerings (ICOs)? The role of economic drivers and social identity on funding choice',[3] Schückes and Gutman quote an entrepreneur comparing the 'simplicity of issuing tokens to starting a web shop'; something that has become highly accessible with tools like Shopify. This simplicity created an influx of projects that usually would not have the opportunity or ability to get funded.

As thousands of projects started conducting token sales, it gradually became clear that many lacked serious teams or realistic business plans and relied on industry hype to profit from unsophisticated investors. As a result, ICOs attracted regulatory scrutiny, most notably from the US SEC.[4] However, some unquestionable success stories were launched in the ICO bubble. For example, Bancor, 0x and Aave raised $153 million, $24 million and $16.2 million, respectively, in the ICO boom in 2017.[5] [6] [7]

DeFi Summer

The true explosion in DeFi occurred in 2020, the 'DeFi Summer'. According to DeFi Pulse, the value of digital assets locked into DeFi grew from less than $1 billion in 2019 to over $15 billion at the end of 2020.[8] Kickstarted by Compound, a decentralized lending protocol, many projects launched liquidity mining programs to attract users to their protocols. Liquidity mining programs aim to solve one of DeFi's obstacles: lack of liquidity. In simple terms, users who deposit assets into a liquidity pool are rewarded with additional tokens, usually in the form of the platform's native token. By providing additional rewards, platforms encourage more users to add liquidity to the pools, making it more attractive for traders. Liquidity mining was originally introduced in 2019 by Synthetix (a synthetic asset protocol), but it was only popularized in 2020.

The popularity of such programs led to the launch of numerous new projects and a period of tremendous growth. Users had a busy summer moving assets between different pools and platforms, searching for the highest yield; often called 'yield farming'. This behaviour demonstrated early on that, while highly effective, such programs do not solve the liquidity issue in the long term.

This period was also marked by rapid innovation and the adaptation of existing ideas, which was only possible due to the open-source feature of many projects. SushiSwap, for example, was created as a fork from Uniswap with added community features. A bold move, SushiSwap's vampire attack on Uniswap become one of the most talked-about events in the DeFi space.

SUSHISWAP AND THE VAMPIRE ATTACK

In August 2020, a pseudonymous developer, known as Chef Nomi, forked the code of Uniswap to create SushiSwap. This new decentralized exchange was similar to Uniswap but added 'community-oriented' features, such as a governance token, SUSHI and staking rewards.

When creating SushiSwap, Nomi recognized that liquidity was essential to make it a success. But, it would be difficult to incentivize users to provide liquidity to a new platform when they could do it for an established and tested one like Uniswap. So, Nomi engineered an aggressive move to divert liquidity from Uniswap to SushiSwap: users would receive not only transaction fees but also SUSHI tokens in exchange for providing liquidity. However, to start earning SUSHI, users had to deposit Uniswap LP tokens.

Such an approach proved effective, and by the time the migration was over, SushiSwap had gained $810 million worth of tokens, roughly 55 per cent of Uniswap's liquidity. This migration of liquidity from Uniswap to SushiSwap was called a vampire attack.[9]

The SushiSwap saga took a controversial turn when Chef Nomi unexpectedly sold his entire stake in SUSHI for ETH, prompting a 73 per cent crash in the price of the SUSHI token and creating a massive backlash.[10] This ultimately led to Nomi transferring ownership of the project to Sam Bankman-Fried, then CEO of well-established FTX. Bankman-Fried, in turn, transferred the control to a multisignature address that was controlled by developers.

In a surprising twist, Chef Nomi later returned the $14 million worth of ETH and apologized to the community. Chef Nomi is no longer associated with the SushiSwap project and, despite its controversial beginnings, SushiSwap has since established itself as a significant player in the DeFi market.

Uniswap, while initially disrupted, later released its own governance token, UNI. This was a pivotal step that helped to re-engage and reward Uniswap's community. To combat similar attacks in the future, Uniswap v3, launched in 2021, included a two-year business licence. This licence acted as a time delay for commercial use of the code. After two years, any project can build on or take from it.

Hacks, volatility and chain reactions

Most recently, the years of 2022 and 2023 were marked by hacks, volatility and crashes.

One of the earliest events was the collapse of the Terra ecosystem in 2022, when Terra's stablecoin, USTC, lost its peg. Within 24 hours, its market cap dropped from over $40 billion to $500 million as users fled, a similar effect to a 'run' on a bank.[11] This collapse created a chain reaction resulting in Three Arrows Capital (a crypto hedge fund), Voyager Digital and Celsius (a centralized lending company) declaring bankruptcy.

Later in the year, the market was shocked again with the FTX and Alameda Research collapse, resulting in another domino effect. As a result, BlockFi (a centralized lending company) declared bankruptcy, and others faced liquidity issues, including Gemini and Digital Currency Group.

Both these events showcase how DeFi is interconnected with centralized companies and the traditional financial system. Liquidity, for example, one of the obstacles to DeFi's growth, is often provided by centralized companies or crypto funds.

This interconnection can be seen both ways. In March 2023, USDC stablecoin lost its peg to the dollar after disclosing that a substantial amount of its cash reserve was deposited in Silicon Valley Bank, a bank in distress at the time.

NOTE ON DeFi

One of the complexities and obstacles to Web3 is the many acronyms and terms used in this space and the fact that they can have different meanings depending on the context and user. Maybe due to it still being an evolving industry, terms and meanings are still being agreed.

DeFi is one of those terms that can create confusion. Sometimes, it is used to refer to the ecosystem of new players that revolve around cryptocurrencies. It can also be used to refer to financial applications that are built on the blockchain.

In this book, we refer to DeFi as the latter. In my view, the problem of using DeFi to refer to this ecosystem of new players is that it misses the point that not all companies in this new industry are decentralized.

In this new ecosystem, we have two new players: CeFi and DeFi. The critical difference is in the first component of the word, centralized vs decentralized. We will look at both players so you can understand the key differences.

And while you do not need to know by heart all the characteristics that compose DeFi, it is important to understand that there are different products and models in Web3, each one with its own risks and opportunities, from both the user perspective and as a leader thinking about partnerships and collaborations.

Centralized finance (CeFi)

Centralized finance (CeFi) platforms rely on blockchain as the under-lying infrastructure and provide a wide range of cryptocurrency-related financial services. However, CeFi typically involves a central entity that governs and manages the platform, just like private companies. It tends to comply with regulatory requirements and provides a degree of security since it holds the user's private key. Many CeFi platforms have a user interface that is friendly and similar to Web2 apps, often appealing to users transitioning from traditional finance to crypto or Web3.

While CeFi can look a lot like traditional financial institutions, they are not the same. TradFi is comprised of centuries-old traditional institutions, while CeFi represents new companies focused on Web3 services and products.

While the distinction between DeFi and CeFi is not always understood, they represent two very different concepts and business models. CeFi serves as a bridge between the traditional model and new concepts and technologies.

Let's look at an example by considering two exchanges: Coinbase and Uniswap.

Exchanges

Coinbase is a centralized exchange (CEX) platform, in which users can buy, sell and trade cryptocurrencies. The user experience is very similar to traditional services, with a sleek and user-friendly interface and customer support. Coinbase holds custody of users' assets and operates as an intermediary between buyers and sellers.

In contrast, Uniswap is a decentralized exchange (DEX) platform. Unlike Coinbase, before interacting with Uniswap, users must first set up a self-custodian wallet (a wallet where they have full control over their assets). On Uniswap, transactions are not overseen by a central authority but are executed autonomously via smart contracts.

In summary, Coinbase provides a streamlined experience at the cost of centralized control, while Uniswap empowers users with financial autonomy but has a steeper learning curve and higher risks.

Let's extend the example to consider stablecoin issuers.

Stablecoin issuers

Circle is a CeFi entity, operator of the stablecoin USDC, which is pegged to the US dollar. Circle oversees the issuance and redemption of USDC, maintaining a reserve of fiat currency to back every USDC in circulation. USDC reserves are held in the management and custody of leading US financial institutions, including BlackRock and BNY Mellon. Circle is regulated as a licensed money transmitter under US state law, just like PayPal, Stripe and Apple Pay.

On the flip side, MakerDAO is a DeFi protocol and the issuer of the DAI stablecoin, also pegged to the US dollar. DAI is generated through a system of smart contracts on the Ethereum blockchain, where users over-collateralize their crypto assets to mint DAI. This decentralized approach eliminates the need for an intermediary. The protocol's governance is handled by governance tokens, MKR token holders, who vote on various parameters to ensure the stability of DAI.

Unlike Circle, where the reserves are managed centrally, MakerDAO's operation relies on algorithmic and community-driven governance to maintain the peg of DAI to the US dollar. While Circle offers a level of trust and ease akin to traditional financial systems, it centralizes control and decision-making. In contrast, MakerDAO facilitates a decentralized and autonomous environment, promoting financial sovereignty at the cost of a more complex user experience.

Some CeFi companies, while starting with one use case, often expand to provide services across a number of use cases based on customer appetite. Ripple, for example, initially focused on payment solutions, has since expanded its offerings significantly. In 2023, Ripple acquired Metaco, a custody company, launched a central bank digital currency (CBDC) platform and expanded its liquidity services.

Eric van Miltenburg, SVP Strategic Initiatives at Ripple, shared the vision of the company with me:

> Our position has always been to help institutions to realise the benefits of blockchain and crypto. It can be difficult for traditional institutions to enter the space because of a lack of expertise, relevant partners or technology capabilities. We have cultivated that experience, knowledge and partnerships required to help them on this journey.

> We started with payments, realising the true promise of blockchain, the instant movement of value. But the intention was always to go beyond that and create a holistic platform where traditional companies can access any crypto needs they have when it comes to financial use cases.

Ripple's strategy is, in essence, being that bridge between blockchain and traditional institutions. More interestingly, even though Ripple started with the payments use case, it now covers almost all of the use cases discussed in Part Two of this book, including custody, payments and tokenization. This is a good example of how all the building blocks will come together and how companies are evolving based on technology and customers' appetites.

Decentralized finance (DeFi)

Decentralized finance (DeFi) promises to replicate traditional financial services (savings, loans, trading, insurance and more) in an open, decentralized, permissionless and autonomous way.

In DeFi, no central authority or intermediary entity holds or controls users' assets. Instead, participants manage their private keys and assets directly via non-custodial wallets.

The open-source nature of the code allows anyone to inspect, fork and innovate. A source of democratized innovation by any ecosystem participant, protocols can be mixed and matched to unlock unique combo opportunities. At the same time, recycling assets and smart contracts on different applications adds to the complexity of an already complicated market and the risks underlying its applications.

In terms of governance, many protocols adopt a decentralized approach, empowering the community to participate in the decision-making process via governance tokens. Community engagement is pivotal to ensure network effects, where the value of the network increases with the growing number of participants.

While some concepts may sound futuristic, many DeFi applications are already live. Borrowing and lending applications like Aave, MakerDAO and Compound (discussed in Chapter 6), exchange protocols like Uniswap, insurance and asset management solutions are some well-known examples. However, in practice, this industry is still nascent and not every component of the vision is yet delivered.

Decentralized governance challenges

DeFi protocols do not tend to start fully decentralized from day one. Instead, most DeFi protocols start as centrally controlled projects, with a small group of founders and core development teams, often funded via venture capital in exchange for tokens. Initially, that core team holds the admin key to the protocol and makes the most important decisions about the design of the same, including the level of fees, voting thresholds and other decisive points. The protocol is then deployed and starts operating independently based on the rules incorporated into the project's code. Later on, the decision-making power is distributed to communities of stakeholders through the creation of governance tokens.

Decentralized autonomous organizations (DAOs) tend to operate using a basic one-token, one-vote model. These governance mechanisms are crucial to make decisions about protocol changes, hiring developers, and even changing governance frameworks. For example, protocols may use their governance process to determine the amount of collateral required to borrow money, to allocate funds for the platform's development, or even to hire someone to audit their code.

It should be noted that disagreements about governance decisions can also occur. In such situations, forks and network splits can materialize, which can lead to investors losing both investments and confidence in DeFi protocols. Additionally, forks can create regulatory challenges as they may result in new cryptocurrencies with differing legal and tax implications.

The community-driven model aims to empower individual participants, creating a sense of ownership and direct involvement. Additionally, by dispersing the governance decisions by a range of participants, the risks associated with the central points of failure can be mitigated. Not controlling the protocol also has liability and tax implications.

In practice, however, at the current state of DeFi development, there are several limitations to such governance models, and many critics, including Camilla Russo, founder of Defiant, say that the industry is playing a 'decentralization theatre'. In a thought-provoking article for Coindesk, Camilla reflects that currently, 'the vast majority of protocols retain the ability to "God Mode" and unilaterally make changes to the protocol'. She describes how Web3 promised 'that users would be owners of the internet; of the applications they interact with and the financial services they use. They would be able to have a say on how things are run and on what decisions are made, and this would be done through holding the protocols' native tokens.'[12] However, that promise has not been fulfilled.

Often, governance tokens are concentrated in a small group of holders, such as early investors and developers, leading to a concentration of power instead of democratization. One recent study found that among the top 10 proof-of-stake platforms by market capitalization, the top 10 validators held between 23 per cent and 88 per cent of the stakes, while the top 50 held between 47 per cent and 100 per cent of the stakes.[13]

Most individuals are also treating governance tokens as 'a proxy to owning a stock', with voting turnout levels being reported as low, allowing investors with a very small proportion of the total supply of governance tokens to swing the vote significantly.

Another criticism is that DeFi protocols are not fully decentralized if they can be stopped when hacks and issues occur. Some founders or developer teams tend to retain an admin key at the early stages of the protocol to be able to correct flaws or bugs, upgrade it or pause/shut it down (a killer switch).

Undoubtedly, as DeFi continues to evolve, so will governance models. One interesting new experiment has been driven by the founder of MakerDAO. Trying to fix some of the issues just discussed, Rune Christensen, the founder of MakerDAO has submitted a proposal to MakerDAO to split the existing governance into smaller teams. While nowadays all decisions are made by the one DAO, the proposal aims to split responsibilities and decisions across subDAOs. Maker subDAOs would be specialized and smaller groups that could make decisions quickly. They would operate with their own governance tokens and have a reduced number of stakeholders voting on each proposal. In simple terms, instead of having all the community members voting on all proposals via the main DAO, there would be different subDAOs, in which different proposals and decisions would be made. While each subDAO would operate autonomously, they would still have to periodically report to the main DAO to ensure alignment with the broader governance framework of MakerDAO. The new proposal aims to reduce DAO governance fatigue, the 'central issue' of DAOs, according to Rune Christensen.[14] The proposal has been approved by MakerDAO and is currently being implemented.

Financial inclusion challenges

DeFi aims to democratize financial systems, making it possible for anyone, anywhere, to access such services, especially underserved communities, who either do not or cannot access financial markets in their current state. Currently, most DeFi applications do not ask for any personal or financial information (like a credit score), so anyone with a smartphone and internet connection can be eligible for a loan (if they have collateral). Transactions are instantaneous (settlement processes are done automatically by the technology), rates tend to be lower since processes are automated, and the fee kept by the application (to pay miners/validators and others) is smaller.

However, financial inclusion is still limited, given the technologies' complexity and the technical capabilities and infrastructure required for such networks. For example, most people do not have the sophisticated knowledge and understanding of DeFi to be able to open up a self-custody wallet.

Additionally, the anonymity (or pseudonymity) and lack of customer due diligence and completion of other AML/CFT processes by most DeFi applications give rise to risks of money laundering, terrorism financing and other illicit use, facilitating misconduct.

Although transactions are traceable and verifiable on-chain, they are anonymous or pseudonymous, without recourse to the identity of the participant. If, for example, funds are taken, or hacks occur, while one can see in which wallets those funds are, it is impossible to know the identity of the wallet's owner, and there is no legal recourse. A colleague often uses the analogy of an iPhone theft, in which one can see where the iPhone is, but there is no legal recourse to recover it.

Future of DeFi

For a long time, DeFi has grown on the outskirts of the financial system without raising much attention from traditional financial professionals or regulators. However, that is changing, with regulators considering how this industry could be regulated.

But what could the future hold for this industry?

Regulation

There are two schools of thought in this space. Some believe that DeFi in its existing form (decentralized and unregulated) will thrive and either overthrow financial services or exist alongside it. Maximalists argue that regulators do not understand DeFi and will hinder innovation. 'Unpopular opinion perhaps: I think we'll have failed if DAOs need to register as LLCs in five years,'[15] argued Anish Agnihotri, an independent researcher working in MEV in 2021.

Others believe that DeFi will transform and adopt some characteristics of traditional models, enabling it to be adopted widely by enterprises and institutions. For example, in 2021, there was a discussion at MakerDAO about whether it should change and adopt some of the characteristics of existing models. In short, participants were discussing whether or not MakerDAO should register as an entity in the US and find a way to pay taxes.[16] This is an ongoing discussion for MakerDAO and other DAOs in DeFi.

The latter vision seems to align with the view of many experts in the industry.

Morgan McKenney, former CEO of Provenance Blockchain Foundation, doesn't believe that DeFi companies will be able to materially scale or become mainstream without operating in a regulated context. Clarity of regulation in her view is a critical enabler for sustainable growth:

> Pure DeFi models are illustrating a totally different way of operating. However, for the industry to go mainstream and companies to become big relative to the financial system, DeFi will need to operate in a regulated context, meaning, for example, doing KYC, AML, and transaction screening. And that can be achieved by partnering with providers that can support meeting those regulations and requirements.
>
> Some parts of blockchain-enabled financial services will likely remain centralised in the near to medium term given the overall nascency of the market, for example, liquidity provision marketplace providers like Coinbase.
>
> Finally, for TradFi to successfully leverage blockchain at scale to support their business, operations and clients, significant engagement, dialog and collaboration will be required with both regulators and policy makers over the next decade.

A similar perspective is shared by Dante Disparte, Chief Strategy Officer and Head of Global Policy at Circle:

> Throughout my career in this market, I have been fortunate enough to have a unique perspective, allowing me to observe and actively participate in the majority of public and private conversations involving central banks, senators, members of Congress, and governments on a global scale. It has become abundantly clear there is simply no shortcut.
>
> There is no pathway for the crypto economy to serve its actual stated purpose of democratising access to finance, self-sovereign identity and digital property rights to billions of people by ignoring public policy and public authorities.
>
> I came to Circle from Libra because I felt a sense of unfinished work and purpose. If we as leaders have a chance to bend the arc of Moore's law in favour of humanity, then we can't quit when it gets tough; we actually should stay the course.

And there's no world where this innovation will unlock its trillions and serve its billions on the edges of being well-regulated. Companies will have to work with public stakeholders.

Many stablecoins failed or lost all of their value because they ignored the pre-existence of, for example, e-money rules. A very prototypical framework for regulating payment stablecoins in Europe, the United States or Asia.

Right from Circle's founding in 2013, the company has prioritised working closely with regulators. Ahead of USDC's launch, Circle had obtained all the necessary licences, comparable to those held by established platforms like PayPal, Stripe, and Apple Pay. This approach has been central to Circle's success in building a reliable, enduring and trustworthy product in USDC.

There is a misconception that stablecoins and crypto are unregulated and there are no rules, a Wild West of Internet banking.

And that is not true. It may not be regulated perfectly or in a globally harmonised manner, but there's no question that the rules are pretty clear around the movement of money, even if it's the movement of money on the Internet.

Circle has forty-eight state banking supervisors who regulate the company and examine the business every single year. As a precondition of maintaining good citizenship in their jurisdictions, we get examined, and they have full authority to stop our activity.

Circle has always taken the regulation-first posture. We answer every single consultation about policy harmonisation and regulatory harmonisation. All over the world.

Disintermediation or adoption?

DeFi started as a movement to disintermediate intermediaries. However, the cost efficiency and innovations brought by the new protocols have interested those intermediaries. DeFi has lower marginal costs, compared with traditional financial institutions (banks and nonbanks), in both emerging and advanced market economies, according to an IMF analysis.[17] Such efficiency and reduction of costs are due to operations being automated through smart contracts, avoiding the high labour and operational costs of traditional financial institutions.

So, instead of disintermediating incumbents, DeFi could actually be used as an automation framework for traditional institutions. Project Mariana, for example, tested the possibility of using novel concepts from DeFi for interbank foreign exchange markets. Spearheaded by the Bank for International Settlements (BIS) in collaboration with the central banks of France, Singapore and Switzerland, the project demonstrated technical feasibility.

PROJECT MARIANA

Bringing DeFi concepts with centralized models

Project Mariana explored how the future of foreign exchange (FX) trading and settlement could look in a world where central banks issued CBDCs, and financial market infrastructures include elements of DeFi.

The proof-of-concept tested the use of AMMs to automate interbank FX processes and cross-border payments through improved transparency and reduced settlement risk. Note that, typically, interbank FX processes and cross-border payments use the order-book process of matching buyers and sellers.

During the experiment, the AMM pooled the liquidity of a hypothetical euro, Singapore dollar and Swiss franc (wholesale CBDCs) with innovative algorithms enabling spot FX transactions to be priced and executed automatically and settled immediately.

'Project Mariana pioneers the use of novel technology for interbank foreign exchange markets. It successfully demonstrated that it is feasible to exchange wholesale CBDC across borders using novel concepts such as automated market makers,' noted Cecilia Skingsley, head of the BIS Innovation Hub, about the results of the experiment.[18]

Given the nascent nature of the industry, BIS Innovation Hub and its global partners will continue research and experimentation.

While the project was purely experimental and does not indicate that any of the involved central banks intend to issue CBDC or endorse DeFi, it showcases how the next generation of financial market infrastructures could assimilate these cutting-edge innovations.

Nitin Gaur, Global Head of Digital Assets and Technology Design at State Street, also believes that traditional institutions will use the new innovative technologies and concepts:

> I view the DeFi world sitting as an automation framework. Whatever DDC (Depository Trust and Clearing Corp) and broker leaders do, we can have a smart contract to do those things, but somebody has to be behind the smart contract to guarantee the quality of service.
>
> For example, broker-dealer networks, custodians, DTCC/Clearing house or Depository Trust and Clearing Corp currently ensure that if you click 'buy', that 'buy' goes through behind the scenes. There are a lot of controls and functions that take place to guarantee the service completion as expected.
>
> Companies will no longer do all the heavy lifting, their cost structures will be reduced, their overall business valuation will be reduced, but they will be able to provide new services.
>
> Everything will be transactional, including machine-to-machine transactions, which is what we have been discussing with IoT (Internet-Of-Things). The velocity of transactions will also go up. In adhering to the ethos of Web3.0, which is creator led economy, will lead to a framework of hyper-financialization as unbankable assets will take tokenised form and existing rails will not only be able to handle diversity of assets but also be stretched to handle the exponential growth of transaction volume.
>
> So, I do see the ability for us to have Lego blocks (DeFi) to really revolutionise the financial system, except that it will not be autonomous. It will be a distributed automated organisation as opposed to a decentralised autonomous organisation. DeFi will play an active role in digitising our financial system, not necessarily the token-based model that the crypto ecosystem is viewing.
>
> The decentralised automated organisations will be the new financial intermediaries.

DeFi, CeFi and TradFi: interconnected systems

While DeFi is currently largely self-contained, the lines between DeFi, CeFi and TradFi are gradually blurring. As players start to integrate and complement each other, new opportunities and challenges arise.

Dependence on centralized infrastructure

While not broadly advertised, some of the decentralized ecosystem relies on centralized services for certain operations. This reliance was underscored in 2020 when Infura experienced downtime, impacting several DeFi protocols.[19] Infura is a centralized infrastructure provider, part of Consensys, crucial for many DeFi services to connect to blockchain networks like Ethereum.

In an article for *Forbes*, Richard Brown, CTO at R3, advocates that the convenience and superior service provided by such centralized platforms often outweigh the purist decentralized approach, making them a valuable part of the DeFi ecosystem.[20]

Liquidity from traditional avenues

Liquidity is a crucial aspect of any financial market, determining its efficiency and functionality. In DeFi, individuals provide liquidity via pools, yield farming and other programs, but a substantial element comes from centralized institutions. Centralized exchanges often act as bridges, allowing liquidity to flow from traditional markets to DeFi protocols. The growing interest in and adoption of crypto-assets by institutional investors and other traditional finance providers (for example, payments providers) have led to the creation of permissioned versions of DeFi, with whitelisting of participants in a compliant manner.

Traditional finance convergence

As traditional financial institutions continue to explore DeFi, a convergence in both worlds will emerge.

For instance, in 2021, the European Investment Bank (EIB) issued a digital bond on the Ethereum blockchain, marking a significant step towards integrating blockchain technology within traditional finance frameworks. This digital bond issuance, led by Goldman Sachs, Santander and Société Générale, showcased a practical institutional use case for blockchain, further bridging the gap between traditional finance and DeFi.[21]

The use of stablecoins in DeFi protocols also enhances the link between DeFi markets and traditional finance. While increased stablecoin use can boost DeFi adoption, it also presents a major vulnerability, especially if a stablecoin loses its peg, leading to severe stress in decentralized exchanges and mass liquidations in liquidity pools.

Such interconnectedness is expected to grow through the use of tokenized assets as collateral in DeFi, allowing traditional financial institutions to unlock liquidity and obtain leverage on pre-existing assets through DeFi.

Growing interconnections between TradFi, CeFi and DeFi will increase the importance for user and market safeguards in DeFi.

Future outlook

In recent years, a confluence of macro and technological trends has contributed to the exponential growth of DeFi. Initially, DeFi's offering focused on exchanges and lending and borrowing as core concepts. But, over the years, DeFi's offerings have evolved with the creation of new products, adoption of stablecoins and acceptance of tokenized assets as collateral.

DeFi has already revolutionized some old paradigms, like the role of central entities in financial services. By bypassing intermediaries, DeFi protocols have the potential to speed transactions and lower costs. An IMF study noted, 'The marginal cost of DeFi is much lower than the other banks and nonbanks in both advanced and emerging market economies, meaning DeFi is cost-efficient in lending.'[22]

However, the stories of hacks and fraudulent activities underscore the inherent risks and vulnerabilities tied to the nascent state of the industry, exacerbated by the lack of a regulatory framework.

As DeFi, CeFi and TradFi institutions become increasingly inter-connected, a proactive regulatory stance is imperative to mitigate negative spillovers and to harness the innovative potential of DeFi responsibly. Many experts in the DeFi industry are now embracing the need for such regulatory clarity.

'The huge difference between the primordial soup of DeFi building and DeFi in the real world is that now you have to engage with regulation and laws,' said Rune Christensen, the founder of MakerDAO, in a plenary session organized by the World Economic Forum. Christensen acknowledged that DeFi's entry into real-world financing might proceed significantly slower than the march of progress that took the niche market segment to a $100 billion valuation.[23]

But DeFi is not sitting and waiting for external frameworks to be provided. Concentrated efforts to create shared principles and best practices are already ongoing. The launch of the Tokenized Asset Coalition (TAC) in 2023 is another example of CeFi and DeFi players working together to provide clarity and transparency to the industry. Founded by Aave Companies, Circle, Coinbase, Goldfinch and others, the TAC encompasses education on asset tokenization, advocacy for best practices to ensure a compliant environment, and adoption by building scalable on-chain infrastructure.[24]

Such initiatives showcase the future of this industry, in which all players will work together to create frameworks that safeguard the user and market.

SUMMARY OF KEY POINTS

- Decentralized finance (DeFi) promises to replicate traditional financial services (savings, loans, trading, insurance and more) in an open, decentralized, permissionless and autonomous way.

- In DeFi, no central authority or intermediary entity holds or controls users' assets. Instead, participants manage their private keys and assets directly via non-custodial wallets.

- DeFi has revolutionized the old paradigm of centralization. By bypassing intermediaries, DeFi projects are speeding transactions and lowering costs.

- The ethos of DeFi carries the promise of democratizing financial markets, but the complexity of the solutions, poor user experience and governance design are restricting their adoption.

- Centralized finance (CeFi) platforms rely on blockchain as the underlying infrastructure and provide a wide range of cryptocurrency-related financial services. Given its user-friendly interface, CeFi often appeals to users transitioning from traditional finance to crypto.

- DeFi, CeFi and TradFi institutions are becoming increasingly interconnected. A proactive regulatory stance is imperative to mitigate negative spillovers and to harness the innovative potential of DeFi responsibly.

Endnotes

1 M McSweeney. SEC filing shows that Uniswap raised $11 million in June, *The Block*, 6 August 2020, theblock.co/linked/74182/sec-filing-uniswap-funding-june (archived at https://perma.cc/3CFA-6U3X)

2 C Russo. What is decentralized finance?: A deep dive by The Defiant, coinmarketcap, 2021, coinmarketcap.com/academy/article/what-is-decentralized-finance (archived at https://perma.cc/SH7M-629T)

3 M Schückes and T Gutmann. Why do startups pursue initial coin offerings (ICOs)? The role of economic drivers and social identity on funding choice, Springer Link, 4 May 2020, link.springer.com/article/10.1007/s11187-020-00337-9 (archived at https://perma.cc/2P9E-TMKQ)

4 D Morris. Coindesk turns 10: The ICO era – what went right?, CoinDesk, 1 June 2023, coindesk.com/consensus-magazine/2023/06/01/coindesk-turns-10-the-ico-era-what-went-right/ (archived at https://perma.cc/EA7T-3L82)

5 Messari. Bancor profile, messari.io/project/bancor/profile (archived at https://perma.cc/ZK5Q-7YCF)

6 Messari. Aave profile, messari.io/project/aave/profile (archived at https://perma.cc/JFG7-BFDM)

7 S Higgins. Decentralized Exchange Protocol 0x raises $24 million in ICO, Coindesk, 17 August 2017, coindesk.com/markets/2017/08/17/decentralized-exchange-protocol-0x-raises-24-million-in-ico/ (archived at https://perma.cc/9D7H-JRKA)

8 Wharton Blockchain. DeFi beyond the hype, May 2021, wifpr.wharton.upenn.edu/wp-content/uploads/2021/05/DeFi-Beyond-the-Hype.pdf (defipulse.com; *The Defiant*) (archived at https://perma.cc/FX7Z-5K54)

9 Cryptopedia. SushiSwap and vampire attacks in decentralized finance (DeFi), 5 October 2023, www.gemini.com/cryptopedia/sushiswap-uniswap-vampire-attack (archived at https://perma.cc/8AYR-54ZN)

10 D Palmer and N De. 'I f**ked up': SushiSwap creator Chef Nomi returns $14M dev fund, CoinDesk, 14 September 2020, https://www.coindesk.com/tech/2020/09/11/i-fked-up-sushiswap-creator-chef-nomi-returns-14m-dev-fund/ (archived at https://perma.cc/4B7W-54N9)

11 A Cuthbertson. 'I lost my life savings': Terra Luna cryptocurrency collapses 98% overnight, *The Independent*, 13 May 2022, independent.co.uk/tech/terra-luna-ust-crypto-price-crash-b2076655.html (archived at https://perma.cc/MGC4-UKRL)

12 C Russo. Crypto's theater is becoming more surreal, Coindesk, 14 August 2023, coindesk.com/consensus-magazine/2023/08/14/cryptos-theater-is-becoming-more-surreal/ (archived at https://perma.cc/QP9E-JT22)

13 I Makarov and A Schoar. Cryptocurrencies and decentralized finance (DEFI), Working Paper 30006, NBER Working Paper Series, 2022, www.nber.org/system/files/working_papers/w30006/w30006.pdf (archived at https://perma.cc/5JRM-LLWV)

14 J Kubinec. Maker subDAO branches out beyond Ethereum, Blockworks, 21 September 2023, blockworks.co/news/maker-endgame-sub-dao-governance-gnosis-dai (archived at https://perma.cc/TW8J-J9ZY)

15 B Dales. MakerDAO ponders the unthinkable as members debate incorporation and paying taxes, *The Defiant*, 12 October 2021, thedefiant.io/makerdao-taxes-incorporation-debate (archived at https://perma.cc/E984-9RZZ)

16 B Dales. MakerDAO ponders the unthinkable as members debate incorporation and paying taxes, *The Defiant*, 12 October 2021, thedefiant.io/makerdao-taxes-incorporation-debate (archived at https://perma.cc/E984-9RZZ)

17 T Adrian. Cryptocurrencies and decentralised finance, 24 June 2022, imf.org/
en/News/Articles/2022/06/24sp083022-cryptocurrencies-and-decentralized-
finance (archived at https://perma.cc/FGR5-H4DZ)

18 BIS. Project Mariana: BIS and central banks of France, Singapore and
Switzerland successfully test cross-border wholesale CBDCs, 28 September
2023, bis.org/about/bisih/topics/cbdc/mariana.htm (archived at https://perma.
cc/8NXW-MYLX)

19 Y Khatri. Ethereum infrastructure provider Infura is down, crypto exchanges
begin to disable ETH withdrawals, *The Block*, 11 November 2020,
theblock.co/post/84232/ethereum-infrastructure-provider-infura-is-down
(archived at https://perma.cc/7EBH-W8S7)

20 R Brown. The convergence of CeFi And DeFi: The banks' big opportunity,
Forbes, 27 April 2021, forbes.com/sites/richardgendalbrown/2021/04/27/
the-convergence-of-cefi-and-defi-the-banks-big-opportunity/ (archived at
https://perma.cc/B9DZ-B2RM)

21 M Young. Ethereum on a high after European Investment Bank's $121M
digital bond news, *Cointelegraph*, 28 April 2021, cointelegraph.com/news/
ethereum-on-a-high-after-european-investment-bank-s-121m-digital-bond-
news (archived at https://perma.cc/J4S8-LZK8)

22 T Adrian. Cryptocurrencies and decentralised finance, 24 June 2022, www.
imf.org/en/News/Articles/2022/06/24/sp083022-cryptocurrencies-and-
decentralized-finance (archived at https://perma.cc/FGR5-H4DZ)

23 O Avan-Nomayo. DeFi needs regulatory clarity to interface with 'real-world'
finance, experts say, *Cointelegraph*, 7 April 2021, cointelegraph.com/news/
defi-needs-regulatory-clarity-to-interface-with-real-world-finance-experts-say
(archived at https://perma.cc/4XWR-5BZF)

24 T Bradford. Industry leaders announce groundbreaking tokenized asset
coalition, Businesswire, 7 September 2023, businesswire.com/news/
home/20230907033750/en/Industry-Leaders-Announce-Groundbreaking-
Tokenized-Asset-Coalition (archived at https://perma.cc/S8PN-KTGM)

10

Investments in Web3

MEET ANDREESSEN HOROWITZ (A16Z)

Marc Andreessen led the team that created Mosaic, one of the first internet browsers, in 1990, before co-founding Netscape, an internet browser, where he hired Ben Horowitz. Later, the pair co-founded Opsware, a software company HP bought in 2007 for $1.6 billion.[1]

Over the years, they found that they worked well together, with Horowitz being more people-oriented and Andreessen being the more technical of the two. Interestingly, according to Andreessen, part of their success is due to Horowitz having essential qualities that he lacks, like good management skills and character judgement.

The two initially dabbled in the venture capitalist world as amateur angel investors. In four years, they funded 36 startups with their own money, with the largest investment being around $200,000. Before launching their firm, they had already invested $10 million of their personal net worth into approximately 50 tech startups, among them well-known companies such as Twitter, Facebook and LinkedIn.[2]

In 2009, they officially opened the doors of their new investing company called Andreessen Horowitz, also known as a16z (there are 16 letters between the 'a' in Andreessen and the 'z' in Horowitz). Their idea was to reinvent the venture capital (VC) industry by building a large team of experts focused on providing hands-on operational assistance, a different approach from the then-traditional VC model, which primarily involved financial investment and strategic guidance. They also bet widely on marketing, launching a16z with great fanfare, a different approach from the traditional VC model of doing little to no marketing.

In 2011, Marc Andreessen famously wrote an op-ed for *The Wall Street Journal* titled 'Why software is eating the world', in which he predicted that software companies would disrupt traditional industries as never seen before.[3] Adopting this perspective, in 2013, a16z made an early investment in Coinbase. At the time, Coinbase was focused on a very small market that was relatively unknown to investors in the public market. Such early investment underscored a16z's ability to identify markets with the potential for exponential growth and companies that could remain at the forefront of a new global revolution.

In 2018, a16z officially announced the formation of a $350 million fund to invest in crypto companies and protocols. In the pair's introductory blog post, they showed a belief in the power of the software but noted that the industry was still early and often dismissed as a toy. However, they believed that the industry would develop extremely quickly since it is a pure software movement, with no dependency on a hardware buildout, and due to the increasing influx of talent and open-source model. 'For those of us who have been involved in software for a long time, it feels like the early days of the internet, web 2.0, or smartphones all over again,' they said in the fund announcement.[4] Interestingly, reading the post today, it feels as if it was written recently, showcasing how long it takes for technology to make an impact.

Since then, a16z has dug deep into crypto and launched four crypto funds. The most recent was announced in May 2022. The announcement stated that, since the rise of computing, there have been major computing cycles every 10 to 15 years; the PCs in the 1980s, the internet in the 1990s and mobile computing in the 2000s. a16z believed that the next cycle would be driven by blockchains. 'We believe blockchains will power the next major computing cycle, which we call crypto or web3,' stated the announcement. The fund totalled $4.5 billion, with approximately $1.5 billion dedicated to seed investments and $3 billion to venture investments.[5]

Over the years, the team has invested across the Web3 landscape, including DeFi, Web3 games, social media, self-sovereign identity, layer-1 and -2 blockchains, DAOs and NFTs. In 2023, a16z announced it would open its first international office outside the US, in London. At the time of the announcement, there was increased scrutiny by US regulators while at the same time the UK Government was trying to become a 'crypto hub'. 'We are

thrilled to open our first international office in a jurisdiction that welcomes blockchain technology and is committed to creating a predictable business environment by pursuing regulations that both embrace
Web3 and protect consumers,' said Chris Dixon, founder and managing director of a16z,[6] showcasing how regulatory clarity can move businesses, capital and talent.

The company was one of the first and loudest venture capital companies that wholeheartedly embraced this new industry from the start. Both founders with backgrounds in technology see parallels with the early days of the internet and invest in it with a long-term strategy and vision. Their investments were unique from day one, and they truly embraced the innovation brought by Web3. In fact, a16z teams are often seen participating in discussion on DAO forums and often accept token rights, instead of the traditional model of receiving shares/equity in exchange of funding.

Recently, other established VC companies also started to focus on Web3, many starting with small ad-hoc investments and only later creating specific funds. Sequoia Capital, for example, launched a $500–600 million crypto-focused fund in 2022, its first sector-specific fund since its founding in 1972. Sequoia has been investing in crypto since 2015 in both equity and token deals, but only now is taking a more active role.[7]

A new breed of VCs is also emerging, founded by Web3 industry leaders, who made profits in the early days and now have available funds, focusing specifically on Web3 and its myriad opportunities. For example, Paradigm was founded by Fred Ehrsam, co-founder of Coinbase, with Matt Huang to focus on early-stage crypto and blockchain projects. Many exchanges also established incubators and accelerators, such as Binance Labs, which incubates early projects and takes a percentage of tokens in exchange for funding.

How traditional players are betting on Web3

STANDARD CHARTERED INVESTING AND BUILDING WEB3 COMPANIES

In 2018, Standard Chartered established SC Ventures, a forward-thinking division committed to promoting innovation, investing in disruptive financial technology and exploring alternative business models. SC Ventures is dedicated to rewiring the DNA of banking through four pillars: Online Economy & Lifestyle, Digital Assets, World Trade & SMEs and Sustainability. Its multifaceted approach encompasses venture capital investments, a venture-building component and an innovation lab, all under one roof.

Listening to customer demand, SC Ventures focused on digital assets from day one, enabling institutional-grade infrastructure. Alex Manson, CEO of SC Ventures, shared with me about SC Ventures' focus on digital assets:

> We think that digital assets including, but not limited to, cryptocurrencies are here to stay. Therefore, institutional adoption is inevitable, but for institutional adoption to occur, there needs to be institutional-grade infrastructure. Which in my mind does not exist today.

Over the past two years, SC Ventures has rolled out a course for employees in co-operation with Oxford University to develop knowledge and expertise in digital assets. There are now over 300 people who have completed the training. In the UK, SC Ventures launched a crypto custodian, Zodia Custody, in partnership with Northern Trust, as well as a crypto trading platform, Zodia Markets, in partnership with BC Group. Early in 2023, SC Ventures also launched SWIAT, a settlement and trading platform, in collaboration with Landesbank Baden-Württemberg (LBBW), DekaBank and Comyno.

Besides building ventures, SC Ventures has also played a key role as an investor in some of the leading Web3 companies. Minority investments were made to strategic partners, namely Ripple, 24x and Metaco (exited after Ripple acquired Metaco for $250 million). In late 2023, SC Ventures announced a digital asset joint venture investment company in partnership with SBI Holdings, in the United Arab Emirates (UAE). The joint venture will focus on investing in companies across the digital assets spectrum, including market infrastructure, risk and compliance tools, DeFi, tokenization, consumer payments and the Metaverse. UAE was recognized as becoming a hub for fintechs in the digital assets space due to its strengthening infrastructure and talent.

SC Ventures, a leader in financial innovation, has already made its mark with several successful ventures and a multitude of strategic investments. As Alex Manson, CEO of SC Ventures, shared with me, the company still sees a vast landscape of opportunities ahead:

> We are not done building infrastructure, there are other bits and pieces needed. Custody is important, exchange is important, settlement is important, and the next big thing is tokenisation. The tokenisation of various assets ranging from financial securities to real estate.

In late 2023, SC Ventures launched Libeara, a tokenization platform, which will enable the creation of a tokenized Singapore dollar government bond fund for accredited investors.

Buy, build, invest or partner?

Digital applications power modern financial institutions. IT and innovation teams support companies keeping up to date and leveraging the latest technology and developments in the industry. And while the 'buy vs build' discussion, often seen in the media, may lead some to think this is a binary option, the reality is that traditional institutions often adopt all methods: buy, build, invest and partner.

Executives adopt different strategies based on a number of factors. A well-established strategy is building internal core functions and partnering for non-core activities. Again, this is not a clean-cut strategy either. Budget, time and market maturity will all play a role in the decision. Let's say that, for example, an institution decided to digitize one of its core functions. While it may have the talent and budget to build the solution internally, the cost and time of building internally is higher than buying an external solution, given there are strong and mature solutions available. In that case, the institution may decide to buy the solution instead of building internally. Through acquisitions, the institution also obtains valuable IP and absorbs the expertise of the new technology and solution, which is often absent within legacy companies. For example, in 2021, Mastercard acquired CipherTrace, a cryptocurrency intelligence company, to 'combine the technology, AI and cyber capabilities of both companies to differentiate its card and real-time payments infrastructure.'[8] For other areas, Mastercard has decided to partner instead. For example, in order to expand its cryptocurrency payment card programme globally, Mastercard has partnered with a number of crypto firms, including Binance, Nexo and Gemini.

Executives should consider all tools available to innovate and leverage new technologies and solutions. Investment in startups is another tool that traditional institutions often use. While some organizations may do it as part of their innovation or IT offering, others have dedicated teams, such as Corporate VC, or CVC teams. Investments are not a new tool. Many traditional institutions have been using investments for years to get exposure to new technologies while outsourcing risk.

Executives can use investment as a strategic tool to get (indirect) exposure to this nascent industry while mitigating risks. In May 2022, a total of 61 banks invested at least once in this space, according to the Blockdata report.[9] Since regulatory clarity is still lacking in many countries, many executives have chosen to fund innovators pushing the frontier rather than attempting to disrupt the industry themselves. Institutions often invest in startups that deliver the infrastructure, security and core solutions, like custody and tokenization, needed for Web3. For example, Citi Ventures, J.P. Morgan and Goldman Sachs participated in Blockdaemon's funding rounds (Citi invested in Series C and the others in Series B of the blockchain infrastructure company).[10]

During times of higher market volatility, institutions may reduce the number of funding rounds they participate in. However, they will still invest by narrowing their scope to companies that provide the core functions for activities that are always needed, such as cybersecurity, compliance and risk. Citi and Paypal Ventures, for example, invested in Series B of TRM Labs, a blockchain tool that helps financial institutions monitor, investigate and mitigate crypto fraud and financial crime.

How tokens could change investment

Historically, institutional gatekeepers like venture capital, accelerators, investment banks or private equity companies tightly controlled access to capital and ideas in the private markets. Retail investors or entrepreneurs faced high barriers in raising funds or sourcing deal flows.

Web3 innovations like token sales, ICOs, initial DEX offerings also called IDOs (a crowdfunding method in which a project launches a token through a DEX) and decentralized crowdfunding platforms enable communities and projects to raise funds directly from their communities. Instead of pitching to a small group of VCs or institutions, founders can market opportunities to a global network of believers in their vision. Likewise, retail investors can gain exposure to early-stage projects and asset classes that were previously inaccessible without the right connections.

'Tokens can be viewed as the next evolution of shares traded on a stock exchange. In traditional markets, the democratization of access to the stock market through platforms like Robinhood and eToro has given retail investors the ability to organise themselves into communities that can further their investment thesis beyond the market rationale,' Andrei Grachev, co-founder of DWF, told *Cointelegraph*.[11]

More than democratizing initial investment, communities will have a say in how future capital raises are performed and who can participate, switching the traditional investment dynamic.

VCS PITCH TO SUSHISWAP

On July 21, 0xMaki, a semi-anonymous and core contributor of SushiSwap, put a proposal forward to the community to raise capital from more traditional institutional venture investors by selling a portion of SUSHI tokens held in its treasury. The proposal included a potential sale of up to $60 million of Sushi tokens, at a 20–30 per cent discount, from the treasury to 21 VCs as strategic investors.[12]

The SushiSwap community was strongly opposed to providing discounted SUSHI tokens to VCs. Many were sceptical about how these VCs would truly add value to SushiSwap. Some were concerned that the VCs would prioritize their own profits, as opposed to the project's long-term growth. 'Sushiswap is a blue chip in the DeFi project and has a constructive governance structure. It is a big mistake to proceed if this proposal is approved,' the SushiSwap community criticized.[13]

In response to the community concerns, VCs engaged in discussion with the community, pitching their strengths and the value they would bring to the table. At one point, Lightspeed Ventures created a new proposal that provided a non-dilutive price for tokens (in other words there wouldn't be dilution in existing ownership) and offered the community the same opportunity to participate as the VC.

Over one month, the community held passionate discussions, with 62 comments on the public governance board, six public community calls, all hosting 400–500 community members each, and countless tweets and news articles. All of this was coordinated by a project that had never raised money from venture investors and had no CEO and no board of directors.[14]

In the end, the decision was made to shelve the deal as the community continued to work towards a solution that could be brought back to a decentralized vote.

Tokens represent a pivotal shift in funding over the last decade, characterized by greater speed and simplicity and broader stakeholder inclusion and alignment. Imagine this: instead of receiving a traditional share certificate, digital or otherwise, your investment in a company is represented by a token. These tokens come with pre-coded restrictions on their transfer and sale, defined at the time of investment. Yet, this innovation also faces some challenges. One significant concern is the lack of (or uncertainty in) regulatory or legal framework in some countries. For example, tokens may not carry any legal or enforceable rights to the company revenue or could be classified as securities with legal requirements. In the US, for example, if a token grants profit or dividend rights, it can be deemed an unregistered security by the SEC, violating disclosure rules.

Do VCs own Web3?

Even though there are alternatives for funding in Web3, the big pie of investments is still done from centralized entities. In 2021, Jack Dorsey, co-founder of Twitter, got into a heated discussion on X, about Web3 funding. 'You don't own web3,' he tweeted. 'The VCs and their LPs do. It will never escape their incentives. It's ultimately a centralised entity with a different label.'[15] His view was that, although the Web3 ethos was based on decentralization and community, it was still primarily controlled by centralized entities since a considerable amount of the funding is provided by VCs, who, in return, receive tokens.

In 2023, this debate resurged when a16z deployed all 15 million of its UNI tokens to vote against the proposal of deploying Uniswap v3 on the BNB chain.

IS UNISWAP OWNED BY VCS?

In February 2023, OxPlasma Labs submitted a final governance proposal to deploy the latest Uniswap iteration on the BNB chain, a decentralized and public blockchain powered by Binance. At the time, Uniswap v3 was active on Ethereum, Polygon, Arbitrum, Optimism and Celo blockchains and the addition of BNB aimed to leverage the high speed and lower fees of the chain and compete against Pancake Swap, itself a fork of Uniswap v2.[16]

A few days later, a16z used its substantial holding of 15 million UNI tokens to oppose the move. UNI is Uniswap's native token, which doubles as a governance token, letting users vote on key proposals. The core of the disagreement between a16z and other parties involved the choice of the cross-chain bridge for the deployment. The proposal suggested using the Wormhole bridge, which was backed by another VC called Jump Crypto. a16z signalled that it would prefer to use LayerZero instead, a bridge protocol backed by the VC firm.

The considerable vote from a16z sparked debate on X. CZ (Changpeng Zhao), the Binance founder, asked his audience of 8.1 million followers if 'Uniswap was controlled by a16z' and Chris Blec, a DeFi researcher, said to his audience that a16z 'decided on what future Uniswap versions look like', adding that a16z 'controlled the treasury'.[17]

However, such reactions may have been overstated. Twenty-four hours later, votes from several other 'whales' counterbalanced the a16z voting, notably 5.76 million from Compound Labs' Robert Lesher, 4.92 million from GFX Labs and 3.5 million from Blockchain at Michigan.[18]

This debate raised an interesting question about ownership and decentralization in Web3. The reality is that the democratization vision is challenging to achieve in practice. Even if startups do not accept VC funding and instead opt for ICO or token sales, the community that can actually participate in such token sales is also restricted. First, they need to have the money available to invest. Second, they need to have the expertise or even awareness of this industry. And simply, there is still only a small group of individuals who understand the technology in the first place.

If it goes against the ethos of Web3, why would companies still look for investment from VC Firms?

VC investment provides legitimacy to the companies, which is particularly important in the Web3 industry. Before investing in companies, VCs conduct extensive due diligence, including assessing the project's technical viability, market demand, competitive environment, token economics and regulatory issues. This process is stricter than ICOs and other ways of crypto fundraising that have much lower barriers to market entry. Often, a website and a whitepaper are all that is needed to sell tokens or launch an ICO.

VCs can also introduce a sizable amount of financing in one go instead of small funding amounts from retail investors. In addition to funding, VCs often offer strategic advice, connections to the industry, and expertise to support the project's success and help handle regulatory obstacles.

As a leader, partner and investor in Web3 companies, you should understand who composes the cap table of the companies you are engaging with. That information will provide you with clarity on decision-making and ownership of the company.

Investing in decentralized projects

Investing in the Web3 space represents a paradigm shift from traditional models. At the heart of this transformation is the emergence of community-centric ecosystems and the integral role of tokens as both investment vehicles and utility enhancers within these networks.

Tokenomics

In Web2, founders tend to initially raise funds from their friends, family and angel investors. As they continue to expand the business, they engage with VCs for pre-seed, seed and series A, B, C and D rounds, eventually leading to an IPO (initial public offering) or acquisition. Through each round, investors inject capital in exchange for equity and, sometimes, a seat on the advisory board. However, the capital remains locked up for years until a liquidity event, such as an IPO or acquisition, occurs.

The investment narrative in Web3 can be different, if investors in Web3 companies receive tokens as a part of their investment, instead of traditional equity. These tokens, which can be bought and sold on exchanges, introduce market capitalization as the project is being built, providing investors with more flexibility and liquidity alternatives. Liquidity refers to the ease with which an asset or security can be converted into cash at market price. In essence, while in equity-funding deals investors need to wait for an IPO or acquisition, think five to ten years; with token-funding deals investors can sell their tokens after lock-up periods, typically one to two years, and recoup investment much faster.

Token economics, aka tokenomics, plays a vital role in the valuation and functionality of Web3 projects. It paves the way for innovative financial structures but can also create potential conflicts of interest, with founding teams having to balance between investors' needs and the border community's interest.

Tokens are usually time-locked, so they can't be sold for a stipulated period, often for one or two years. When the vesting period concludes, investors face a conundrum. They can either choose to sell the tokens, reaping substantial profits but potentially driving down the token price and impacting the community's holdings, or they can opt to retain their tokens. Tokens, in essence, create a new challenge: short-term investor liquidity vs long-term project build.

TIGER GLOBAL SELLS BRAINTRUST TOKENS

In 2021 Tiger Global, a big investment firm, made significant investments into private tech companies. One notorious investment was made into Braintrust, a crypto-powered recruitment company. In return for the investment, Tiger Global received BTRST tokens, which are Brainstrust native tokens used as a currency and reward system for the users. The tokens had a multi-year lock-up period.

In 2022, amid collapses of Terra, FTX and others, the crypto market took a downturn, with the total market cap decreasing as much as 70 per cent. Tiger Global, and other VCs, started to face big portfolio losses. To appease and calm their limited partners, who provided the capital for the fund, Tiger Global reconsidered some of its holdings. In January 2023, after the lock-up period expired, Tiger Global started selling large quantities of the BTRST tokens, with support from FalconX (an institutional investment firm). The sale of such significant quantities contributed to a more than 20 per cent decrease in the Braintrust token's price.[19]

This event underscored the intricate challenges faced by VCs: balancing limited partners' needs while supporting a project's long-term strategy. The inherent transparency of token transactions, recorded on public blockchains, means that every sale is visible to anyone, including the project's community members. High-profile events, like Tiger Global selling substantial quantities of tokens, can damage the reputation of VCs in the Web3 community. These actions reinforce the sentiment that VCs prioritize their own short-term profits over the long-term objectives and health of the projects they invest in.

Note that this space is still evolving and there are a few variations of investment models. As discussed, many new Web3 companies will use the token-investment model, the most innovative form of funding. More 'conservative' Web3 companies still use the traditional model of equity-funding, while other companies have adopted a dual model, issuing both tokens and equity – often starting with the traditional route of equity and later adding token sales or ICOs.

Community

In Web3, communities are often at the centre of many projects; they are not just participants but often co-owners of the same. Their influence extends through governance, funding and strategic direction facilitated by tokens.

While previously, VCs would assess business models and support promising founders and their vision, now, VCs need to consider community as a critical metric for investment. A robust and engaged community can lead to a self-sustaining ecosystem, driving both adoption and value creation.

The role of VCs will also change in the sense that they need to adopt the culture and participate in discussions and voting like other community members. Sequoia, for example, has publicly noted that it wants to have a more active role. The recent crypto-specific fund was created to support this and to provide the flexibility to engage more deeply. That means Sequoia will now start staking, providing liquidity, and participating in governance and trading instead of just investing in and holding tokens. 'Our network of builders at Ethereum, Solana, major DeFi protocols, and beyond have urged us to do the same,' Shaun Maguire, partner at Sequoia Capital, told *The Block*.[20]

Investing in Web3 vs Web2

The investment landscape of Web3 is significantly different from Web2. This difference is not just technological but extends to market dynamics and strategic imperatives for investors and founders.

In a recent discussion with Pete Townsend, Managing Director at Techstars Web3 (a pre-seed VC and accelerator), he told me the metrics he uses to evaluate founders. He reflected that, given the existing market size and user base of Web3, he focuses on founders capable of bridging the gap between Web2 and Web3 to grow and succeed:

At the macro level, investing in Web3 is harder because it's a smaller market. While the number of crypto addresses might suggest a broader base, between 350 and 400 million, the reality of daily active users paints a different picture of about 15 million active users (excluding centralised exchanges). If we contrast that with Facebook, for example, a Web2 company, they have 2 billion active users. So, Web3 is a much smaller market.

And so, when investing in Web3, I look for founders who understand that they need to go beyond Web3 users. They need to be able to sell to Web3 and Web2 users. That's why, in the Techstars Web3 programme, we look for three things.

First, we look for those who are building the Decentralised Internet, which includes a broad infrastructure built on blockchain. Sometimes, the technology will slink off into the background, with clients agnostic to the infrastructure solution. In other cases, startups will provide infrastructure to truly decentralised projects.

The second strand is what we call tokenised economies, which is when someone is building a protocol or a dapp on top of an existing protocol. In such cases, a token is required to drive the supply and demand of the services provided on the network. In simple terms, the network will become its own economy, and that's why it's called token economics or tokenomics.

Now, founders need to be able to build something that is truly decentralised because centralised tokens just don't work. To me, tokens issued by projects or companies that have no plans to decentralise are akin to loyalty points. The FTT token issued by the now-collapsed FTX exchange is such an example. And so we focus on those building tokenised economies with a long-term perspective because we need long runways to build fully decentralised networks.

The third piece is those that are helping to onboard the first 1 billion users of Web3 (whether they know it or not). So, these would be consumer applications that happen to be using blockchain technology, which we see a lot of, for example, in FinTech. Several propositions are using stablecoin rails to deliver peer-to-peer payments. Users may think they are transferring U.S. dollars, but behind the scenes, a USDC or USDT dollar-pegged token is being moved to provide instantaneous settlements.

And so, when we invest, we consider all those three strands and whether they will be able to solve real-world problems for those who are not crypto natives. We look for companies that understand how to translate this new world to Web2 customers.

Market maturity

A WATERSHED MOMENT FOR WEB3

On 14 April 2021, Coinbase made history as the first major cryptocurrency exchange to go public via a direct listing on the Nasdaq stock exchange. At the time, this 'watershed' event was seen as finally bringing legitimacy and validation to the industry.

By opting for a direct listing, Coinbase allowed employees and shareholders to sell shares immediately at a market-based price. Other tech companies like Spotify, Slack, Palantir and Roblox have previously used and pioneered direct listing.

Founded in 2012 as one of the earliest US-based crypto platforms, Coinbase experienced meteoric growth by simplifying Bitcoin and Ether purchases for retail investors. By 2021, Coinbase served over 56 million verified users with its fiat-to-crypto onramps and custody solutions.[21] Coinbase had raised more than $500 million from venture capital investors, including Andreessen Horowitz, Tiger Global and Paradigm, who last privately valued it at $8 billion. On the day of the debut, the stock swung as low as $310 and as high as $429. Coinbase ended the day at $328.28, valuing the company at $85.7 billion, more than 10 times its last valuation as a private company.

The successful public debut proved there was investor appetite for a regulated and reputable crypto business catering to traditional institutions and individuals. Of course, scepticism remained as analysts debated Coinbase's lofty valuation compared with incumbents like Nasdaq Inc, with a market cap of $256 billion, and Goldman Sachs, with a market value of $111 billion.[22]

Coinbase represents just a fragment of the Web3 story. Yet, its successful IPO signified a pivotal shift in Wall Street's sentiment of dismissing crypto as a fad to acknowledging this industry as legitimate. Web3 businesses are now considered on a par with other major tech corporations. Since Coinbase's IPO, other Web3 companies have expressed interest in following suit. In late 2023, Circle announced it was considering an IPO in 2024. Circle received investment from financial services firms BlackRock, Fidelity Management and Goldman Sachs and was valued at $9 billion in February 2022.

However, the often-repeated 'we are still early' mantra underscores the industry's ongoing growth and untapped potential. Many more IPOs are expected throughout the next few years while the industry matures and establishes its market presence.

In my discussion with Pete Townsend, Managing Director at Techstars Web3, he mentioned this vision of vast and untapped opportunity in this space:

Amara's Law states that people always overestimate the impact of technology in the short run and underestimate its impact in the long run. And I totally believe that. I got into this industry in 2016, inspired by what I saw on page 2 of the Bitcoin whitepaper in 2014. I was figuring out blockchain at the same time as a few of my former TradFi (traditional finance) counterparts, and we were all thinking the same thing. If blockchain can operate this fluidly for Bitcoin, imagine what it could do for financial markets more broadly. A lot has happened since 2014 and my interests in blockchain and web3 go way beyond the financial markets now, but it's still only been 15 years since the launch of Bitcoin.

The dawning of the internet age was in the 90s. We are now 30 years on and see how much has happened. Imagine what's going to happen between 2024 and 2040 in this space. It's mind-blowing. We have so far to go and much more to do.

Future outlook

In the early stages of Web3, there was a rush of token sales. Many projects would pre-sell a token and then promise to bring a product to market. However, most of those projects could not deliver, and often the token's value dropped to zero. The market has since matured, with builders and investors bearing the scars of the excess and now designing their projects differently. Instead of just issuing a token, modern projects seek to build and validate a product through the engagement of its community before releasing a token. Some are even scrapping the idea of a token altogether unless it serves a clear purpose.

Pete Townsend, Managing Director at Techstars Web3, has seen this change first-hand:

We did our first programme in 2021, at the height of the bull market. Back then, I met founders who had raised significant amounts of capital but had no product, nothing built. And I would always be puzzled as to why they were pitching to me. You can call it hubris or naivete, but all that came crashing down in the first half of 2022.

All the founders we brought on in the first programme had the opportunity and vision to benefit from a token. We could see how a token would bring value to the business. However, when we finished the programme in July of 2022, there was no market for those tokens. So, everybody had to pivot, and not necessarily pivot their product, but their fundraising strategy. We went from 'we will launch a token to raise 1 to 3 million to build our product over the next year' to 'we have got to build something, we have got to get that product into customer's hands, and then we are going to use that traction to raise money. And we will raise a bit, and then we will go get some more traction, and we will go back and raise again.'

This change has meant that at the end of 2021 and early 2022 that we were considering founders whose vision was to build a network, and that network required a token to operate. But now that we have seen where Web3 is going, we returned to the original premise of just looking for excellent founders. Don't get me wrong, we were looking for excellent founders in 2021. But we were also looking for excellent founders whose product proposition could bring a token to market.

Now, through the benefit of experience, we are steering projects away from launching tokens unless absolutely necessary to operate the network. Tokens can bring more pain to your project and create a lot of unnecessary noise and distraction, so if one is not really needed then just leave it aside.

This recent shift in the market reflects a market maturity, with founders moving towards a product-centric approach. Despite fluctuations in investment driven by macroeconomic factors, investor sentiment and other variables, the industry's growth remains robust, and investors are still optimistic. 'We are very much long-term investors in this space. We are not a fly by night – come in, and try to get a quick hit and move on because our core business is obviously long on the entire industry,' said Yibo Ling, the Chief Business Officer of Binance Labs, the VC arm of Binance exchange, during an interview with CoinDesk.[23]

Investment in Web3 represents an evolving landscape where traditional funding players, VCs, accelerators and financial institutions intersect with innovative concepts such as token raising and decentralized governance. Funding markets and models are evolving to align with this new decentralized ecosystem and to take advantage of new investment opportunities. While some VCs have invested in innovative companies with decentralization at heart, most financial institutions are still taking conservative bets in companies aligned to their business.

SUMMARY OF KEY POINTS

- Traditional institutions use a combination of buy, build, invest and partner methods to keep informed and leverage the latest technology and developments in the industry. Many have invested in Web3 startups focused on infrastructure, security and core solutions.

- Token sales, ICOs, initial DEX offerings (also called IDOs) and decentralized crowdfunding enable communities and projects to raise funds directly from their communities, democratizing investment.

- Investing in the Web3 space represents a paradigm shift from traditional models, with the emergence of community-centric ecosystems and the integral role of tokens as both investment vehicles and utility enhancers within these networks.

- Investors are focused on founders that are creating impactful solutions and capable of bridging the gap between Web2 and Web3 to grow and succeed.

- The market has matured from the early days of token issuance. Modern projects are focused on building and validating a product instead of releasing a token.

Endnotes

1 a16z. Ben Horowitz bio, a16z.com/author/ben-horowitz/ (archived at https://perma.cc/Q896-WDRG)

2 History computer. Andreessen Horowitz: The history of Silicon Valley's kingmakers, 29 November 2022, history-computer.com/andreessen-horowitz-guide/ (archived at https://perma.cc/4K9D-ZG5R)

3 M Andreessen. Why software is eating the world, a16z, 20 August 2011, a16z.com/why-software-is-eating-the-world/ (archived at https://perma.cc/4Z7U-262Q)

4 a16z. Introducing a16z crypto, 2018, a16z.com/introducing-a16z-crypto/ (archived at https://perma.cc/2P29-9WBF)

5 C Dixon. Crypto Fund 4, a16z crypto, 25 May 2022, a16zcrypto.com/posts/announcement/crypto-fund-four/ (archived at https://perma.cc/4H3B-YK52)

6 Reuters. Andreessen Horowitz to open its first international office in London, 12 June 2023, www.reuters.com/business/finance/andreessen-horowitz-open-its-first-international-office-london-2023-06-12/ (archived at https://perma.cc/2FLQ-87KA)

7 Y Khatri. Sequoia Capital is launching a $500-600 million crypto fund to invest in tokens, *The Block*, 17 February 2022, theblockcrypto.com/post/134578/sequoia-capital-new-crypto-fund-tokens (archived at https://perma.cc/PCA9-MHGU)

8 Mastercard press release. Mastercard acquires CipherTrace to enhance crypto capabilities, 9 September 2021, mastercard.com/news/press/2021/september/mastercard-acquires-ciphertrace-to-enhance-crypto-capabilities/ (archived at https://perma.cc/4FYG-KUU7)

9 Blockdata. Top banks investing in crypto and blockchain May 2022 Update, 15 June 2022, www.blockdata.tech/blog/general/top-banks-investing-in-crypto-and-blockchain-may-2022-update (archived at https://perma.cc/V3NX-BST9)

10 Blockdata. Top banks investing in crypto and blockchain May 2022 Update, 15 June 2022, www.blockdata.tech/blog/general/top-banks-investing-in-crypto-and-blockchain-may-2022-update (archived at https://perma.cc/V3NX-BST9)

11 R Sadykova. Crypto VC: Token investing and the next bull run with Digital Wave Finance, *Cointelegraph*, 4 October 2023, cointelegraph.com/news/crypto-vc-token-investing-bull-run-dwf (archived at https://perma.cc/D2SW-JBQS)

12 Sushiswap forum. [Withdrawn] Sushi phantom troupe – strategic raise, 2021, forum.sushi.com/t/withdrawn-sushi-phantom-troupe-strategic-raise/4554 (archived at https://perma.cc/C3LV-MP87)

13 J Ye. Crypto Funds pitching to the community? Feat. SushiSwap, 23 July 2021, medium.com/despread-global/crypto-funds-pitching-to-the-community-feat-sushiswap-4216104d788 (archived at https://perma.cc/T5CZ-DNWN)

14 J Dorman. Sushiswap (SUSHI) treasury raise: Proof decentralized governance works, 17 August 2021, www.ar.ca/blog/sushiswap-treasury-raise-proof-decentralized-governance-works (archived at https://perma.cc/6M6F-F35G)

15 J Kastrenakes. Jack Dorsey says VCs really own Web3 (and Web3 boosters are pretty mad about it), *The Verge*, 21 December 2021, www.theverge.com/2021/12/21/22848162/jack-dorsey-web3-criticism-a16z-ownership-venture-capital-twitter (archived at https://perma.cc/6XQG-8YRB)

16 Protos Staff. Uniswap votes to launch on Binance's centralized BNB Chain, 24 January 2023, protos.com/uniswap-votes-to-launch-on-binances-centralized-bnb-chain/ (archived at https://perma.cc/F8F7-XWEM)

17 M Koopsen. 'Uniswap controlled by a16z?': Crypto Twitter split over VC firm's governance move, Decrypt, 6 February 2023, decrypt.co/120653/uniswap-controlled-a16z-crypto-twitter-split-over-vc-firms-governance-move (archived at https://perma.cc/X5BP-2MSK)

18 M Koopsen. 'Uniswap controlled by a16z?': Crypto Twitter split over VC firm's governance move, Decrypt, 6 February 2023, decrypt.co/120653/uniswap-controlled-a16z-crypto-twitter-split-over-vc-firms-governance-move (archived at https://perma.cc/X5BP-2MSK)

19 L Schwartz and A Sraders. 'Token projects have to eat that sh*t every day': Crypto VCs face a harsh reality in the bear market, *Fortune Crypto*, 1 June 2023, fortune.com/crypto/2023/06/01/crypto-venture-capital-harsh-reality-bear-market-tokens/ (archived at https://perma.cc/CX88-JDNK)

20 Y Khatri. Sequoia Capital is launching a $500-600 million crypto fund to invest in tokens, *The Block*, 17 February 2022, theblockcrypto.com/post/134578/sequoia-capital-new-crypto-fund-tokens (archived at https://perma.cc/XLM5-J6A4)

21 A Levi. Coinbase closes at $328.28 per share in Nasdaq debut, valuing crypto exchange at $85.8 billion, CNBC, 14 April 2021, cnbc.com/2021/04/14/coinbase-to-debut-on-nasdaq-in-direct-listing.html (archived at https://perma.cc/3ASQ-JVYT)

22 *The New York Times.* Coinbase valued at $86 billion in 'landmark moment' for crypto, 14 April 2021, nytimes.com/live/2021/04/14/business/stock-market-today (archived at https://perma.cc/AVH7-HVDE)

23 B Betz. Binance's VC arm, with over 200 investments, focuses on 'explosive' potential for Web3, CoinDesk, 11 May 2023, coindesk.com/business/2023/05/11/binances-vc-arm-with-over-200-investments-focuses-on-explosive-potential-for-web3/ (archived at https://perma.cc/R4YB-GX9R)

11

The regulatory perspective of Web3

$580 million. Such news triggered a wider sell-off, similar to a bank run, placing immense pressure on FTX to meet the sudden demand for customer withdrawals. Due to a lack of funds, FTX eventually halted customer withdrawals altogether.[2]

In need of rescue, FTX started looking for buyers. On 8 November, Binance's CEO offered to acquire FTX but pulled out 24 hours later due to serious issues identified during due diligence related to how FTX had been conducting itself, implying serious governance issues. Without a way forward, on 11 November, FTX filed for Chapter 11 bankruptcy protections. Sam Bankman-Fried was arrested in the Bahamas and subsequently extradited to the US on charges including wire fraud and money laundering. In late 2023, the trial of FTX was one of the most-watched fraud trials in years.

In 2023, Sam Bankman-Fried was found guilty of all seven counts of fraud and conspiracy to commit fraud, the jury delivering its verdict after less than four hours of deliberation.

'Sam, what have you done?' tweeted Sean Ryan Evans, host of the *Bankless* podcast. This tweet reflected the sentiment felt across the industry. Bankman-Fried was a very well-respected figure in the industry by other founders, the press and the regulators. The failure created a ripple effect in the industry and across the globe due to FTX's global nature and presence.

The fraud committed by Sam Bankman-Fried was 'traditional' fraud and not crypto fraud – commingling and embezzling customer funds. Simply put, he moved client funds from FTX to be used in trading at Alameda, venture capital investments, political donations and other personal gains. Some have debated that financial regulation could have prevented such fraud, which had nothing to do with crypto, blockchain or digital assets. Whether traditional or crypto fraud, the reality is that this event added even more scepticism to the industry and spurred calls for regulation.

Calls for regulation

Over the past decade, the meteoric rise of cryptocurrencies and Web3 activity has posed new and complex challenges for regulators tasked with protecting consumers and the financial system. As the industry grew from a small digital experiment into a $1 trillion global industry in 2022,[3] so did the interest from regulators and supervisors. Fuelled by recent hacking and fraud stories such as Terra-Luna, Celsius and FTX, efforts to regulate this industry have moved to the top of the policy agenda.

The emergence of digital currencies, including the release of the Bitcoin paper in 2009, was partly a response to concerns about traditional banking systems, and brings an interesting question: *How does one regulate a movement that, by design, resists central entities?*

Maximalists of the Web3 ethos of decentralization argue that decentralized technologies cannot and should not be regulated, while others claim regulation is required and welcomed but should not halt innovation. This debate will continue as the industry develops further.

Regulators typically play a crucial role in protecting customers and safeguarding market integrity by setting standards and enforcing rules. However, heavy-handed regulation runs the risk of stifling beneficial innovation or pushing activities underground, a tricky balancing act between risks and rewards. So far, regulators worldwide have adopted different approaches, with countries such as Switzerland and Singapore seen as the trailblazers, welcoming new companies and products while defining clear rules and regulations. At the other extreme, countries including China have banned cryptocurrencies altogether.

The industry is not only complex but global at its heart. Companies based in one jurisdiction are able to provide products and services for clients across the globe. Thus, international coordination is required to offer level-set rules and requirements that go across countries instead of individual, siloed efforts. Some work to coordinate response at a global level has been developed. The Financial Stability Board

(FSB) and International Monetary Fund (IMF) published a joint paper that highlighted recommendations and standards to address financial stability, financial integrity, market integrity, investor protection, prudential and other risks derived from crypto-assets.[4] However, the agreement and implementation of a global framework will take time, given the different stakeholders and agendas at play. The coming years will determine whether regulators can find the right calibration between protection and innovation at a global level.

Why do we need regulation?

Before we dive deeper into regulation, let's take a step back and consider the role of financial regulation. As the World Economic Forum states, 'the primary aim of financial regulation is to support financial stability, transparency, protection for consumers and investors and a level playing field for different market participants.'[5]

Recent failures like the Terra-Luna stablecoin collapse and fraudulent activities on FTX emphasized the urgent need for policies that protect consumers and prevent abuse and malpractices. Such stories not only hurt existing consumers but also keep new consumers at bay, holding off mainstream adoption. Trust is one of the most used words in financial services. And for mainstream adoption, consumers will need to be able to trust that new companies have their best interests at heart and that they will be protected. Regulation will be essential to protect consumers and cement a trustworthy reputation of the Web3 industry as a safe place to invest and participate.

Web3 innovation also brings additional complexity and broader implications to the financial markets. The IMF, for example, argues that the adoption of stablecoins could replace official currencies and, as a result, significantly impact countries' monetary and fiscal policies. In a similar vein, the IMF raised concerns with the implementation of Bitcoin as a legal tender by El Salvador, stating that it was 'not against' the implementation of Bitcoin but saw 'macroeconomic, financial and legal issues' with its adoption.[6] It is too early to understand the real implications of adopting Bitcoin as a legal tender, but several authorities are closely monitoring El Salvador's actions to understand the local and global impacts.

Finally, clear requirements can level the playing field for companies building in this industry. The existing regulatory uncertainty can create significant risks for companies, with unexpected changes in regulation resulting in fines, extra taxes, or having to rethink business models and countries of operations. Such environments make it extremely difficult for businesses to plan for the future.

'No regulation, please'

To ensure we have a balanced view on this topic, it is important to consider for a moment the opposing perspective. The ethos of Web3 leans towards innovation, decentralization and financial freedom. Regulation is often viewed as an impediment to these principles. Many in the Web3 community believe that regulation is not required, arguing that it will stifle innovation and discourage developers and entrepreneurs from building new products and services.

Many highlight that the nature of the technology provides a sufficient framework to manage and mitigate risks. Mechanisms of financial and non-financial incentives are often put in place to encourage desired behaviour and discourage malicious actions. Such incentives can be considered a form of self-regulation, with good platforms and services naturally rewarded with more users, while bad actors will be weeded out over time. One example of such an incentive is the fact that, in some blockchains, users who are responsible for checking and validating transactions, called validators, are financially rewarded for verifying transactions but can lose their tokens for approving malicious actions. The theory is that if these incentives are well designed, they can effectively regulate the behaviour of participants without the need for external enforcement.

Some idealists go one step further and argue that 'code is law'. In their view, the code that runs blockchain networks should be treated as law. The rules and logic embedded in the code govern how the systems operate and offer a new paradigm of trust and agreement, so traditional legal frameworks and regulatory bodies are deemed redundant, if not obstructive. Ethereum Classic describes the code of a smart contract as the 'ultimate arbiter of the outcome of an on-chain interaction, as opposed to some overriding force from outside the network'.[7]

While the idea of a perfectly neutral, self-patrolling system is appealing, high-profile mistakes and hacks have cast doubts on the idea that code is a sufficient form of regulation on its own. If a smart contract is poorly written or has a bug, it can result in unearned profits, all while technically following the law of the code. In short, there are no do-overs, bailouts or refunds. What's more telling is how this belief was challenged during The DAO Hack, in which ultimately the actions were reversed, and the code was not law, but human.

THE DAO HACK

At the beginning of May 2016, a few members of the Ethereum community announced the inception of 'The DAO', which was also known as Genesis DAO. The DAO was built as a smart contract on the Ethereum blockchain, a pure decentralized autonomous organization (DAO).

The DAO was meant to operate like a venture capital fund for the crypto and decentralized space. In essence, the platform would allow anyone with a project to pitch their idea to the community and potentially receive funding from The DAO. In order to raise funding to start the project, the DAO team pioneered a new decentralized funding model. During its creation, there was a period in which anyone was allowed to send Ether to a unique wallet address in exchange for DAO tokens. This crowdfunding innovative approach was an unexpected success, managing to gather 12.7 million ETH, worth around $150 million at the time.[8]

However, a month later, on 17 June, the project's fate changed drastically. Flaws in the DAO's code enabled a hacker to drain funds from The DAO. In the first few hours of the attack, 3.6 million ETH were stolen, the equivalent of $70 million at the time, leaving investors out of pocket. After multiple discussions to find a solution for the bug and to recover the lost funds, a radical solution was proposed. What if they rewound time through a 'hard fork'? A hard fork of the entire Ethereum blockchain would not only fix the bug, but create something much more radical: an 'irregular state change'. In simple terms, the hard fork would take back all the hacked funds and return them to their owners, as if nothing had happened.

This led to a heated discussion between two strongly ideological sides. On one side were investors who wanted their money back and Ethereum pragmatists who saw the potential for reputational damage. They believed Ethereum would not be taken seriously if the hacker kept the hacked funds. On the other end were those against a hard fork. To them, using a hard fork was not just cheating but a betrayal of the entire ethos. Under the 'code is law' ethos, blockchains and rules supersede courts and nation-states, so, if you use bugs in the code to exploit or hack, you earned it.[9]

In the end, the Ethereum community controversially decided to perform a hard fork and restore the stolen funds, violating the blockchain's immutable record. This caused a rift, with two new chains now live. Ethereum Classic (ETC) continued on the original chain, preserving the hack's integrity, and Ethereum (ETH) was a new chain created as a result of the hard fork. Ethereum is the more popular of the two, and the one you will probably hear about.

The idea of an incentive-based approach and self-regulation is an interesting one that offers a new perspective on how systems could be organized and governed. This is a perspective that goes beyond technology and reconsiders long-held assumptions about governance and the status quo. The traditional social norm in financial services is to have laws and entities that provide supervision and enforcement of those laws. However, in this new model, regulation is enforced by the technology challenging the norm.

While an interesting perspective, this new model is not working perfectly, as we have seen from recent hacks and attacks. While bad actors are being eventually weeded out after such stories, the industry's reputation has been continuously damaged as a consequence, and many innocent investors have lost significant savings. Hacks, risks and fraud stories were less of a concern in the early days, when the industry was relatively closed, and users understood the risks, but this is no longer the case. The industry is growing exponentially due to increased institutional adoption, retail interest and integration between traditional financial markets. With higher stakes and more consumers involved in the industry, consumer protection is becoming paramount.

Balanced view

The extreme view that no regulation is needed at all is only shared by a small group of individuals in the industry. Most stakeholders in the Web3 and financial technology sectors recognize that while excessive regulation can stifle innovation, a complete absence of regulation can lead to significant risks, including fraud, financial instability and loss of consumer trust. This understanding has led to a growing interest in self-regulation and collaborative approaches.

Many experts are proactively defining and adopting new standards and practices to ensure further transparency, security and ethical behaviour. A recent example occurred after the collapse of FTX, in which the community came together and identified Proof of Reserves as a critical standard. Proof of Reserves is the process of verifying that the customer assets held by a cryptocurrency exchange or financial institution correspond to the number of assets the company holds in reserve on behalf of the customers. Proof of Reserves would have provided transparency about FTX's actual asset holdings, potentially preventing the misuse and movement of customer funds. Proof of Reserves is now being voluntarily adopted across the industry, including the largest exchanges worldwide: Kraken, Binance, Bitmex, Derebit, Kucoin and OKX.

Many companies and founders are going one step further and actively working with regulators and policymakers. This collaboration is not new; in fact many have been doing so for years. However, they highlight that regulators must find the right balance between regulation and innovation. Too much regulation could lead companies to move to offshore locations, while too little regulation may result in increasing risks for consumers and investors, lack of accountability and the potential for unethical practices.

In the wake of the FTX collapse, Brian Armstrong, CEO of Coinbase, wrote an op-ed for CNBC where he highlighted that the lack of regulatory oversight in the Bahamas created a situation in which companies like FTX could take 'dangerous risks' with no repercussions. In the piece, he called for 'sensible' regulation that encouraged innovation while protecting customers. Too 'heavy-handed' regulation could have the opposite problem of driving companies to offshore locations (like FTX). 'Those of us who care about the future of crypto want to create sensible regulation for centralised exchanges and custodians in the U.S. and other regions,' Armstrong noted.[10]

Challenges in regulating Web3

New, fast-paced technological advancements are adding multiple layers of complexity to the regulatory landscape. Artificial intelligence, for example, has been one of those emerging technologies in the news, with regulators and leaders raising concerns about potential risks that may arise if regulation and rules are not considered. Such concerns and attention took place after the technology emerged into the public domain and was being used and built by many.

Artificial intelligence is not unique. Quantum computing, for example, is another technology that is being developed and studied in closed environments, but, once released, it could disrupt global industries and countries. The challenge regulators face is how to keep up to date with such new emerging technologies that are transforming our economy, society and daily lives. Many are stretched with resources and multiple priorities while trying to acquire the talent and learn the new skills required to meet these challenges.

The Web3 industry and its technology are among those emerging areas that are challenging regulators worldwide. Given its fast-paced and evolving nature, applying existing regulatory frameworks or developing new ones in a timely manner has been challenging. The innovation and complexity of the new products and services require a deep understanding of the technology to be able to regulate effectively. The fact that there isn't a global terminology makes matters even more complex. For example, terms such as digital assets, cryptoassets or crypto tokens are often used interchangeably, with definitions and taxonomies based on the perspective (technical, functional or legal) in which these assets are analysed. Monitoring the markets is also difficult due to patchy data and the thousands of new actors, such as validators and protocol developers, who may not be subject to typical reporting requirements.

On top of all of that, Web3 poses a unique set of challenges owing to its decentralization, borderless nature and anonymity. Unlike traditional finance, some solutions in Web3 have no centralized entities. Instead, governance and control are diffused across participants. Regulators, used to clear jurisdictional authority and identifiable entities and stakeholders, now face the challenge of defining where the accountability lies and how they can impose standards.

Who is accountable in a decentralized system? Should developers be expected to deliver risk management standards or protect client interests?

The borderless nature of Web3 creates jurisdictional nightmares. Protocols operate globally, free from geographical constraints, posing unique challenges to regulators establishing and enforcing local laws.

How does one country enforce its laws on a decentralized exchange with no central operating location?

Many DeFi protocols allow for anonymity or pseudonyms. The ability for free speech and to provide financial inclusion is at the centre of the Web3 ethos. Lending protocols like Aave and Compound, for example, allow individuals the freedom to access financial services pseudonymously. Users' identities are represented by their wallet's public key, an alphanumeric string of letters and numbers, instead of their names or ID information. Such solutions provide user privacy but can pose a direct challenge to developing and enforcing regulatory efforts.

Hester M Peirce, US SEC Commissioner, discussed the complexities of regulating this industry in a speech at the Duke Conference organized by Duke University in the US. In her speech, she noted that the DeFi industry is primarily driven by code developers and individual users, making it difficult to monitor and enforce regulation: 'Regulating people who write code is more difficult from a practical and legal perspective, including because it would impinge on free speech and would raise fairness issues since open-source coders cannot exercise control over how their code is used.'[11]

Even with all those challenges and considerations, some regulators have filed complaints and sued decentralized entities, surprising the industry. In the US, for example, the recent CFTC case against the Ooki DAO set a new precedent that every single voting participant and developer in a decentralized protocol could be found liable for illicit activities. While this is a significant action that might make developers and Web3 individuals pause before they continue developing and building, it is unclear how regulators will enforce such actions considering the global, decentralized and anonymity characteristics of DAOs.

COMMODITY FUTURES TRADING COMMISSION (CFTC) WINS ITS LAWSUIT AGAINST OOKI DAO

In 2019, developers Tom Bean and Kyle Kistne founded the bZeroX protocol, a centralized platform that accepted margined and leveraged retail commodity transactions (similar to a trading platform). However, in November 2021, the protocol was hacked and drained of $55 million after suffering two smaller hacks in 2020. Perhaps due to media attention, later in 2021, the founders transferred control of the protocol to a DAO, which subsequently renamed itself as Ooki DAO.[12]

The CTFC complaint goes one step further and argues that the founders transferred control to the community in an attempt to circumvent the law. The formal complaint quotes a statement allegedly made by one of the founders:

It's really exciting. We're going to be really preparing for the new regulatory environment by ensuring bZx is future-proof. So many people across the industry right now are getting legal notices and lawmakers are trying to decide whether they want DeFi companies to register as virtual asset service providers or not – and really what we're going to do is take all the steps possible to make sure that when regulators ask us to comply, that we have nothing we can really do because we've given it all to the community.[13]

In September 2022, the CFTC charged bZeroX and its founders, and claimed the company had offered leveraged and margin trading products to US persons without registering as a designated contract market (DCM) or a futures commission merchant (FCM). Not wanting the case to drag on, the founders offered to settle, paying a $250,000 fine.[14]

However, the CFTC didn't stop there. It also filed a complaint against the Ooki DAO, sending shockwaves through the industry. Similar to bZeroX, the CFTC claimed that Ooki DAO was running an unregistered crypto futures trading facility. The Commission stated that every Ooki token holder who had participated in DAO governance votes was in fact liable for the DAO's conduct.

This case was one of the first times a government agency had gone after a DAO and its token holders. Before this case, the prevailing belief held by the industry players was that DAOs and decentralized platforms were mostly protected from regulatory scrutiny due to their decentralized nature.

In June 2023, after the Ooki DAO failed to respond to the lawsuit, the judge called this 'strategic nonparticipation' and sided with the CFTC. The judge also ordered Ooki DAO to pay $643,542 in penalties, cease its operations and shut down its website permanently.[15]

How and whether the CFTC will seek to enforce this judgement remains to be seen. In fact, the CFTC has already confronted a similar challenge when it tried to serve the lawsuit because Ooki DAO didn't have a business address. The lawsuit was sent through the chatbot on the DAO's website, a move that the court upheld over objections from the crypto industry.

The major challenge is to find the balance between protection and innovation. Overly restrictive regulations could not only slow down the pace of technological advancements but also lead to companies relocating to countries with favourable regulatory environments.

Existing frameworks

The regulatory frameworks and approaches towards blockchain and Web3 vary globally, reflecting each region's unique economic, political and technological landscapes. Considering selected major markets provides insight into the unfolding regulatory landscape.

Switzerland

Switzerland has long been recognized for its favourable and clear regulatory environment for crypto and blockchain companies. Zurich has worked hard to brand the region as 'Crypto Valley' with a clear regulatory framework for digital assets. 'You can deny it, or you can face it. We always said we have to face it because these things are coming if we want or not,' said Dolfi Müller, the former mayor of Zug, regarding the emergence of cryptocurrency and blockchain technology.[16]

The clear regulatory environment is the reason why Switzerland continues to attract various blockchain projects and companies. Ethereum, for example, one of the most famous blockchains, was created from a small apartment in Zug. 'It was like a shoe box. A family house. People were living there on mattresses, almost like a hostel,' said Bernd Lapp, an early member of the Ethereum Foundation's advisory board.[17]

European Union

The EU has recently made strides and is often used as an example of how to create a unified approach across multiple jurisdictions. The Markets in Crypto-Assets (MiCA) Regulation offers a customized regulatory structure that applies to all 27 EU member states and draws on existing regulation where appropriate; e-money being one example. The EU has also updated existing regulations to encompass this new industry. For example, it has extended the travel rule, already applicable in traditional finance, to crypto transactions, stating that any crypto transaction, above a certain threshold, must include the customer personal information. Additionally, Virtual Asset Service Providers, called VASPs, must sanction screen the counterparty customer and perform due diligence on the counterparty VASP.

United Kingdom

In the UK, regulatory bodies have been progressively outlining frameworks and rules to govern the Web3 space, indicating a determined effort to create a structured and clear regulatory environment. In 2022, the UK government announced a plan to make the UK a global 'crypto hub'. Prime Minister Rishi Sunak, at the time Chancellor of the Exchequer, offered in a statement his clear vision for Web3:

> It's my ambition to make the UK a global hub for cryptoasset technology, and the measures we've outlined today will help to ensure firms can invest, innovate and scale up in this country. We want to see the businesses of tomorrow – and the jobs they create – here in the UK, and by regulating effectively, we can give them the confidence they need to think and invest long-term. This is part of our plan to ensure the UK financial services industry is always at the forefront of technology and innovation.[18]

The UK has so far adopted the 'same risk, same regulatory outcome' principle, with the government expecting Web3 activities to meet the same regulatory standards expected of similar traditional financial services activities.

United States

In the United States, the legal and regulatory landscape is characterized by a complex interplay between federal and state laws. Federal laws apply across the entire country and are enacted by the federal government, while each individual state has its own set of laws and regulatory frameworks. Businesses need to navigate both sets of laws to ensure compliance.

FEDERAL STANCE

Tensions between the industry and the US regulators, which had been growing throughout the years, increased substantially in 2021, when Gary Gensler was appointed chair of the Securities and Exchange Commission. The SEC has argued that almost all cryptocurrencies should be classified as securities, like stocks traded on Wall Street, which would force companies to register with the SEC and be subject to strict disclosure requirements. In 2022, after the collapse of FTX, a new round of enforcement actions was used to assert regulatory jurisdiction over the blockchain and digital asset industry.

In its 2022 fiscal year, the SEC filed 760 total enforcement actions,[19] which included a large number of charges against the crypto industry. The same year, the SEC significantly expanded the Crypto Assets and Cyber Unit, previously known as the Cyber Unit. This enforcement activity continued in the first half of 2023, with the SEC charging a number of well-known companies, including Kraken, for operating an unregistered securities exchange, broker, dealer and clearing agency.[20]

The 'regulation by enforcement' practice in the US uses legal actions, such as lawsuits or fines, to set precedents and guide industry behaviour. Regulatory authorities argue that, although the Web3 industry is based on a new technology, it violates existing laws around securities, commodities and money laundering. Therefore, companies should be made liable.

While enforcement actions are necessary to address fraud and market manipulation issues, this approach has created additional uncertainty, with institutions subject to existing rules rather than new tailored ones and discussions dragging on in court for years. This has potentially led to more confusion and exponential legal expenses. Brad Garlinghouse, CEO of Ripple, estimates that the company will have spent $200 million defending itself against a lawsuit initiated by the SEC.[21]

Such uncertainty seems to be halting US innovation and leadership in Web3. Coinbase estimates that the US share of global Web3 development has already dropped from 40 per cent to 29 per cent in the last five years.[22] Additionally, several companies have suspended their Web3 offering in the US. Revolut announced in 2023 that US customers would no longer be able to buy crypto. 'As a result of the evolving regulatory environment and the uncertainties around the crypto market in the US, we've taken the difficult decision, together with our US banking partner, to suspend access to cryptocurrencies through Revolut in the US,' a Revolut spokesperson stated.[23]

STATE REGULATION

As discussed, unlike many countries where financial regulations are dictated at the national level, the US features a unique system in which individual states have significant autonomy in creating and enforcing their own laws. Circle, for example, has to report to 48 state banking supervisors who regulate the company and examine the business every single year.

Among this mosaic of different state laws, one state stands out as a trailblazer and is often described as the most crypto-friendly place in the United States: Wyoming.

WYOMING, THE CRYPTO-FRIENDLY STATE

Wyoming, famed for its vast landscapes and cowboy heritage, is the nation's least-populated state, with 2.3 times more cattle than humans. Despite this traditional backdrop, Wyoming has distinguished itself as a pioneering force in the development of cryptocurrency and blockchain laws in the United States.

At the centre of the transformative story is Caitlin Long. Originally from Wyoming, she interned at the state legislature as a University of Wyoming student. Later, she decided to leave her hometown to pursue a career on Wall Street, with Credit Suisse and Morgan Stanley. In 2017, Caitlin witnessed the birth of Bitcoin and decided to donate some to her old University. To her surprise, the University of Wyoming politely declined. The issue was that a state money-transmitter law required any entity accepting Bitcoin to hold an equal value in dollars in reserve. Such experience led her to return to her hometown and approach state legislators with a vision to make Wyoming a hub for digital asset businesses. In Wyoming, she found some familiar faces. 'One of the legislators was still there, believe it or not, 27 years later,' she recalls. 'The stars just aligned.'[24]

From 2018 to 2019, Wyoming passed more than 13 new laws laying the foundation of its digital asset regulation. Since then, the work has continued with a number of new laws passed every year. Notably, the state has recognized a new kind of bank, a special-purpose depository institution (SPDI), which is a regulated custodian for crypto assets. Kraken and Custodia Bank, later founded by Caitlin, are among a handful of firms that have acquired SPDI status since 2020.

Wyoming also became the first state to regulate DAOs and recognize them as limited liability companies (LLCs). In one of its most ambitious endeavours, the state enacted the Wyoming Stable Token Act, authorizing state authorities to issue a stablecoin backed by dollars or US Treasury bonds.

Despite such progress, challenges persist, among them the ongoing legal battle for the fate of SPDIs. In 2023, Custodia Bank was denied access to Federal Reserve banking services, preventing the bank from operating normally under the federal regulation.

While most US states have taken cautious steps towards integrating blockchain and cryptocurrencies into their financial systems, Wyoming has boldly positioned itself at the forefront of this technological revolution. This approach reflects a larger strategic vision to diversify the state's economy beyond its traditional industries, like mining and agriculture, and to establish itself as a hub for technological innovation.

Future outlook

While Web3 idealists argue that the nature of the technology provides a sufficient framework to manage and mitigate risks, most experts in this space are not only open to regulation but are actively working with regulators to ensure more clarity for the industry.

In a discussion with Diogo Mónica, co-founder and President of Anchorage Digital, he told me how he has worked with regulators and why that work is important:

Many institutions need regulatory clarity in order to participate in the digital asset class. That is why we decided to pursue a federal bank charter from the Office of the Comptroller of the Currency in the first place. As the only federally chartered digital asset bank, Anchorage Digital Bank plays an important role in building bridges between traditional and decentralised finance.

By providing rules of the road, thoughtful regulation can support further institutional engagement in the asset class. Consider, for example, our federal bank charter from the OCC. As a federally chartered bank, Anchorage Digital Bank is required to keep all assets in segregated, on-chain vaults. The segregation of client and firm funds is a legal requirement and forms the basis of bankruptcy protections for our institutional client base.

The industry still needs greater regulatory clarity from lawmakers in Washington. Key issues on our radar include market structure reform, stablecoin regulation, and the classification of assets (for example, what is a security versus what is a commodity). At Anchorage Digital, we are proud to call for greater regulatory clarity from lawmakers in DC.

In recent years, such discussions and work between regulators and the Web3 industry have increased across the world. Many new regulators started to pass laws for crypto and digital assets, such as MiCA in Europe. However, even the most crypto-friendly countries have mainly regulated only small parts of the industry while a significant number of crypto-related activities still remain a grey area (for example NFTs and DeFi). This approach reflects the complexity of this emerging industry. Regulators tend to focus first on areas that are similar to existing systems, such as centralized finance, and follow with further discussions and consultations on more decentralized and new models. Decentralization is indeed one of the biggest challenges for regulators used to regulating, monitoring and collaborating with centralized entities.

'Is this protocol or project truly decentralized?' is one of the first questions many regulators will consider. For protocols and projects with some form of centralization (like a user admin privilege), regulators may be able to deploy existing frameworks. However, the challenge arises when we consider more decentralized institutions and protocols. This will be undeniably an area of focus over the next few years.

SUMMARY OF KEY POINTS

- Exponential growth of the industry, and recent fraud and hack stories, moved efforts to regulate this industry to the top of the policy agenda.

- Web3 idealists advocate for the 'code is law' philosophy, asserting that the nature of the technology provides a sufficient framework to manage and mitigate risks, without the need for external regulation.

- The extreme view that no regulation is needed is only shared by a minority. The majority of experts support regulation and have been collaborating with regulators for years, emphasizing the importance between regulatory oversight and fostering innovation.

- Web3 poses unique challenges to regulators given its fast-paced and evolving nature, decentralization, globalization and anonymity.

- Web3 regulatory frameworks and approaches vary across the globe. Switzerland, the EU and UK are considered favourable due to their clear regulatory environment. The US legal and regulatory landscape is a complex interplay between federal and state laws.

- While progress has been made in providing frameworks to the Web3 industry, significant crypto-related activities remain grey areas. In the future, regulators will continue to expand frameworks and laws to cover the more decentralized products and services.

Endnotes

1 M Lewis. *Going Infinite: The Rise and Fall of a New Tycoon*, Penguin, London, 2023.

2 *The New York Times*. Why did FTX collapse? Here's what to know, 10 November 2022, nytimes.com/2022/11/10/technology/ftx-binance-crypto-explained.html (archived at https://perma.cc/RRF9-CBU6)

3 CoinGecko. Total crypto market cap chart, www.coingecko.com/en/global-charts (archived at https://perma.cc/82J5-WVTL)

4 FSB. FSB and IMF outline comprehensive approach to identify and respond to macroeconomic and financial stability risks associated with crypto-assets, 7 September 2023, www.fsb.org/2023/09/fsb-and-imf-outline-comprehensive-approach-to-identify-and-respond-to-macroeconomic-and-financial-stability-risks-associated-with-crypto-assets/ (archived at https://perma.cc/B8TF-5VAF)

5 World Economic Forum. Cryptocurrency regulation is changing. Here's what you need to know, 20 July 2022, www.weforum.org/agenda/2022/07/cryptocurrency-regulation-global-standard/ (archived at https://perma.cc/8RTY-6Q2U)

6 BBC News. World Bank rejects El Salvador request for Bitcoin help, 17 June 2021, bbc.co.uk/news/business-57507386 (archived at https://perma.cc/S7GK-WXNT)

7 Ethereum Classic. Code is law, 22 February 2022, ethereumclassic.org/why-classic/code-is-law (archived at https://perma.cc/YP78-HBHP)

8 S Falkon. The story of the DAO – its history and consequences, Medium, 24 December 2017, medium.com/swlh/the-story-of-the-dao-its-history-and-consequences-71e6a8a551ee (archived at https://perma.cc/6NMG-BTNL)

9 D Morris. CoinDesk turns 10: 2016 – how The DAO Hack changed Ethereum and crypto, Coindesk, 9 May 2023, coindesk.com/consensus-magazine/2023/05/09/coindesk-turns-10-how-the-dao-hack-changed-ethereum-and-crypto/ (archived at https://perma.cc/4YPZ-T9J6)

10 B Armstrong. Op-ed: Crypto markets need regulation to avoid more washouts like FTX, says Coinbase CEO Brian Armstrong, CNBC News, 11 November 2022, cnbc.com/2022/11/11/op-ed-crypto-markets-need-regulation-to-avoid-ftx-type-situations.html (archived at https://perma.cc/46GZ-PKTN)

11 H Peirce. Outdated: Remarks before the Digital Assets at Duke Conference, 20 January 2023, sec.gov/news/speech/peirce-remarks-duke-conference-012023 (archived at https://perma.cc/FL3F-46PK)

12 T Tolka. The end of the Wild West for decentralized crypto trading, Disruption Banking, 12 September 2023, www.disruptionbanking.com/2023/09/12/the-end-of-the-wild-west-for-decentralized-crypto-trading/ (archived at https://perma.cc/42SD-7S89)

13 CFTC. Complaint for injunctive and other equitable relief and civil monetary penalties under the Commodity Exchange Act and Commission Regulations, 2022, storage.courtlistener.com/recap/gov.uscourts.cand.400807/gov.uscourts.cand.400807.1.0.pdf (archived at https://perma.cc/4HLH-EF86)

14 N Wang. CFTC penalizes blockchain protocol $250K, files action against successor DAO, Coindesk, 22 September 2022, coindesk.com/policy/2022/09/22/cftc-penalizes-blockchain-protocol-250k-files-action-against-successor-dao/ (archived at https://perma.cc/FP3C-488Z)

15 E Napolitano. CFTC wins lawsuit against Ooki DAO, Coindesk, 12 June 2023, coindesk.com/policy/2023/06/09/cftc-wins-lawsuit-against-ooki-dao/ (archived at https://perma.cc/6MH6-LWTE)

16 J Wilser. Zug: Where Ethereum was born and crypto goes to grow up, Coindesk, 27 June 2023, coindesk.com/consensus-magazine/2023/06/27/zug-where-ethereum-was-born-and-crypto-goes-to-grow-up/ (archived at https://perma.cc/XS3X-ME9S)

17 J Wilser. Zug: Where Ethereum was born and crypto goes to grow up, Coindesk, 27 June 2023, coindesk.com/consensus-magazine/2023/06/27/ zug-where-ethereum-was-born-and-crypto-goes-to-grow-up/ (archived at https://perma.cc/XS3X-ME9S)

18 HM Treasury. Government sets out plan to make UK a global cryptoasset technology hub, 4 April 2022, gov.uk/government/news/government-sets-out-plan-to-make-uk-a-global-cryptoasset-technology-hub (archived at https:// perma.cc/33FU-L2LL)

19 US SEC. Press release: SEC Announces Enforcement Results for FY22, www.sec.gov/news/press-release/2022-206 (archived at https://perma. cc/9SVK-R892)

20 US SEC. Crypto assets and cyber enforcement actions, 2023, www.sec.gov/ spotlight/cybersecurity-enforcement-actions (archived at https://perma. cc/28WV-8GEH)

21 R Browne and A Kharpal. Crypto companies are playing poker with the SEC as agency cracks down on the industry, CNBC News, 14 May 2023, cnbc. com/2023/05/15/crypto-companies-coinbase-ripple-are-playing-poker-with-the-sec.html (archived at https://perma.cc/4KJU-N4Z8)

22 Coinbase. Just the facts: A regulation by enforcement only approach is hurting American leadership, jobs, and innovation, 11 September 2023, www.coinbase.com/blog/just-the-facts-a-regulation-by-enforcement-only-approach-is-hurting-american(archived at https://perma.cc/85U6-XA3U)

23 M Meichler. Revolut to shutter US crypto operations due to 'regulatory environment', Decrypt, 4 August 2023, decrypt.co/151272/revolut-shutter-us-crypto-operations-due-regulatory-environment (archived at https://perma.cc/ NR9Z-8AHY)

24 M Aspan. How Caitlin Long turned Wyoming into crypto country, *Fortune*, 29 July 2021, fortune.com/2021/07/29/caitlin-long-wyoming-crypto/ (archived at https://perma.cc/A4JZ-NZRW)

PART FOUR

Moving forward

12

Industry changes needed for mainstream adoption of Web3

Do you know how the internet works? How about your phone?

In 2019, a survey was conducted in the US to test people's knowledge about the internet, and found that 1 in 3 people in the US could not explain how the internet actually functions. Some of the most creative explanations of how the internet works included 'it just does', 'under the oceans' or 'through pipes'.[1] Similarly, most users have no idea how their phone works, even though they spend so much time looking at it. One recent report found that adults in the US check their phones, on average, 344 times a day (i.e. once every four minutes) and spend almost three hours daily looking at it.[2] While they might not know how it works, they do know the value they can get from using their phone to pay for the bus, pull up their airline ticket for check-in, text a friend and order food online. Web3 mainstream adoption will be similar; the technology will fade into the background while the benefits, outcomes and experiences will become the focus. Citi says we will have reached successful adoption of Web3 when it 'has a billion-plus users who do not even realize they are using the technology'.[3]

The adoption of this new technology will also occur in different forms. Different use cases and users will accept the more decentralized and open infrastructure, while others will require a centralized form. For example, while some users may be happy with having a self-custody wallet and bearing the risks of 'being a bank', others will prefer a third-party custody wallet for security. Imagine clients that have all their savings spread across cryptocurrencies, maybe for their child's education. For such an important savings account, they may not want to hold the wallet keys. If something terrible happens to them, for example a fatal accident or unexpected heart attack, and they take the keys of the wallet with them, the kids won't be able to access the wallet and, as a consequence, the savings. Instead, in this situation, they may want to use a third-party provider for the wallet in which they know they are protected if something happens to them.

Jess Houlgrave, CEO of WalletConnect, believes choice will be essential for mainstream adoption:

> Some in the ecosystem believe that mass adoption is when everyone holds crypto and manages their own keys (self-custody). But, for me, the vision for mass adoption is when a lot more is abstracted away from the end user. Web3 is about providing people with choices and the ability to manage their data. They may decide to give their data to other people, delegating some of that responsibility. And that is part of the choice that Web3 has to offer.
>
> I just hope that the implementation doesn't lose the fundamental values of Web3 and simply recreates our existing systems in a more technologically efficient way. I hope that when people build those better experiences, they still embed the values of openness and self-sovereignty in that technology.

So, how far from mainstream adoption are we?

If we compare Web3 with the internet evolution, we are still in its dial-up phase. I remember the early days of the internet, where access was done primarily through a dial-up connection. A horrible loud sound would indicate that you were connecting to the internet, and you needed a dedicated phone line, meaning no one could use the phone while you were on the internet, which led to many arguments in households. The user experience was terrible, with sites taking forever to load. Then, as the internet evolved, a distinct space emerged that was marked by legally ambiguous, illicit and questionable activities. This realm became known as the 'dark web'.

Currently, the user experience in Web3 is also slow and complex. One needs to set up self-custodial wallets with new concepts like private and public keys and seed phrases, and connect wallets with decentralized applications (DApps), which poses challenges for new users. While the industry talks about being frictionless and trustless, the experience is neither. Just as the transition from dial-up to broadband required infrastructure development and user experience improvement, the move to mainstream adoption depends on regulatory frameworks that foster innovation while protecting the end user, better user experiences and technological advancements.

Regulation

'The chief challenge of institutional adoption is regulatory scrutiny and outlooks,' states McKinsey.[4]

As discussed in Chapter 11, the regulatory landscape is evolving, with regulators across the world beginning to issue guidance. While initial guidance is a step forward, many areas, including DeFi, DEX and DAOs, are still not covered, leaving entities to operate in grey areas. Additionally, there is still a significant lack of consistent regulation across jurisdictions, creating complexities for companies operating at a global level.

Ultimately, regulation will provide legal clarity for financial institutions to participate while protecting consumers from unstable experiments. A balance between regulation and innovation will be needed to ensure the industry is not over-regulated, stifling innovation.

Eric van Miltenburg, SVP, Strategic Initiatives at Ripple, believes that regulation, while needed, should be created in collaboration with the ecosystem:

> Regulation is helpful in terms of setting a level playing field, encouraging competition and protecting consumers, but it shouldn't be so prescriptive that it stops innovation. That is the fine line that a lot of regulators are trying to walk at the moment – some more successfully than others.

MiCA, for example, is a great success story. Having such comprehensive regulation for such a large geographic area sets the bar for other jurisdictions, and also gives us something to evolve over time. We now have regulations in place that we can look to build on. Execution will be key, of course. It is important that regulation is created in partnership with the industry and that a principles-based approach is used, as opposed to being too arbitrary and/or prescriptive.

User experience

Simplifying the Web3 user experience (UX) will play a crucial role in mass adoption.

Currently, onboarding is highly complex, with users often asked to jump through too many hoops up front, like setting up a self-custody wallet, remembering seed phrases and purchasing cryptocurrency. And all of that happens before the value of Web3 is made clear.

Once onboarded, users often encounter jarring experiences and endless jargon. Simple transactions can have unknown waiting times and high costs. For example, unlike the fixed fee structure used in conventional payment systems, the amount paid to process each transaction in Ethereum, called gas fees, largely depends on the number of participants looking to execute transactions at any given time. And it can take, typically, from 15 seconds to 5 minutes for ETH transactions to be completed.[5]

Moving value between centralized and decentralized words also proves challenging. Users can spend a significant amount of time and money converting to and from cryptocurrencies, having to pay substantial fees each time. Users will only adopt Web3 en masse when they can manage and exchange assets as part of their portfolio, which will be composed of on-chain and off-chain assets.

Is it safe to do this? What do I do with my seed phrase? How am I supposed to do that? What does this mean? Oh good, where is my money?

Does this sound familiar? This is a typical user journey of someone who is used to the sleek Web2 user experience, heard of this thing called 'crypto' and wanted to explore it. However, as you can see, the experience is a far cry from the sleek and intuitive experience of Web2.

Most people do not understand the technology and jargon used, but many are actually aware of and curious about what 'crypto' means. In 2022, a Coinbase ad presented during the Super Bowl commercials went viral. So many people scanned the QR code that the website temporarily crashed.[6] So, interest is there, but the friction and learning curve associated with most Web3 apps are restricting new user adoption.

Don't Make Me Think, a book by Steve Krug, states that good software lets users accomplish their tasks easily and directly, without frustration.[7] If we can achieve that in Web3, user adoption will increase substantially.

Ongoing efforts to improve UX

Aware of the steep learning curves and complex interfaces, many Web3 companies have recently launched wallet standards and user-friendly interfaces.

BINANCE SELF-CUSTODY WALLET

In 2023, Binance, a centralized exchange, announced the launch of a Web3 self-custody wallet. The Binance self-custody wallet aimed to create a bridge with Web3, allowing a user-friendly gateway for users to interact with the DeFi ecosystem.

The self-custody wallet uses multi-party computation (MPC), an advanced security technique. It removes the need for users to manage or memorize seed phrases, providing a secure and smooth onboarding opportunity for users who want to explore DeFi without having to worry about losing their key.

The wallet aimed to meet the demand for a simple, convenient and secure way to experience the world of Web3. During the announcement of this new wallet, CZ, the founder of Binance, noted, 'Binance's Web3 Wallet lowers the barriers of entry for users to achieve full self-custody of their assets, and it is an important, convenient bridge towards DeFi empowerment. Ultimately, our priority is to ensure users can explore Web3 with us within a user-friendly and protected environment.'[8]

This launch put Binance alongside other major centralized exchanges like Coinbase and OKX, which have launched similar Web3 wallet solutions.

Other companies are indirectly pushing user experience further by providing robust developer tools and resources. By focusing on developer enablement, these companies are fostering an environment where innovative applications can be built with greater efficiency and effectiveness.

WALLETCONNECT

Founded in 2018 by Pedro Gomes, WalletConnect, an open-source protocol, began with a simple idea: to allow mobile wallet users to easily connect to desktop apps through the magic of the QR code.

WalletConnect has become the standard for connecting in Web3, enabling developers to connect over 500 wallets to their DApps. From a user experience perspective, no matter which wallet you may use, you can connect using a QR code.

Jess Houlgrave, CEO of WalletConnect, shared the company's vision with me, explaining:

We are focused on making it easier for people to be onboarded and for developers to build those great experiences. WalletConnect started because many wallet providers began to emerge, yet apps couldn't interoperate with them without hardcoding multiple integrations. This complexity for developers meant that users were limited in their choice of wallet. WalletConnect was therefore designed with user choice in mind – to enable users to use the wallet of their choice, by making it easy for developers to interoperate with a vast

> *range of wallets. For the user, it's as simple as logging into an application by scanning a QR code with their phone.*
>
> Recently, WalletConnect also created an email embedded wallet, so users can create and manage a wallet without having to think about seed phrases; instead, the onboarding is done by using their email, a simple, easy and well-understood way to log in.

Why is user experience still so bad?

You might be wondering why the user experience is still so bad. After all, bad UX is a well-known issue in Web3.

The open-source model and decentralization ethos, while promoting innovation and collaboration, paradoxically contributes to a lack of centralized coordination, leading to diverse standards and protocols and complicating efforts to create a unified and seamless user experience. Additionally, Web3's relative infancy means development has been primarily focused on the core protocol functionality. Given the rapid pace of technological evolution, projects are constantly evolving, with new hurdles emerging as quickly as older ones are resolved. Such fast-paced development often prioritizes back-end advancements over front-end usability, resulting in technically sound interfaces but not user-friendly experiences.

Graham Cooke, a Google alumni, founder and author, describes in his book *Web3: The end of business-as-usual* a protocol-app dynamic during the internet evolution that exemplifies the current status in Web3. In his analysis, he noticed that in Web1 there was 80 per cent focus on developing protocols and only 20 per cent focus on developing applications. Web1 was all about creating the 'train tracks'; the creation of protocols that facilitated data connections and computers connecting with computers, with the emergence of emails, transfer files, HTTP and so on. In Web2, there was a protocol–app inversion. Eighty per cent of Web2 was application, and 20 per cent was protocol development. The vast majority of capital and talent focused on how to use the existing protocols instead of creating new ones. UX became king as apps were built on top of the protocols.[9]

This analysis is directly comparable with what we are seeing with Web3 and explains why the current focus is on building robust protocols instead of user-friendly applications. The industry is still building the 'train tracks' needed before there is a shift to creating easy-to-use applications, which use those tracks to deliver user value.

Technology and infrastructure

In terms of technology and infrastructure, there are three key areas that require improvement before mass adoption: scalability, interoperability, and security and privacy.

Scalability

In financial services, scalability means the ability to handle more customers, more transactions and more data efficiently. Traditional banking infrastructure is designed to scale up, with databases upgraded according to demand requirements.

However, blockchain, the technology underpinning Web3, faces unique scalability challenges. As the interest in and adoption of Web3 have increased over the past few years, blockchain networks have struggled to scale, unable to handle an increasing number of transactions while maintaining the same performance. Ethereum, for example, has faced challenges in supporting high transaction volumes, resulting in congestion, slower transaction times and high gas fees (transaction fees).

For mainstream adoption in finance, blockchain technology needs to be able to support transaction volumes comparable with existing banking systems in a low-cost and secure way. To put it in perspective, Visa states that it can execute more than 65,000 transactions per second (TPS) while Ethereum handles on average 12 TPS and Bitcoin manages around 7 TPS.[10]

Aware of this challenge, many in the industry have been working on scalability solutions. Ethereum, for example, is currently being upgraded to enhance the speed, efficiency and scalability of the Ethereum network. New Layer 1s, the blockchain base layers, such as Solana, have also emerged, focused primarily on providing higher throughput and lower costs.

SOLANA

In 2017, Anatoly Yakovenko founded Solana, but the network and its native token, SOL, only went live three years later, in March 2020. Since then, Solana has been growing significantly due to its high throughput and low transaction costs, attributes that have propelled the platform in the ecosystem.

In 2022, Alkesh Shah, head of digital asset strategy at Bank of America, gave the highest praise to Solana, saying that due to its low cost, speed and scalability, 'Solana could become the Visa of the digital asset ecosystem.' However, he noted that such scalability would be achieved while impacting decentralization and security, referring to previous outages: 'Solana prioritises scalability, but a relatively less decentralised and secure blockchain has tradeoffs, illustrated by several network performance issues since inception.'[11]

Such trade-offs are known as the blockchain trilemma, a term coined by Vitalik Buterin, founder of Ethereum. The blockchain trilemma notes that it is harder for blockchain networks to achieve all three properties: scalability, security and decentralization. Instead, blockchain networks tend to prioritize two of those properties at the expense of the third one. For example, Bitcoin prioritizes decentralization and security at the expense of scalability, with transactions being slow but the network extremely secure.

In 2023, Visa announced it would use Solana as a settlement layer for its cross-border USDC stablecoin payments. This strategic decision was influenced by Solana's high throughput, low costs and fast transaction times. In the announcement, Visa stated, 'the Solana blockchain sees 400 millisecond block times, averages 400 transactions per second (TPS) and typically surges to more than 2K TPS across a variety of use cases during periods of peak demand.'[12]

Later, in 2023, Solana was again in the news with the announcement of Firedancer, a new validator developed to enhance Solana's performance and scalability. During tests, Firedancer was able to process 1.2 million TPS, showcasing its potential to bolster Solana's infrastructure for large-scale applications.[13]

Additionally, a set of new off-chain solutions have emerged. Layer 2s are built on top of Layer 1s (base layers like Ethereum) and aim to address scalability and efficiency issues. In simple terms, Layer 2 means that some of the work that would be performed by the main chain, the Layer 1, can be moved to the second layer. Eventually, the transactions are added to Layer 1, where they are secured in the blockchain ledger and history. However, truly efficient, secure and stable scaling solutions in crypto are hard to achieve. Bridging assets across Layer-1 and Layer-2 ecosystems can create an increasingly confusing and insecure environment.

While new solutions and blockchains are created and upgraded to solve the scalability issue, it is likely that we will not have one single blockchain for everything. Instead, different blockchains will work for different use cases.

Interoperability

As new blockchain networks and apps are developed each year to meet the needs of specific industries and use cases, interoperability is becoming paramount. There are already more than 100 Layer-1 blockchains and several Layer-2 and Layer-3 networks. Given the wide variety of the ecosystem, it is vital that blockchains are able to communicate with other networks, back-office systems and external data sources. Blockchain interoperability refers to the capacity of different blockchain systems to exchange data, messages and digital assets.

Currently, transactions are straightforward only if both parties are on the same blockchain. Interoperability would simplify cross-chain transactions, making it easier and more efficient for entities to perform transactions. This is particularly crucial in the financial services industry, where different financial players operate on various blockchains and legacy systems.

Similarly, users who own different types of cryptocurrencies need to use a variety of wallets and exchanges to manage each type. With true interoperability, users could manage all their assets from a single platform, simplifying asset management and enhancing security.

Now, imagine that you could not transfer money smoothly from one bank to another, or that you could not send a message to friends and family because they used a different provider. Just as interoperability facilitated smooth transfers and communications across different networks, a similar principle can greatly benefit the blockchain ecosystem.

Despite the apparent need for interoperability, it still remains a challenge. Each blockchain is built with unique standards and code bases, creating barriers for seamless interoperability. Marcel Harmann, founder and CEO of THORWallet, shed light on this issue in a discussion with *Cointelegraph*. In the interview, he noted that each base-layer protocol, like Ethereum, is designed to facilitate secure data exchange only within its own ecosystem, due to the embedded smart contracts. Transferring assets outside the network would require a blockchain to trust the state validity of another blockchain. Marcel continued by highlighting that each blockchain employs its own consensus mechanism: 'Consensus mechanisms on each blockchain decide the canonical history of all the transactions that were validated. This produces extremely large files that must be processed with each block and can only be viewed in the specific language native to the blockchain.'[14] Therefore, interoperability between blockchains encompasses more than just the exchange of assets, also understanding and processing the history of another blockchain, which is a complex and challenging task.

On top of these, security and privacy are also major challenges when it comes to interoperability. Ensuring data is securely transferred and properly validated when moving between different blockchain networks can be challenging. This is a crucial task, not only for privacy reasons but also to safeguard the overall security and integrity of these transactions, underpinning the trustworthiness and reliability of blockchain.

Aware of this challenge, many in the industry are focused on creating several techniques to enable interoperability, with numerous new projects underway. Projects like Polkadot and Cosmos are often referred to as key examples of cross-chain interoperability protocols built specifically to support communication between networks.

POLKADOT

In 2013, a number of people gathered to launch a blockchain platform called Ethereum. Among them was Gavin Wood, co-founder and CTO of the Ethereum Foundation, who had developed Solidity, the programming language for writing smart contracts that lies at the heart of Ethereum.

Gavin Wood ended up leaving the development team at Ethereum and eventually founded Polkadot in 2016. With Polkadot, Gavin wanted to create a new multichain ecosystem that would serve as a bridge to other blockchains, doing away with what he described as 'a patchwork of independent and isolated legal systems of the internet'.[15]

One year later, Polkadot raised funds through an initial coin offering, which was one of the most successful at the time, raising around $ 145 million.[16] However, it faced a setback when a significant portion of these funds were frozen due to a hack into Parity Technologie, one of the key development teams behind Polkadot. Eventually, Polkadot was launched in 2020 in a smooth and staged rollout.

Polkadot is an innovative multichain network designed to enable different blockchains to interoperate seamlessly. At its core, a central base layer, called the relay chain, allows different blockchains connected to it to pass data and value to one another.

Polkadot allows developers to build customized application-specific blockchains, known as parachains, within its ecosystem. These parachains are independent, fully fledged blockchains with their own logic, features and validators. All parachains connect to the relay chain.

Polkadot's relay chain act as the main chain of the system, serving as the central hub governing the entire Polkadot ecosystem. Its primary role is to facilitate cross-chain interoperability and communication between the internal (parachains) and external blockchains. Additionally, the relay chain is responsible for upholding network security and maintaining the system's underlying consensus protocol.

In order to connect with external blockchains, Polkadot uses Bridges, a method often used in this space to connect multiple networks but which has suffered its own security challenges, with hacks often occurring.

In addition to projects like Polkadot, the blockchain sphere has seen the emergence of other significant interoperability solutions. One notable example making strides in financial services is Chainlink's Cross-Chain Interoperability Protocol (CCIP).

Chainlink, already well known in the industry for its decentralized oracle network that connects on-chain and off-chain systems, ensures that smart contracts receive accurate and timely information from the real world. Chainlink CCIP was successfully launched in 2023 as an expansion of the Chainlink ecosystem. In essence, CCIP is a cross-chain communication layer that enables seamless and trustless transfer of data and value across blockchains.

In 2023, Chainlink collaborated with Swift, the global financial messaging network, on an interoperability experiment. The project aimed to explore the feasibility of enabling financial institutions to use their existing back-end systems to interact with tokenized assets and transact across both public and private blockchains. Initial findings of this experiment were promising, with Swift and Chainlink's CCIP demonstrating that it can provide a single point of access to multiple networks.[17] While still early days, this experiment is interesting given that it connects legacy systems with the new blockchain ecosystem.

Interoperability is critical to unlocking the full potential of Web3. First, it will allow users to move their assets between networks without any issues, making a much more seamless experience with lower barriers to entry. Second, it will allow for the ecosystem to become more interconnected, increasing liquidity across networks and allowing the possibility of creating new services and products.

Security and privacy

Robust security and privacy protections are non-negotiable in heavily regulated industries like finance. Concerns over existing security and privacy breaches pose challenges for Web3 adoption.

Blockchain's security arises from cryptography and distributed architecture, but vulnerabilities still exist that need addressing before mainstream adoption. Smart contracts encode complex financial logic, but bugs have led to exploits draining millions. For example, The DAO was hacked due to vulnerabilities in its code base, resulting in $70 million of ETH being stolen.[18] Several exchanges have suffered breaches, and fraud continues to be a risk, with various 'rug pulls' and Ponzi schemes, while KYC and AML procedures are often lacking.

User privacy is also a concern. Transactions are recorded on a public ledger, making it possible for anyone anywhere to view transaction history and associate this with specific addresses. Such a lack of privacy raises concerns for users who wish to keep their financial transactions private and makes them susceptible to hacking, fraud and scams.

To address such concerns, Web3 developers are exploring the use of privacy-enhancing technologies like zero-knowledge proofs (ZKPs) and decentralized identity systems. ZKPs allow for the secure sharing of data without exposing the actual data itself. For example, a ZKP can cryptographically prove an Ethereum user has enough funds to pay for a transaction without exposing their wallet balance. Decentralized identity systems allow individuals to control their digital identity and the associated data rather than relying on a centralized authority to manage and store their personal information. Both technologies enable regulators to identify and act on malicious on-chain activities while protecting user data.

Some experts are looking at options to create privacy at the blockchain level, Midnight, for example, is an interesting and recent development in this space.

MIDNIGHT

In 2013 at the launch of Ethereum, alongside Vitalik Buterin and Gavin Wood, was Charles Hoskinson. Charles held the position of CEO briefly but left the project in 2014 due to disagreements about its governance.

Wanting to take a more structured academic approach, Charles went on to found Input Output Hong Kong (IOHK), a blockchain research and development company with the goal of creating a blockchain platform that would solve problems found in previous crypto projects. Cardano, the first blockchain to be founded on peer-reviewed research and developed through evidence-based methods, was launched in 2017.

In 2022, IOHK announced it was creating a data protection-based platform called Midnight to allow users to operate more freely and securely by safeguarding sensitive personal and commercial data. 'The platform will use zero-knowledge cryptography and a combination of private and public computation, creating a trustless ecosystem that safeguards sensitive personal and commercial data,' stated the announcement.[19]

In 2023, Midnight launched with a limited number of places available for early development and networking access.

In a discussion with Mauricio Magaldi, Head of Product for Midnight, he emphasized the benefits of combining public blockchains and data privacy:

> Imagine if any business could run their operations without the risks and the costs associated with data protection or security? By bringing together the public nature of blockchains with the selective disclosure of information made possible by the use of zero-knowledge technologies at the protocol level, data protection is now possible for both web3 natives and enterprises.

Web3 infrastructure needs to continue to evolve to become more robust. Overcoming privacy and security challenges is crucial for the wider adoption and successful integration of Web3 with financial services. This evolution will entail not only technology advancements but also a higher focus on ensuring regulatory compliance and cultural change in risk perception.

Mauricio Magaldi continued:

The immutable data available in public blockchains can serve as a feature for permissionless composability, yet it can also be seen as a bug, because most industries are regulated and required to comply with data protection and secrecy requirements, such as GDPR in Europe and the banking secrecy act in Brazil. Combining the network effects of public chains with the ability to enable individuals and companies to manage the visibility for their data and metadata is the holy grail of blockchain adoption in regulated industries.

Will Web3 ever have a 'ChatGPT' moment?

At the end of 2022, ChatGPT (a large language model-based AI chat-bot) was launched and quickly amassed over a million users. Such mass adoption took Facebook ten months and Netflix three years to match.

Since then, the tech and finance worlds have been abuzz with the idea that Web3 needs a similar breakout moment, a 'ChatGPT' moment. Satya Nadella, the CEO of Microsoft, showed his support for blockchain at the World Economic Forum in 2023, stating 'Blockchain is a technology that has a set of use cases, we at Microsoft support it today. A distributed database is a good thing, it has its uses.' However, he feels the sector is still not showing full potential: 'But you need to have the killer apps, what is the use case that gets broad adoption, what is the ChatGPT moment for blockchain?'[20]

While I understand the sentiment behind Web3 needing a defining moment, I believe focusing solely on this narrative misses a crucial point. Blockchain, like the internet, is a foundational technology that powers applications, often invisibly, in the back end. Its relevance to the end users lies not in the technology itself but in the use cases, benefits and outcomes it enables. For institutional adoption, I like to compare it to a cloud implementation. In that sense, no one talks about what cloud provider they use or that they are using a cloud-powered product, unless they are part of the IT team.

Jess Houlgrave, CEO of WalletConnect, considers two distinct use cases: the acquisition of cryptocurrencies and the usage of blockchain as a technology. And similarly, she doesn't believe there will be a 'ChatGPT moment' for either:

> Crypto, as an asset class that people can store value in, in itself is consumer-facing. Individuals hold Bitcoin and crypto. My personal view is that it is likely to continue to grow because it's a hedge against the failure of institutions around the world today. But I don't think it will have a 'ChatGPT' moment.
>
> The rest of it, the way we move stablecoins around the world, how we manage our identity, provenance and digital ownership, all of these, are going to be built on that technology. They are deep infrastructure, and so it is not something that most consumers should or ever will need to know. In the same way, most consumers can't explain how the TCP IP protocol works for the Internet. They just use the Internet and applications that deliver them value. That will be the same with crypto, customers will get value because they have a better app experience or because it's cheaper, more secure or more supportive of their privacy.
>
> For mainstream adoption of web3, we need to shift the discussion from the technology itself to the tangible benefits and outcomes it delivers. The industry needs to build products that consumers want and need. By focusing on real-world applications and their impact, we can better illustrate the transformative potential of blockchain and foster its broader acceptance and integration.

Future outlook

When speaking with Dante Disparte, Chief Strategy Officer and Head of Global Policy at Circle, about where we are in the Web3 journey, he quoted Winston Churchill, saying that we are nearing 'the end of the beginning'. For Dante, the successful adoption of this industry is driven by two major categories:

One of them is institutional adoption. Which you could argue is represented by the interest of established firms, whether large global financial institutions like JP Morgan or large global asset managers like Blackrock and many in between. Those organisations are still somewhat on the sidelines. But, that wave of institutional adoption could represent unlocking trillions of dollars of new investment and capital flows and connectivity between digital assets and the real economy. That adoption is still early.

The next category is the race to a billion users. If you consider technology adoption charts, on one axis, you have time; on another axis, you have the share of the population using the new technology. If we plotted crypto and Web3 in that technology stack, we would still be very early in terms of time and adoption.

To unlock institutional adoption and the billion-person everyday participation in the digital asset economy, the technology has to fade into the background. I wrote an article in *Forbes* in 2018, it feels like it was one thousand years ago, titled 'When We Stop Talking About Blockchain, We Can Change The World With It,' [21] and my arguments remain the same today. When was the last time you went to an Internet conference and spoke about hardware, software and physical routers?

Web 3 and crypto are still very early because the technology is a protagonist as opposed to the outcomes that markets and people care about. The quest for the trillion dollar unlock, and billion-person adoption remains the objective.

Despite all the technical complexity and unanswered questions, the potential for Web3 is undeniable. Many of the existing issues are already being researched and resolved by the industry. Regulators are providing further regulatory clarity (even if it is unequal across the globe), and companies are building new solutions to solve technology issues and simplify the user experience.

As my friend Dante Disparte says, as we have moved from dial-up to broadband and from broadband to always-on financial services, the tech starts to fade into the background. In reality, many companies already use blockchain technology in the back end but do not advertise it to their clients. This is simply a sign of a maturing industry.

SUMMARY OF KEY POINTS

- The successful mass adoption of Web3 will occur when it 'has a billion-plus users who do not even realize they are using the technology' as per Citi's report.[22]

- Web3 is still in its dial-up phase. The move to mainstream adoption depends on technological advancements, better user experiences, and regulatory frameworks that foster innovation while protecting the end user.

- As discussed in Chapter 11, the regulatory landscape is evolving, with regulators worldwide starting to issue guidance. A balance between regulation and innovation will be needed to ensure the industry is not over-regulated, stifling innovation.

- Simplifying the Web3 user experience will play a crucial role in mass adoption. Some companies are already focused on providing wallet standards and tools for developers to create user-friendly solutions.

- Scalability in financial services is often measured via number of transactions per second (TPS). While Visa can execute more than 65,000 TPS, Ethereum can only handle on average 12 TPS and Bitcoin around 7 TPS. Blockchain needs to solve its scalability challenges to be able to handle financial markets.

- Robust security and privacy protections are non-negotiable in heavily regulated industries like finance. Concerns over existing security and privacy breaches pose challenges for Web3 adoption.

Endnotes

1   T Sandle. Survey: Just how much do we actually know about the internet?, *Digital Journal*, 3 November 2019, digitaljournal.com/social-media/survey-just-how-much-do-we-actually-know-about-the-internet/article/561061 (archived at https://perma.cc/QS6A-WRLT)

2   A Ruggeri. How mobile phones have changed our brains, BBC, 3 April 2023, bbc.com/future/article/20230403-how-cellphones-have-changed-our-brains (archived at https://perma.cc/RS6E-FP7Z)

3   Citigroup. Money, tokens, and games, 30 March 2023, citigroup.com/global/insights/citigps/money-tokens-and-games (archived at https://perma.cc/5W5D-NSJH)

4   Mckinsey. Web3 beyond the hype, 26 September 2022, mckinsey.com/ industries/financial-services/our-insights/web3-beyond-the-hype (archived at https://perma.cc/7GLE-LC3W)

5   A Sergeenkov. How to check your Ethereum transaction, 11 May 2023, coindesk.com/learn/how-to-check-your-ethereum-transaction/ (archived at https://perma.cc/URJ5-CA9E)

6   C Gartenberg. Coinbase's bouncing QR code Super Bowl ad was so popular it crashed the app, 14 February 2022, theverge.com/2022/2/13/22932397/ coinbases-qr-code-super-bowl-ad-app-crash (archived at https://perma. cc/3776-ANBA)

7   S Krug. *Don't Make Me Think: A common sense approach to web usability*, 2nd edn, New Riders, 2005.

8   A Sarkar. Binance launches Web3 wallet for its 150M registered users, *Cointelegraph*, 8 November 2023, cointelegraph.com/news/binance-web3-wallet-launch-120-million-registered-users (archived at https://perma.cc/ NMW5-DA4B)

9   G C Cooke. *Web3: The end of business-as-usual*, Whitefox Publishing, 2022.

10 Visa Crypto Thought Leadership. A deep dive on Solana, a high performance blockchain network, 2023, usa.visa.com/solutions/crypto/deep-dive-on-solana. html (archived at https://perma.cc/Z7DS-LMN2)

11 J Benson, Solana could beat out Ethereum to 'become the Visa' of crypto: Bank of America, Decrypt, 12 January 2022, decrypt.co/90334/solana-could-beat-ethereum-visa-crypto-bank-america (archived at https://perma.cc/ DR8R-2XM3)

12 Visa. Visa Expands Stablecoin Settlement Capabilities to Merchant Acquirers, 9 May 2023, usa.visa.com/about-visa/newsroom/press-releases. releaseId.19881.html (archived at https://perma.cc/3FNU-WWPE)

13 Tau. What is Firedancer? Explore Solana's new validator client, Alchemy, 20 January 2023, alchemy.com/overviews/what-is-firedancer (archived at https:// perma.cc/EJ5F-2ZCE)

14 A Clarke. Why interoperability is the key to blockchain technology's mass adoption, *Cointelegraph*, 28 August 2022, cointelegraph.com/news/ why-interoperability-is-the-key-to-blockchain-technology-s-mass-adoption (archived at https://perma.cc/33GM-YVWM)

15 B Pimentel. An Ethereum co-founder is now on a crusade against 'crypto nationalism', protocol, 30 September 2021, protocol.com/fintech/polkadot-ethereum-gavin-wood (archived at https://perma.cc/3CTD-QULR)

16 S James. Polkadot: The history, Medium, 24 March 2022, medium.com/@ samueluj23/polkadots-history-is-intertwined-with-the-development-of-ethereum-5be40d58753d (archived at https://perma.cc/NP27-XDXP)

17 Swift press release. Swift unlocks potential of tokenisation with successful blockchain experiments, Businesswire, 31 August 2023, businesswire.com/news/home/20230831212747/en/Swift-Unlocks-Potential-of-Tokenisation-With-Successful-Blockchain-Experiments (archived at https://perma.cc/HP53-NUP3)

18 Cryptopedia. What was The DAO?, 5 October 2023, www.gemini.com/cryptopedia/the-dao-hack-makerdao (archived at https://perma.cc/25FN-KF5M)

19 F Sanchez. IOG announces new blockchain to protect data and safeguard technology freedoms, 18 November 2022, iohk.io/en/blog/posts/2022/11/18/iog-announces-new-blockchain-to-protect-data-and-safeguard-technology-freedoms/ (archived at https://perma.cc/BKM2-7VNR)

20 B McGleenon. Microsoft boss: 'Blockchain needs a ChatGPT moment', Yahoofinance, 17 January 2023, uk.finance.yahoo.com/news/microsoft-blockchain-chatgpt-124532476.html (archived at https://perma.cc/D98X-UDHT)

21 D Disparte. When we stop talking about blockchain, we can change the world with it, *Forbes*, 28 March 2018, forbes.com/sites/dantedisparte/2018/03/28/when-we-stop-talking-about-blockchain-we-can-change-the-world-with-it/?sh=376c721b1037 (archived at https://perma.cc/5FXH-2PB9)

22 Citigroup. Money, tokens, and games, 30 March 2023, citigroup.com/global/insights/citigps/money-tokens-and-games (archived at https://perma.cc/5W5D-NSJH)

13

Web3 and the future of finance

REVOLUTIONIZING CAR SALES

How often can you sell a car? Until recently, car sellers in Brazil could sell the same car multiple times. At 9 am, the first client would go in, look at the car and make the payment, leaving the client believing they had successfully bought the vehicle. However, before the vehicle's registration documents had been updated to reflect the sale, a second client would be brought in to buy the same car. Unaware of the previous transaction, the second client would look at the car and decide to buy and pay for the same car. And the story would go on.

It sounds like an unbelievable story, but it was shared with me by a Brazilian colleague about what he saw happening in Brazil. The fraudulent sale of the same car was only possible because there was a time gap between the sale of the car, meaning the payment, and the administrative update of its registration, the delivery – leading multiple buyers to be deceived into buying a vehicle that had already been sold. However, Web3 adoption is changing this story, providing Brazilians with a safer way to negotiate and acquire cars, real estate and other goods and services.

In 2021, LIFT Challenge Digital Real Edition was launched. This was a special edition of the LIFT lab, in collaboration with the Central Bank of Brazil. The challenge aimed to assess use cases related to the issuance of a CBDC, a digital Brazilian real expected to be launched in 2024, and its technological feasibility. As part of the challenge, a proposal from Santander Brazil and a Web3 infrastructure provider called Parfin was selected. The proposal included the conversion of vehicles and real-estate ownership titles into digital format (i.e. tokenization) to improve negotiation efficiency through a delivery versus payment (DvP) method.[1]

In 2022, Santander created a minimum viable product (MVP) and presented the demo platform to the central bank. Through a marketplace, tokenized vehicles could be sold and bought by clients. The payment, in CBDC, was secured in an escrow account, for a few seconds, while the smart contract validated the rules (e.g. Was the car previously sold?). Once all rules were validated, the car's ownership was transferred to the buyer, and the funds were released to the seller. All steps were automated via smart contracts and done in a few seconds or minutes.[2] This experiment showcased the potential of tokenization for DvP transactions, ensuring security, efficiency and trust.

Santander is looking to expand the experiments further by using real clients and exploring the use of the tokenized asset, the car, as loan collateral.

The LIFT challenge programme also evaluated solutions for three other use cases: payment versus payment (PvP) related with exchange between currencies, the use of the Internet of Things (IoT) for direct settlement and the use of DeFi protocols in a compliant way. It is a brilliant example of how Web3 could be used in the not-so-distant future across the globe. Countries with less-developed banking infrastructure might leapfrog, showcasing the future of finance. This could be similar to what we have seen with other technologies, where, for example, some African countries bypassed traditional banking systems and went straight to mobile banking.

The bigger picture

In May 2022, Christine Lagarde, President of the European Central Bank, told a Dutch television show that cryptocurrencies are 'worth nothing'.[3] She is not alone in thinking this way. Often, leaders across the globe declare that 'crypto' is dead and that Web3 is simply a fad. But, what those critics are missing is the big picture. They are too focused on the speculation use case of the asset instead of considering the different developments and use cases in this space. More importantly, they are only considering their existing regulatory, social and economic environments.

There are three key aspects of Web3 that are driving change and have proven opportunities potential for the future: trading and speculation of cryptocurrencies, digital currencies used as a store of value, and infrastructure changing the fabric of financial services.

Trading/speculation

The rise and fall in the value of cryptocurrencies, like Bitcoin and Ethereum, have attracted both retail and institutional investors seeking profit from market volatility. In the early days, numerous stories of individuals getting rich from Bitcoin drew media attention and made headlines. However, Web3 has evolved into more than an investment or speculation asset. In reality, the investment component is just a small part of the opportunity.

Store of value

Especially important in some developing and emerging countries, where there is a lack of confidence in the legal tender or central banks, is the fact that savings in digital currencies are not only attractive but a safeguard. Cryptocurrencies have been regarded as the future for a digital store of value, a safe haven in times of economic uncertainty, such as inflation and currency devaluation.

The decentralized nature of these digital assets also means that they are not controlled by any single entity or government, which is essential for those seeking independence from traditional financial systems.

In a discussion with John D'Agostino, Senior Advisor for Partnerships and Strategy for Coinbase Institutional, he highlighted how crucial a store of value is in certain countries and will be part of the future of finance:

We are somewhat spoiled here in the US. No matter your view on the government at any point in time, they do not tend to break into your house and use force to take your assets. That happens in other parts of the world. And if you fall on the wrong side of the government, in those places, the banks are useless to you, and the law is useless to you. You can buy diamonds or gold and try hiding them somewhere, but that's heavy and inconvenient. And so, in such situations, immutable, fungible digital assets as a store of value are quite useful.

For anyone concerned about inflationary pressure because of money printing in the US and Europe, the fixed supply could help solve that problem. So it's not perfect, but it's the best thing I have seen.

John noted that the creation of a store of value is not new. Indeed, billionaires have used wine, art and sports teams to store value for years:

Stradivarius violins are another fascinating example. Their value has increased consistently for a very long time. But there have been multiple studies that show Stradivarius violins are not superior to cheaper, modern violins. But a relatively small community of, very wealthy, people and companies decided they have value, so they became a store of value. Sports teams, many of which consistently lose money, are another example. Now, in an increasingly digital age, why wouldn't a uniquely digital store of value exist?

Infrastructure

Perhaps the most significant but less visible aspect of Web3 is its infrastructure. This encompasses the underlying blockchain technology, DApps, smart contracts and other protocols that form the backbone of Web3. From new forms of money to new tokenized assets, such infrastructure is not only enabling a new set of applications but is also changing the fabric and ecosystem of financial services, and changing the roles, responsibilities and business models of existing players.

Will we need banks?

Given the potential for disruption and disintermediation of existing players, one must consider what the future could look like. *Will we even need banks in the future of finance?*

This intentionally provocative question is not just rhetorical in today's rapidly evolving landscape. It invites us to consider the shifting dynamics in finance and what the future could look like.

What would indeed compel retail clients to transition from traditional banking incumbents to DeFi platforms? What would make you comfortable to move all your money from an incumbent bank or challenger bank into the world of DeFi?

More than just a simple and easy user experience, it is about achieving a level of 'peace of mind'. Currently, if something goes wrong, you can call, text or email someone at the bank, who will promptly help you. If the bank goes into bankruptcy, you are still covered by various financial protection schemes. Now, let's imagine a scenario in which DeFi meets both requirements. *Would this be enough to persuade retail clients to transfer all of their funds to a custody wallet to leverage DeFi products?*

The answer is not straightforward. In 2013, UK account holders tended to remain with their banks longer, 17 years, than they would stay in their marriage, which lasted on average 11 years.[4] A decade later, we are seeing a generational shift. Millennials and Gen Z are more open to changing their banking providers, driven by technology adoption and value perceptions. However, older generations still tend to be loyal to their original banks. Additionally, the profile risk is also important to consider. Many individuals are risk-averse when it comes to their finances and like to keep their accounts in 'traditional' banks, perceived as safe and trustworthy.

Given this backdrop, it does not seem likely that DeFi will completely overtake traditional banks to become the sole future of finance. Instead, we are heading towards a more diversified financial ecosystem in which all players (incumbents, fintechs, CeFi and DeFi) coexist, each catering to clients with distinct needs and risk appetites.

This future will likely witness a growing number of partnerships and collaborations between DeFi, CeFi and incumbents. CeFi and DeFi are bringing innovation to financial services, while the large financial institutions bring their brands, trust and distribution. Such partnerships will lead to an evolution of financial services with a convergence of traditional assets and digital assets.

Additionally, as the industry matures and new regulation is defined, there will be an increased focus on risk management, governance and customer protection. Experienced leaders from financial services or other regulated sectors are being hired by Web3 startups, bringing the experience of building in a safe and compliant manner.

Ultimately, the form and role of banks as we know them today will change.

Past, present and future

METRO BANK

In the summer of 2010, the first high-street bank to open in the UK in over 100 years opened its doors in Holborn, right in the centre of London.

Metro Bank was founded by the US businessman Vernon Hill, along with co-founder Anthony Thomson (who later left Metro Bank to form digital challenger Atom). Speaking at the branch opening ceremony, Vernon Hill told reporters, 'Britons are dying for revolution in the banking business, focused on service, and we are here to provide it.'[5]

Metro Bank's strategy focused on making the customer experience of banking more akin to going shopping. At the centre of the brand were physical branches, called Stores, which were bright and colourful (blue and red) to give the impression of a retail experience. They were open seven days a week, from 8 am until 8 pm, for customer convenience. Metro Bank even encouraged customers to bring their dogs into branches, keeping water bowls available for companions.

Throughout the years, Metro Bank continued its expansion, and by 2023 had more than 76 branches and 2.7 million customers.[6] It was an interesting strategy of opening branches while others were closing them. However, behind the colourful branches, Metro Bank started to show signs of financial distress. In 2019, Metro Bank was rescued, raising £375 million via issuing new equity and, in 2023, it secured a last-minute rescue deal after its share price plunged following concerns over its finances.[7]

While the rescue has calmed the market for now, serious concerns about the bank's viability have surged. Metro Bank has found it challenging to attract customers away from the established brands, continuing to invest heavily in a branch network while the incumbents are dramatically cutting back their own branch networks.

Co-founder Anthony Thompson describes the branch model as 'outdated' and the future of Metro Bank as 'challenging'. Anthony left Metro Bank in 2013 after disagreements with the board about the branch strategy. 'I saw the biggest change in consumer behaviour in my life in the market data as I was looking at – this move from traditional banking, branch-based banking, to digital, and mobile in particular,' he told *City A.M.* 'It was very clear to me that the strategy of retail only had to change. I shared my views with the board, and the board didn't share those thoughts and felt the branch strategy still has legs, and that was the point in which I stepped down.'[8]

When was the last time you set foot in a bank branch?

Metro Bank is an excellent example of a bank that has struggled to understand the evolution of customer needs and technology advancements. Yes, 20 years ago, people used to go to physical branches, with workers filling up branches at lunchtime, trying to complete their banking needs during the branch's opening hours. However, banking has changed over time, and, with the advent of online and mobile banking, most clients do not go to branches, but instead bank online. This trend was even more pronounced after the global pandemic in 2021 shutting down numerous physical bank branches throughout the globe and making clients move online.

Old grandiose buildings that previously held banks are now being reused for other purposes, such as hotels, houses or even arts and entertainment. In Northern Ireland, for example, a performing arts company is now occupying the former Northern Bank building. 'There are two old bank vaults still intact in the basement, which we have converted into a recording and streaming studio,' the artistic director at Accidental Theatre told the BBC, adding that the thick walls made for excellent soundproofing.[9]

The form and role of a bank have changed in the last decade and will change again in the next. Leaders and executives at the forefront of finance must ensure they understand the potential for changes and technologies that will be disrupting it.

Web3, as an emerging technology, will be a driver for that change. As an open-source, decentralized technology, it is impossible to 'put it back in the box'. Even more telling are the recent pilots and use cases that have demonstrated real value to both institutions and central banks. What will be the new form of finance? We don't know yet, but change is coming, and leaders who embrace it will be at the forefront of the new finance.

'We have not yet reached land. There is so much more space for innovation and so much uncertainty over use cases,' reflected Kristalina Georgieva, managing director of the International Monetary Fund, in a recent speech noting CBDC work. 'This is not the time to turn back.'[10]

Perception of new technologies

Imagine a world where a robotic companion, sleek and intelligent, not only tidies up your home but also shops for you. It's a crisp autumn morning, and you are lounging on your couch. You say a command, and the robot whirs to life. Its sensors meticulously navigate your home, cleaning with precision.

Let me guess, you are imagining a big-sized robot with eyes like a human, arms outreached, with fingers capable of gripping and manipulating objects, with legs able to move up and down the stairs, wearing a cleaning apron. Interestingly enough, that is the image used in science fiction movies, but it is far from the reality of the robots that are already part of our lives today.

Cleaning robots are small and circular, with bumpers and sensors to navigate your house. They do not have eyes or hands. And while a robot physically going shopping doesn't exist yet, IoT has made strides in shopping convenience. Smart refrigerators can track your groceries and even suggest recipes. You can use Alexa, a cloud-based voice service, to shop on Amazon, manage alarms and greet visitors, all with the power of your voice. New technology forms and appearances tend to differ from those that the human brain imagines. In reality, the form they take is often much simpler and less sci-fi than you would expect.

Similarly, with Web3, it is hard to know for sure what use cases will prevail in the future and how this technology will be used, but one thing is certain: the form will be much simpler than you may think. If we consider IoT technology, as in the example here, it is also being used in combination with Web3.

LIFT CHALLENGE: SMART LOCKER (IOT)

In Brazil in 2021, the LIFT Challenge Digital Real Edition called for innovative projects addressing four key areas: DvP, PvP, the application of DeFi and the integration of the IoT. Bank Capital and the company TecBan responded to this challenge with a unique proposal under the IoT category, focusing on e-commerce and parcel delivery.

Their proposal involved the use of smart lockers to enhance online shopping, reduce fraud and increase inclusion and accessibility for individuals living in remote or hard-to-access locations. This proposal was accepted and developed under the LIFT challenge.

The MVP consisted of an online marketplace website, two physical lockers, one located in Sao Paulo and the other in Brasilia, and the use of a private blockchain network. The user experience was similar to that consumers were already familiar with when doing online shopping.

In simple terms, users would log in to the marketplace and select the product they wanted to buy. For delivery, they would select the closest physical locker and complete the payment, in this case using the Brazil CBDC. The funds (payment) were temporarily held in an escrow account and managed automatically by smart contracts. Once the product was delivered to the physical locker, the user would receive a message with the code to open the locker. Only after the buyer collected their product from the physical locker would the smart contract release the funds to the seller. Note that the smart contract's rules and actions were linked with a physical action, the collection of the product from a locker.

The process offered a familiar online shopping experience with enhanced security. It significantly reduced the risk of fraud, providing a safer and more reliable e-commerce experience. The results of this innovative approach were presented to the central bank at the end of 2022, showcasing the successful integration of technology with physical retail processes. Given positive feedback, the team is continuing to explore this solution further.

The Brazil experiment showcases how the real use cases and solutions are much simpler than you would expect when you hear about crypto. In the UK, Amazon is already providing a similar experience. Products bought online can be either delivered to customer's homes or to physical Amazon lockers available in numerous locations. The difference is that the payment is made automatically, so if the product is not delivered or fraud is committed, the client could lose the money. Often customers need to check refund policies and contact Amazon for help. The use of Web3, in this case, is just a small upgrade in the background that reduces fraud and improves security for the client. From a bank's perspective, it also reduces online banking fraud, which can be a costly factor.

New technologies also tend to make users uncomfortable and sceptical, often afraid of new scams or fraud. Do you remember the first time you used your credit card to pay online? You probably felt discomfort and were not sure that you were doing the right thing or could trust that site. However, online payments have become the most common activity. As more emerging technologies change our existing paradigm and trusted organizations like central banks and traditional banks support such innovations, clients' adoption and acceptance of new technologies will change. Education will be crucial to ensure clients are comfortable adopting such new technologies.

To progress, we need to solve the PR problem

While disruptive technologies always need some time to be accepted by the general public, this industry has created an additional emotional response from the public, with scams, hacks, frauds and bad actors continuing to be the main protagonists. And yes, Web3 currently has problems that we need to fix for this industry to reach its full potential. But I wonder: Why does Web3 have such a bad PR problem?

In a discussion with John D'Agostino, Senior Advisor for Partnerships and Strategy for Coinbase Institutional, he told me that he sees parallels between Web3 and hedge funds, and that we need to elevate responsible voices for this industry to progress:

> Some of the concerns are valid. Sometimes crypto people have this odd tendency to deny it, but there are absolutely bad actors. Some of the characteristics that makes digital assets innovative unquestionably are also useful to bad actors, e.g. the technology is efficient, (mostly) immutable and fungible. But the question is: Is the bad actor problem any worse than everywhere else? I don't think so.
>
> I believe this industry has a massive PR problem, similar to what I saw in Hedge Funds. The archetypal 'hedge fund guy' is, for the most part, not well liked. Bizarrely, the private equity archetype is better viewed. That's odd because they are, more often, the ones leveraging up, cutting staff and selling businesses for parts. All hedge funds do is trade liquid stocks. The problem is crypto did what hedge funds did: it tends to elevate the worst possible people to the position of de-facto spokesperson.
>
> Price volatility without commensurate caution will hurt retail acceptance of digital assets as both investments and for career choices. I taught a class at MIT recently and asked, 'Raise your hand if you are looking at a career in crypto.' Out of about 300 students, only 4 raised their hands. And that surprised me, so I spoke with them afterwards, and they told me their lack of interest was, in part, due to the recent NFT bubble. Many had bought NFTs, or had friends who did, and felt the projects – and community – had let them down. They felt that there was

a systematic attempt from almost everyone in the industry to sell this overvalued trend. Few, they felt, were raising their voices and warning about the risks of NFTs. Interestingly, they didn't feel this way about meme stocks, which lost similar amounts of value. Again – bad PR.

Overall, we need to do a much better job of identifying and shunning bad actors – i.e. self regulating. The question will be: Will the industry drive its own evolution, or will it be forced by the regulators and society?

While the media tends to focus on the volatility of cryptocurrency prices and hacking stories, the experts in the industry are focused on the potential of the technology and forging ahead. As the industry matures, the focus is moving from the hype and price cycles to solutions being built quietly in the background.

In an insightful discussion with Sendi Young, former Europe MD and UK Board Director at Ripple, she reflected on her experience moving from a traditional institution to the Web3 industry and future trends. Referring to the notorious collapse of FTX and its consequent impacts on the industry, Sendi said:

> When I joined Ripple, in June 2021, I realised at the time, that we were at the top of the hype cycle. But then I witnessed the first phase of the sentiment cooling down.
>
> But, it is during these 'crypto winters' when the noise and speculation goes away, that the serious builders working on real world use cases are able to further establish themselves. This is when trends become permanent, primarily through adoption by traditional financial institutions. Traditional institutions are leaning into this space, making investments, and trying to turn pilots into real solutions. When I was speaking to the banks that have been investing in this space for the last 10 years, you could see that they are looking at it from a long-term perspective. In a panel I spoke on, one of the banks' executives said, 'We don't invest in these technologies with a two-day horizon, instead we invest with years horizon. It's not like put your money and take your money the next day when the price of bitcoin drops.'

Sendi believes that there is a real opportunity in this industry, which is now translating into traditional institutions focusing on driving investments and solutions:

If we consider the recent hype around tokenising commercial deposits, it is an implicit acknowledgement from the banks around the potential of the technology. And considering how it could be relevant and applicable to them.

So do I think that the hype has come down? Yes. But is that necessarily a bad thing? No. We are going to have cycles but the space is so broad that it depends on which part of the segment you look at, you can always find opportunities.

Ultimately, I do believe in the premise of the technology, and what it brings. Nowadays, that is a lot more well-understood and accepted, not really questioned anymore.

Leaders are now considering 'How do we make it fit into our business model?', 'How do we generate revenue?' or 'How do we serve our customers?' as opposed to discussing if they should join this innovation. It's no longer a question of 'if' but, 'when' and 'how'.

The quest for Web3 and the future of finance

The future looks promising with so much innovation and experience flowing into this industry. In a discussion with Tyrone Lobban, Managing Director at J.P. Morgan and head of Blockchain & Onyx Digital Assets, he told me how excited he is about the future and potential of this industry, with the Onyx team doubling down on their efforts to pursue innovative commercial solutions enabled by blockchain:

> I am incredibly excited about everything we are doing. I genuinely believe we have such a great opportunity to make a meaningful impact. We just announced our participation in the continuation of Project Guardian, in which we are tackling a significant problem in the Asset and Wealth Management industry with a solution that could meaningfully reduce costs and the overhead of managing discretionary portfolios at scale. We've had positive feedback and interest from that announcement, showcasing the project's potential. It definitely exceeded our own expectations.

As part of our future work, we will continue to tokenise different assets and build up the breadth of products on the Onyx Digital Assets platform. We are doing some early-stage work in the energy space, considering how we can make better use of energy and use blockchain to meet energy goals, for example through carbon credits tokenisation. And we will continue our work around digital identity. It is an incredibly hard problem to tackle, but as a large bank, we are uniquely positioned to work on an identity solution.

In short, we believe the expansion of tokenisation into new product domains and digital identity will help us take strides in our goal of rewiring the financial system.

From a DeFi perspective, experts still believe in its potential to transform finance, increase transparency, create efficiencies and open up access to finance. In a discussion with Stani Kulechov, founder and CEO of Avara, previously Aave Companies, he told me how he sees the future of DeFi:

> (Permissioned) DeFi has the potential to play a role streamlining global payments and settlements making them more efficient, and improving the user experience for financial institutions, businesses and their clients. We expect to see more financial institutions using blockchain technology in the future. Ultimately, this helps to improve the bottom line, and create top line (revenue opportunities) by opening access to new markets.
>
> DeFi is also playing an increasing role in emerging markets, where it is vital to increasing access to financial markets and tools, and to increase economic empowerment. We are seeing a growing number of use cases for DeFi such as crowdfunding and insurance and prediction markets.
>
> The ultimate goal of DeFi is to increase access, provide transparency, speed transactions and lower costs. DeFi removes third parties and legacy approval systems, empowering users with control and custody over their financial assets and enabling direct participation in decision-making over how their funds are managed.

Future outlook

'We are done doing POCs [proof of concepts],' said a senior banker at a conference, 'now we need to scale up.' Over the last decade, the technology has been tested by traditional institutions. They now have numerous proofs that it works and brings benefits, from efficiencies to new products and services. In the next few years, incumbents will focus on scalability and identifying solutions that provide commercial benefits.

Many believe that traditional institutions will adopt their own blockchains and solutions, with tokenization being the star, and an interoperable infrastructure will be adopted at the industry level. In that sense, institutions will be able to select their own infrastructure based on requirements and needs, similar to the existing infrastructure model. Different digital currencies, such as CBDCs, stablecoins and bank deposits, will be adopted and used for internal needs, industry and cross-border activities. For example, deposits may be adopted for internal activities, while wholesale CDBCs are used for cross-border activities.

How will DeFi play in this new world? Some of the innovations created by DeFi are already being tested by central banks and traditional institutions (like AMMs), which could mean such solutions or even protocols being leveraged by traditional players. As both words become more integrated, more liquidity will flow into DeFi and better on- and off-ramps will be created, simplifying the user experience and increasing adoption.

As the industry evolves, regulations must adapt to it at both the country and global levels. For this future to be realized, identity and privacy will be essential. Digital identity will not only provide security but also make the users the owners of their own data, a fundamental principle of Web3.

Impact on traditional institutions

Existing beliefs assume that central authorities must mediate market participation. However, distributed infrastructure provides transparency that could make intermediaries redundant. The role of traditional institutions will change with the Web3 rollout.

The transparency of blockchain will create operational efficiencies, eliminating the need for reconciliation and other operational activities currently in place, and leaner organizations. The new infrastructure's transparency and benefits will change the role of institutions.

A combination of private and public blockchains will be adopted, depending on institutions' risk and regulatory acceptance. (Note that as of January 2024, regulators in the US are not welcoming the usage of public blockchains, leading many institutions to focus on building private blockchains.) However, the 'old rails' will not be replaced overnight. Old and new rails will coexist for a long time within financial institutions across processes, teams and jurisdictions.

Given Web3's new paradigm and other emerging technologies on the horizon, the team's skills will need to be reassessed. Digital skills will replace traditional ones, with the focus on teams to be able to work and leverage new technologies like blockchain, artificial intelligence and analytics software.

Will Defi lead to greater financial inclusion?

The short answer is we don't know.

The industry agrees that expanding access for the 1.7 billion adults excluded from the traditional financial systems is critical. While fintech has reduced the gap and overcome the challenge of physical distance from traditional bricks-and-mortar locations, accessing financial services is still difficult for those without a government identification. DeFi, given its decentralized and openness features, has the potential to overcome this. Nowadays, anyone can create a blockchain wallet, with an internet connection, and access financial services on the blockchain. Emerging markets have been leaders in adopting crypto and stablecoins as a store of value. Individuals are using stablecoins and blockchain rails to send money home (i.e. remittances). Stablecoins were used to send aid directly to Ukrainian refugees after the start of the war in Ukraine.

However, challenges remain. Internet availability, digital literacy and market volatility could limit further adoption. User-friendly designs and localized education initiatives could help bridge these gaps. Existing risks, such as hacks and frauds, and price volatility will need to be fixed upfront, before Web3 is ready to onboard underrepresented and underserved consumers. Further regulatory requirements may reduce the openness of this industry but would provide customer protection, which is essential for vulnerable customers. New forms of identification and online engagement could also be used to onboard consumers into financial services.

Success in this endeavour could make DeFi a tool for greater financial empowerment, but execution remains challenging. Hybrid models blending traditional institutions and DeFi may also be the solution – for example, using DeFi to broaden investment to remote locations. A concerted effort by the industry will be required to maximize financial inclusion.

Embracing the future

When I started to learn about this space, I was surprised by the complexity and breadth of this industry. From the outset, it may seem like it contains a bunch of advocates with extreme views about the world and society. Bitcoin itself was created as part of a backlash against establishment views of finance. The first block of Bitcoin even contained a message saying, 'The Times 03/Jan/2009 Chancellor on brink of second bailout for Banks', referring to a newspaper article about the British government's potential bailout of banks following the 2007–2008 financial crisis and highlighting its anti-establishment characteristics.[11]

However, what I found was a mix of individuals from different backgrounds and with different beliefs. Many with a traditional financial services background jumped into this space after seeing the transformative potential the infrastructure could bring. And yes, some technologies are hyped initially but do not truly mature. However, emerging technologies that do materialize have exponential outcomes and impacts. With Web3, we are discussing the opportunity to reinvent finance and change the rails and currency. How often can you be part of such a transformation in finance?

Although there was once a divide between Web3 companies and traditional players at the start, this gap has begun to narrow. Many institutional players have quietly been learning, testing and developing in the background and are now ready to deploy at scale. But we are still at the start; most of Web3 is yet to be built.

SUMMARY OF KEY POINTS

- Countries with less-developed banking infrastructure might leapfrog to the adoption of Web3, showcasing the future of finance. Brazil is a good example of the potential of this technology, which can be seen by the work performed via the LIFT challenge.

- Often, critics declare that 'crypto' is dead and that Web3 is simply a fad. However, those critics are missing the big picture. Besides speculation, digital assets are used as a store of value in developing countries, and blockchain technology has a recognized benefit in terms of efficiency and creation of new products and services.

- We are heading towards a more diversified financial ecosystem in which all players – incumbents, fintechs, CeFi and DeFi – coexist. Each will cater to clients with distinct needs and risk appetites.

- While the media tends to focus on the hype and price cycles, experts are focused on the technology potential and forging ahead. Traditional institutions are confident that the technology works, given pilots and tests performed over the years, and so are changing their efforts to scaling solutions that can bring commercial value.

- Web3 creates the opportunity to reinvent finance and change the rails and currency. But we are still at the start. Leaders in finance must understand how Web3 will disrupt and how they can adapt.

Endnotes

1 LIFT Challenge, liftchallenge.bcb.gov.br/site/liftchallenge/en (archived at https://perma.cc/L7VB-HYJV)

2 Discussion with Parfin CEO Marcos Viriato, youtube.com/watch?v=8RkxV4MiMew (archived at https://perma.cc/3A42-YVGL)

3 R Browne. Christine Lagarde says crypto is worth nothing, 23 May 2002, CNBC, cnbc.com/2022/05/23/ecb-chief-christine-lagarde-crypto-is-worth-nothing.html (archived at https://perma.cc/MX7H-ZB3P)

4 P Collinson. Switching banks: Why are we more loyal to our bank than to a partner?, *The Guardian*, 7 September 2013, theguardian.com/money/2013/sep/07/switching-banks-seven-day (archived at https://perma.cc/N3AJ-TDSB).

5 A Fawthrop. A history of Metro Bank: Assessing the UK challenger's rise to prominence, 5 February 2019, www.nsbanking.com/analysis/metro-bank-history/ (archived at https://perma.cc/NJ27-WHKE)

6 J Kollewe and J Makortoff. Metro Bank agrees rescue deal with investors, *The Guardian*, 8 October 2023, theguardian.com/business/2023/oct/08/bank-of-england-sounds-out-buyers-for-metro-bank-including-natwest (archived at https://perma.cc/84YG-9CMX).

7 J Kollewe and J Makortoff. Metro Bank agrees rescue deal with investors, *The Guardian*, 8 October 2023, theguardian.com/business/2023/oct/08/bank-of-england-sounds-out-buyers-for-metro-bank-including-natwest (archived at https://perma.cc/42R3-RKLP).

8 C Conchie. Metro Bank founder: I told them branches wouldn't work 10 years ago, *City A.M.*, 12 October 2023, cityam.com/metro-bank-founder-i-told-them-branches-wouldnt-work-10-years-ago/ (archived at https://perma.cc/SK3U-TWPR)

9 BBC News. Bank closures: Bringing high street bank buildings back to life, 13 March 2021, bbc.co.uk/news/uk-northern-ireland-56373503 (archived at https://perma.cc/PD83-HN3W)

10 IMF. The digital finance voyage: A case for public sector involvement, Keynote address, Singapore Fintech Festival, 15 November 2023, imf.org/en/News/Articles/2023/11/15/sp-111423-the-digital-finance-voyage-a-case-for-public-sector-involvement (archived at https://perma.cc/CB3R-NZKR)

11 C Tardi. Genesis block: Bitcoin definition, mysteries, and secret message, Investopedia, 30 November 2023, www.investopedia.com/terms/g/genesis-block.asp (archived at https://perma.cc/L9RU-6NM2)

ACKNOWLEDGEMENTS

I am extremely grateful to the countless people who generously shared their time and expertise throughout this project. I hope this book serves as both a tribute to the collaborative spirit that fuelled its creation and a source of inspiration for the next generation of experts venturing into the transformative landscape of Web3 in financial services.

A special thank you to the experts featured on these pages for sharing their experiences, learnings and invaluable contributions to reviewing drafts and providing essential feedback.

Next, I would like to thank my friends Mike Sotirakos and Tzahi Kanza for dedicating their time to reading and providing feedback on selected chapters. Their insights were instrumental in shaping this work.

A particular appreciation to my partner, Ben Ackland, who not only reviewed chapters but also served as the primary editor for numerous blog posts that paved the way for this ambitious undertaking. Thank you for your continuous support and advice.

Finally, I would like to thank my friends, too numerous to name, with special mention to Sally Yiallouros and Ana Correia for their unwavering cheerleading throughout this journey. To my family, thank you for your continued support and for always encouraging me to pursue anything that I wanted to.

INDEX

Note: Page numbers in *italics* refer to tables or figures.

Looking for another book?

Explore our award-winning
books from global business
experts in Finance and
Banking

Scan the code to browse

www.koganpage.com/finance

More books from Kogan Page

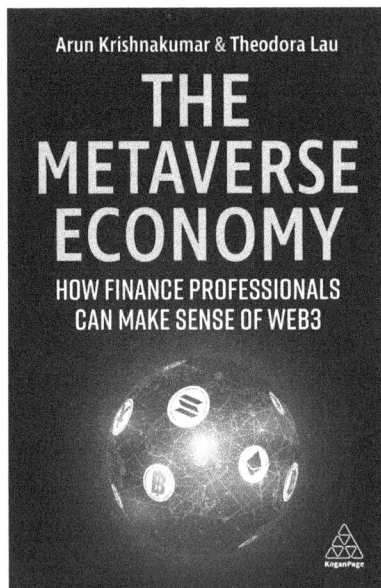

www.koganpage.com

From 4 December 2025 the EU Responsible Person (GPSR) is:
eucomply oÜ, Pärnu mnt. 139b – 14, 11317 Tallinn, Estonia
www.eucompliancepartner.com

www.ingramcontent.com/pod-product-compliance
Lightning Source LLC
Chambersburg PA
CBHW071544210326
41597CB00019B/3120

9 781398 615717